Understanding Lessor Mathematics

Using the latest research, this book provides an insight into how learning in mathematics can be improved through a lesson study approach. This highly practical resource explores the research and theory that underpins lesson study, and shows the significant impact it can have on teacher development.

Divided into ten accessible main chapters that focus in depth on an individual mathematics lesson, each chapter provides research and background to the lesson, an outline of key features, a detailed description and analysis of the lesson in practice, post-lesson discussions and reflections which generalise from the experience, as well as links to helpful resources. Some of the key topics explored include:

- ◆ Fractions
- ◆ Proportional relationships
- ◆ Probability and statistics
- ◆ Geometry
- ◆ Modelling
- ◆ Algebra
- ◆ Dialogic reasoning.

Understanding Lesson Study for Mathematics is the perfect resource for all mathematics teachers, trainee teachers, and professional developers who are looking to develop the use of lesson study in their own practice or for those simply seeking new inspiring ideas for the mathematics classroom.

Rosa Archer, Manchester University, has worked on lesson study for ten years with colleagues from Japan and from England.

Siân Morgan, Manchester University, is a teacher educator, researcher and professional developer with a passion for mathematics education and lesson study.

David Swanson teaches at Manchester University and researches mathematical and pedagogical concept development and critical social perspectives on education.

Understanding Lesson Study for Mathematics

A Practical Guide for Improving Teaching and Learning

Rosa Archer, Siân Morgan
and David Swanson

Routledge
Taylor & Francis Group

LONDON AND NEW YORK

First published 2021
by Routledge
2 Park Square, Milton Park, Abingdon, Oxon OX14 4RN

and by Routledge
52 Vanderbilt Avenue, New York, NY 10017

Routledge is an imprint of the Taylor & Francis Group, an informa business

© 2021 Rosa Archer, Siân Morgan and David Swanson

British Library Cataloguing-in-Publication Data
A catalogue record for this book is available from the British Library

Library of Congress Cataloging-in-Publication Data
A catalog record has been requested for this book

ISBN: 978-1-138-48571-6 (hbk)
ISBN: 978-1-138-48572-3 (pbk)
ISBN: 978-1-351-04828-6 (ebk)

Typeset in Palatino
by Swales & Willis, Exeter, Devon, UK

Contents

Preface

At the heart of this book are ten chapters that focus in depth on an individual mathematics lesson. Each chapter includes some of the thinking behind the lesson, a description and analysis of the lesson in practice and some general understanding developed from the experience.

Each lesson and chapter has been developed through lesson study (LS). All three authors are former teachers and currently teacher educators and researchers at The University of Manchester, and have worked on using LS as a professional development tool for teachers and for pre-service teachers for several years. We have seen that LS can have a significant impact on teachers' development and this book is an attempt to share what we have learned and understood.

The idea of this book was born while we were discussing readings we could share with our pre-service teachers on a particular aspect of mathematics teaching. We could find many densely written academic articles and many descriptions of teaching practice, but very little in between, which related big ideas with classroom practice in a convincing and accessible way. We therefore decided to write our own to share with our pre-service teachers, and we found conducting and reporting on lesson studies to be the perfect vehicle.

The aim of this book is therefore to reflect on research on pedagogy via practical applications and translate research into practice (and vice-versa). Through it we hope readers will develop their understanding of learning and teaching mathematics, and also learn about LS as a method for further development.

What different readers may get from this book

LS, as a professional development tool, has become very popular in the UK and in the US in recent years. However, in our experience, LS is interpreted in many different ways, and sometimes in an overly simplistic and not always helpful way. This book aims to provide sufficient reflections and theoretical background on LS to support those wishing to develop it in their own establishments.

The book includes:

♦ A focus on mathematics pedagogy for mathematics teachers and pre-service teachers

◆ Ten lessons including the research background, planning, reflections and lesson plans in easily accessible writing
◆ A focus on 'difficult to teach topics' and curriculum challenges
◆ Current debates and research translated into practice
◆ A model for conducting, writing up and sharing lesson studies.

The book can therefore be read at many different levels. Teachers and pre-service teachers wishing to develop their pedagogy or introduce new ideas in the classroom could read the lesson plans and lesson reflections and try the lessons themselves. The research-based background to the lesson will help develop their understanding further and support their reflection and analysis. Pre-service teachers can find practical examples of lesson planning and reflection to assist them in these important areas. Those developing professional development courses could share the lesson plans with colleagues and use some of the activities suggested within. Teacher educators could also use some of the activities suggested and use the lesson plans and evaluations as discussion points with students. Pre-service teachers, master's students and undergraduate students on education courses could use the chapters to support the writing of academic assignments.

Recent changes to the national curriculum in the UK and particularly the greater emphasis on mastery within the classroom and problem solving within public examinations are posing new challenges to the various groups discussed above; we hope that the materials found within this book can offer suggestions to support understanding and reflection.

Guidance for readers

Each chapter may be read and used independently. However, those who wish to begin with some further background on lesson study should read the introduction to it in Chapter 1. This introductory chapter is also useful in explaining the structure of the lesson chapters, as the sections closely follow the different phases typically found in lesson study. We should also note here that at times we adapt grammatical tense to these phases in later chapters, using present tense when describing the practical experience of the lesson, so the reader can more easily imagine being present as a 'fly on the wall' in the classroom.

Through the chapters of the book we tell three interrelated stories about mathematical understanding, pedagogy and lesson study. Following the ten chapters on each lesson, in Chapter 12 we draw together and generalise from the understandings we have developed in relation to each, and add some thoughts on lesson study as a form of research.

Overview of chapters

Chapter 1

This chapter outlines the background to and main features of LS, including relevant literature and practical advice for departments or individuals who wish to use LS for their professional development. There are also sections that focus on the typical structure of Japanese lessons and our experience of LS in different contexts, including LS in Initial Teacher Education.

The subsequent chapters have the following parts:

◆ Introduction to the lesson, including the context of the school where it was taught and the focus for the LS
◆ Background to the lesson – pedagogical considerations on a particular aspect of teaching and learning mathematics that draws on research
◆ An outline of key features of the lesson
◆ Lesson reflection and analysis – a description and analysis of the key moments in the lesson
◆ What we have learned – this is an informed commentary on the lesson that focuses on what we (the authors) learned from being part of the LS, linked to the lesson itself and the LS process, and suggests possible next steps
◆ A fully developed and detailed lesson plan with links to resources when appropriate.

Chapters also include the main mathematical content, key mathematical pedagogy and a suggestion for the most appropriate target age range. Most lessons, however, could be adapted for other ages and, where this is possible, suggestions on how to do this will be given.

Some of the chapters will also consider the re-planning, re-teaching and re-reflecting, if re-teaching of the lesson was an important stage of the lesson's development. Vignettes may also be included in some of the chapters, detailing individuals' experiences of working with LS.

Within the chapters (2–11), there are opportunities to reflect and tasks that will enable the reader to develop their own understanding. In what follows we give the chapters headings, mathematical content and associated pedagogy within the lessons. We also include the relevant Key Stage (KS) for each of the lessons.

(For readers outside of the UK, KS correspond to the following age groups: KS2 ≈ 7–11 years old, KS3 ≈ 11–14 years old, KS4 ≈ 14–16 years old, KS5 ≈ 16–19 years old.)

Chapter 2: Perimeter and mastery (KS2/KS3)

This chapter will draw on the literature and current practice related to Singapore Mathematics and develops a model mastery lesson. The research focus for the lesson study was on testing a new problem (anchor task) related to perimeter and compound shapes that would be sufficiently accessible and open, allowing a variety of approaches, and to analyse children's reasoning that emerges from this problem.

Chapter 3: Developing understanding of fraction through context (KS2/KS3)

The materials for this lesson were developed for the NCETM's multiplicative reasoning project and draw on Realistic Mathematics Education. Pupils were asked to consider a real-life context to explore their understanding of fractions. The context allows the teacher to see what the pupils' concepts of fractions are; in particular about the 'whole'. The lesson study research focus was to step back as much as possible and not confirm whether pupil's ideas are correct, verbally and non-verbally; 'hear it and move on', but value all contributions, to encourage pupils' independent knowledge formation rather than over-reliance on the authority of the teacher.

Chapter 4: Proportional relationships and the double number line (KS2/KS3)

The research focus of this chapter is based on the use of the double number line to develop multiplicative and proportional reasoning. Unlike the other lessons in this book the authors were not involved in the planning of the lesson but one was an observer. The lesson was observed as part of a LS cycle in Japan.

Chapter 5: Communicating mathematically about shape (KS2/KS3/KS4)

This lesson adapts a common pedagogical tool to promote dialogue in the classroom where students sit back-to-back and describe a drawing to their partner. The research focus of the lesson study was to look at ways to support learners in communicating mathematically and in bringing to their consciousness how communicating can also help them develop their understanding.

Chapter 6: Constructing deep geometrical understanding (KS3/KS4)

The materials for this lesson are based on Colin Foster's lesson 'Staying on the page'. The lesson supports practice leading to fluency by using some engaging problem solving on centre of enlargement. The research focus for this LS is to observe how embedding practice of centre of enlargement within a wider problem helps develop a deeper relational understanding.

Chapter 7: Modelling through open-ended tasks (KS3/KS4)

This chapter discusses the use of a Bowland lesson 'Outbreak', which encourages students to make mathematical models and decisions within wider moral and practical discussions. The research focus was how teachers can support the development of open-ended tasks without taking away from the openness of the activity.

Chapter 8: Early algebra using real-life scenarios (KS3/KS4)

This lesson is an adaptation of the ICCAMS research lesson 'boat hire' and draws on the related literature on algebraic reasoning. The research focus is on how to use real-life scenarios to support the development of early algebraic understanding.

Chapter 9: Sustaining argument about randomness (KS3/KS4/KS5)

Students' lists of real and imagined coin tossing are used to develop and sustain (friendly) argument which becomes more and more mathematical. The research focus here is on sustaining argument in a classroom with students not generally accustomed to discussion and group reasoning.

Chapter 10: Experimental design: connecting statistics to student experience (KS4/KS5)

In this lesson students take part in an experiment to test the Mozart effect (which claims that listening to music improves performance on reasoning tasks) and then critique the experiment and look for ways to improve it. The primary focus of the lesson study was to see how connecting mathematics to experience in various ways, such as analysing the links between mathematics and music and participating in the experiment to be critiqued, would encourage engagement and influence reasoning.

Chapter 11: Teaching logarithms through problem solving (KS5)

This lesson illustrates how many of the pedagogical ideas developed in earlier chapters can also be used to develop higher level concepts and, in particular, the understanding of logarithms at A level. The lesson study focus here is on understanding to what extent, and how, the lesson helps develop understanding of logarithms through problem-solving.

Chapter 12: Conclusion(s): mathematics, pedagogy, professional development and research

This concluding chapter discusses some of the more general understandings of mathematics, pedagogy and people's (in particular young people's) understanding of mathematics developed within the book. The chapter also spells out how we believe we have been doing research while writing this book, in terms more common to academic literature.

The reader might wish to use the following table as a reminder of who was involved at each stage of the LS process.

Chapter	Who designed the lesson	Who planned the lesson	Who taught the lesson	Who observed the lesson and participated in the post lesson discussion	Teacher's/Teachers' previous involvement with the lesson
2	Two of the authors together with two newly qualified teachers	Two of the authors together with two newly qualified teachers	One of the newly qualified teacher	One of the authors and the other newly qualified teacher	No previous experience of the lesson but experienced with mastery
3	Sue Hough and colleagues (Manchester Metropolitan University)	Two of the authors, one primary teacher and one secondary teacher (schools on same site)	The primary teacher with a teaching assistant	Two of the authors and a secondary teacher	Previous experience in professional development course where lesson was studied in detail and modelled
4	Colleagues from a primary school in Japan, facilitated by IMPULS	Colleagues from a primary school in Japan. This is the only lesson where the authors were not involved in the planning	One of the Japanese primary teachers	Colleagues from an international delegation working on IMPULS (including one of the authors) and several colleagues from the district	No previous experience of the lesson. The lesson was introduced to the international delegates the day before

5	David Swanson	Two of the authors and a teacher	The teacher who is also a head of department. Two pre-service teachers assisted with the teaching	Two of the authors, the teacher and the two pre-service teachers	The tutors / authors had modelled the lesson to the pre-service teachers and had completed a lesson study in HE
6	Colin Foster Loughborough University	First lesson: Two of the authors and an experienced teacher. Second lesson: Two of the authors and a newly qualified teacher.	First lesson: The experienced teacher. Second lesson: the newly qualified teacher	First lesson: 40 pre-service teachers and their tutor. Second lesson: two authors and the teacher	The tutors / authors had introduced and modelled the lesson in a university lecture
7	Bowland	A group of ten pre-service teachers and their university tutor, who is also one of the authors	Two of the pre-service teachers.	The pre-service teachers and their university tutor (one of the authors) together with the classroom teacher	The tutors / authors had introduced the pre-service teachers to the lesson in university but the lesson was not modelled.

(Continued)

Chapter	Who designed the lesson	Who planned the lesson	Who taught the lesson	Who observed the lesson and participated in the post lesson discussion	Teacher's/ Teachers' previous involvement with the lesson
8	Adapted from a lesson designed by Margaret Brown, Robert Coe, Jeremy Hodgen and Dietmar Küchemann	Two of the authors and a pre-service teacher at the end of her training	The pre-service teacher	Two of the authors and a pre-service teacher	The pre-service teacher had participated before in a lesson study cycle on this lesson
9	David Swanson	Two of the authors and a pre-service teacher at the end of his training	The pre-service teacher	Two of the authors and a pre-service teacher. Also, pupil voice was gathered	The pre-service teacher had participated before in a lesson study cycle on this lesson
10	Alan Marshall and adapted by David Swanson	One of the authors with two teachers	The classroom teachers thought one lesson each	One of the authors, the two classroom teachers and a researcher form the university.	No previous experience
11	David Swanson	Two of the tutors and a recently qualified teacher	The classroom teacher	Two of the tutors and a teacher who had trained with us	No previous experience

Acknowledgements

We are in debt to many people, including all the mathematics educators, researchers and groups who designed the lessons that inspired us: Robert Coe (Durham University), the team at Bowland; Colin Foster (University of Loughborough); Jeremy Hodgen (Kings' College London); Alan Marshall (University of Edinburgh); Sue Hough (Manchester Metropolitan University); and Dietmar Kuchemann (University of Nottingham).

The teachers and pre-service teachers who contributed to the planning and teaching of the lessons, and teaching colleagues who very generously allowed us to work with their classes: Callum Adamson; Maddie Barnett; Shaun Barton; Urszula Braun; Malcolm Connolly; Kate Collins; Jon Finch; Sylwia Glazewska; Judy Holdcroft; Gillian Munro; Steven Nixon; Ben Parson and Matt Shurlock. We are also very grateful to the management of the schools who kindly welcomed us into their classrooms: All Saints School, Chetham's School of Music, Connell College, Essa Primary, Falinge Park School, Manor Academy, Priestley College, Sasahara Elementary School, Trinity Church of England High School.

This book would not have been possible without the encouragement and support of our colleagues form Manchester Institute of Education at The University of Manchester. In particular, Rob Buck; Alan Cross; Tom Donnai; Claire Forbes; Bob Hindle; Andy Howes; Narinder Mann; Maria Pampaka; David Spendlove and Julian Williams who reviewed our chapters. We also offer thanks to some of our former pre-service teachers who commented on some of our drafts: Shaun Barton; Judy Holdcroft; Michelle Pang and Dafydd Roberts-Harry. Many thanks also to James Cross and Juste Kruvele for providing the observation sheet in Chapter 5; IMPULS for providing one of the authors with the opportunity to observe several inspirational lesson in Japan; Martin Scott, Head of Department at Trinity Church of England High School, for sharing his wisdom about mastery, and David Rose, Newcastle University, for his helpful comments on Chapter 1.

Most of all, we thank our talented pre-service teachers for continuing to inspire us with their insights and enthusiasm and our families and friends, especially Ian Archer, Shirin Hirsch and Damian Morgan, for supporting and encouraging us while writing this book.

1

An introduction to lesson study

We begin this chapter with a background to lesson study (LS), its origins and current popularity. Also included is a description of the variety of LS 'research foci' that we discuss within the book. This is followed by a discussion of benefits of and risks to LS, the phases of the LS cycle and how to overcome some of the possible obstacles. We provide an overview of a typical Japanese lesson and finally reflect on our experiences of working with LS in a variety of contexts.

Background to lesson study

LS is a long-established research-based approach to the continuing development of teachers' professional practice. It is widely accepted that LS assisted in transforming teaching and learning in Japan from teacher-centred to student-centred learning aimed at developing mathematical thinking and problem solving (Takahashi & McDougal, 2016). It has been used in some form for over 140 years in Japanese schools. Stigler and Hiebert (1999) popularised Japanese mathematics teaching and LS in the US through their book *The Teaching Gap: Best Ideas from the World's Teachers for Improving Education in the Classroom.* Since then, LS has been developed elsewhere including in the West, initially being used in the US and Australia and, more recently, in the UK (Hart, Alston & Murata, 2011).

LS is usually described as some or all of the following: teachers working to research and develop a particular practice (the focus); researching and planning a lesson together; collaboratively teaching and observing the planned lesson; and collaboratively analysing and critically reflecting on that lesson. It is not primarily about perfecting lessons but mainly about researching and developing pedagogical understanding and practice. Ideally, this implies that findings from the lesson will be generalised beyond the immediate context and experience, and understandings will be shared with others through reports and potentially change pedagogy and even the curriculum.

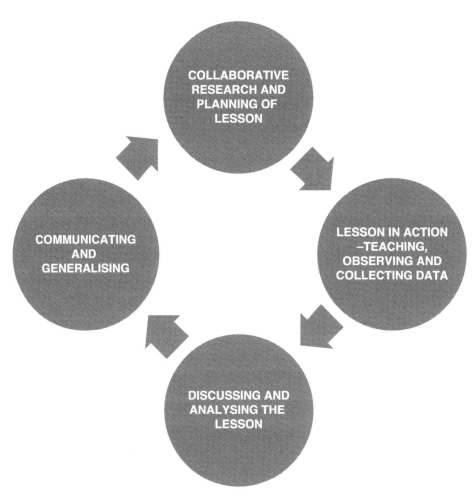

Figure 1.1 The lesson study cycle

In some cases the research lesson is refined and retaught before the stage of communicating and generalising. We will analyse later in this chapter the advantages and disadvantages of re-teaching the lesson in particular contexts. For example, in Initial Teacher Education (ITE) we will see how, in our experience, re-teaching is an essential part of the cycle for pre-service teachers. Fernandez (2010) also advocated the relevance of 'repeated cycles' in LS with ITE students. However in Japan, re-teaching the lesson is not common practice (Fujii, 2014) and some Japanese researchers believe the re-teaching of the lesson to be unethical, since it positions teaching as a science experiment, and children as experimental objects (Seleznyov, 2018).

Teachers begin the LS process by deciding on a LS focus and a problem or content area that they wish to develop. Previous research (Fernandez & Yoshida, 2004; Lewis & Tsuchida, 1998) has indicated the need for an identified focus when conducting LS, the Japanese calling this focus the research goal and the lesson plan the research proposal. Some examples of goals from lessons include 'take initiative as learners', 'be active problem-solvers', 'be active problem-seekers', 'develop scientific ways of thinking' and 'develop their individuality' (Lewis & Tsuchida, 1998, p. 14). Equally goals may be focused round topics that are difficult to teach, such as 'How does one divide fractions?' The research foci for the chapters in this book can be found in the preface.

Hart, Alston and Murata (2011, p. v) highlight that LS is a 'complex professional learning approach' with a variety of interpretations, and thus there is a 'need to identify what is essential for an experience to be LS'. We would agree with this. In the authors' experiences, LS is not just seen differently in different cultures/nations, but also within the same cultures/nations, with participants adapting some of the key elements to suit local conditions. Through this book and the following ten LS cycles, we will highlight various elements within LS, and in Chapter 12, we will analyse our experiences and summarise what may be useful in other contexts.

LS is aimed at developing the pedagogic practice of the profession as a whole, though, of course, in doing so the individuals involved would be expected to develop their own professional practice too. A great deal of time is spent reflecting on how learners think and learn, with general implications for better teaching practice, rather than a focus on the errors of the teacher and how a particular teacher might improve (as in coaching or other more judgemental forms of lesson observation). As Stepanek, Appel, Leong, Mangan and Mitchell (2006, p. 2) say: 'Developing a new approach requires deep thought, inquiry and collaboration with a collective focus on teaching rather than teachers.'

Benefits of lesson study

LS has been seen to develop and support teachers in a non-threatening collaborative way, which is important in the current context in schools in the UK
(and elsewhere) where 'performance management and performativity are so
dominant in schools and in professional learning' (Williams, Ryan & Morgan,
2014, p. 151). LS is essentially a collaborative form of professional development. Cajkler, Wood, Norton, Pedder and Xu (2015) analysed 200 studies into
LS, and they claim/state that there were four principal benefits for teachers:

◆ Greater teacher collaboration
◆ Sharper focus among teachers on students' learning
◆ Development of teacher knowledge, practice and professionalism
◆ Improved quality of classroom teaching and pupil learning
   outcomes.

(pp. 193–194)

We have also observed, by working on LS for several years, that it can provide
a powerful way to develop teachers' mathematical content and pedagogical
knowledge. Teachers question their own content knowledge and pedagogical
knowledge by discussing the lesson plan with colleagues and by reflecting on
learners' responses. Alongside this, LS can help develop a culture of talking
about mathematics between colleagues who, with time, consequently gain
the confidence to discuss content and pedagogy. As we observed above, the
LS process is not aimed at achieving the perfect lesson. Participants engage in
LS in Japan to learn something new and extend their professional knowledge
(Takahashi & McDougal, 2016).

Risks

There are some risks associated with conducting LS cycles and it is important
to note them here in order to be prepared. Norwich and Jones (2014) discuss
two central risks: (1) that those involved in the LS may not fully appreciate
the complexities of the process, particularly if they are new to the practice;
and (2) that 'the LS strategy could be used selectively to make it fit current
practices, perhaps because of external pressures' (p. 152). Such risks might
hinder reflections and observations so they may become more superficial/
surface level and not achieve the deep analysis and reflection needed. We
have observed this particularly when not enough time is dedicated to the

preparatory work. Also, in relation to the second point, in our experience lesson study can be misused as a performativity/accountability tool negating the associated benefits of LS.

We, however, believe that the LS process is beneficial when it can help develop a climate of enquiry within schools, even if initially, for the inexperienced team, the gain might be more limited. LS is not a quick fix; it takes time and dedication and the authors have observed that it works better when school management/leadership are committed to devoting, or at least allowing, time and energy to it.

Different phases of lesson study

In this section we discuss the different elements of the lesson study process, all of which support the development of pedagogical understanding and practice.

> In order to develop expertise, learning by reading, listening and seeing is not sufficient. It also requires learning through planning, doing and reflecting.
>
> (Takahashi, 2015, p. 52)

As we outline the different phases we will include the Japanese names for them since some of these words are commonly used in some LS practice, including in schools in our own context. These phases describe the *Japanese LS model* that is theorised in the literature. This ideal form is not necessarily followed exactly in other contexts or even in all Japanese practice, but the elements described below will always be present in one way or another. Later in this chapter we will describe some variations within the contexts we operate in, and how we have followed these elements within the experiences described within this book.

Select a research focus

As stated above, in order for the LS to be meaningful there must be a chosen research focus for the lesson. The focus allows observers to collect data during the lesson so the discussion can be centred round the research focus instead of being a more general 'what went well' type of reflection. The data collection and analysis of learners' responses allows us to distinguish between a research lesson and a lesson observation (for evaluation or for demonstration). We have included the research focus for all chapters within the preface and within the introduction or lesson outline of each chapter.

Researching and planning the lesson: *Kyozai Kenkyu* and the development of the research lesson proposal

Kyozai Kenkyu literately means 'research of teaching materials' in Japanese:

> *Kyozai – teaching materials*
> *Kenkyu – research*

During this phase teachers get together and use the literature to study the themes related to the chosen topic/focus/problem. This is an opportunity for teachers to deepen their own understanding of the chosen topic and related pedagogy (Stepanek et al., 2006). *Kyozai kenkyu* also involves a study of the curriculum, and requires a reflection on how the selected lesson fits within it, what the children need to know and what they will learn in the lesson and its aftermath. Including provision for this has been identified as a weakness in the teaching of mathematics in English schools, while a lot of thought is given to the sequencing of topics within the Japanese curriculum (Robutti et al., 2016). This phase also involves a study of the literature in order to identify learning issues such as typical misunderstandings and misconceptions around the topic. Existing literature is also used to consider possible tools, manipulatives, or materials that may be used and possible tasks that may be presented to students. This process is what we intend to model, by presenting a background section within each chapter that reviews ideas from the literature related to the lesson. According to Takahashi and McDougal (2016) a LS cycle cannot be successful if this phase of the cycle is overlooked or done too quickly.

In our experience with the ten lesson studies in this book, the main part of this research and planning of the lesson was completed by the authors prior to meeting with the teachers, (as university educators we are immersed in mathematics educational research and this day-to-day practice, and referring to associated literature, informs what we did at this stage). We then met as a *planning team* to further plan the lesson and consider the context; this was generally audio recorded, in order to improve our reflections of the process.

The teachers then created a detailed plan for the lesson, basing their decisions on what they learned (Takahashi & McDougal, 2016). The lesson plan is a research proposal that must include:

◆ The research focus
◆ The needs of all students
◆ The place of the lesson in the sequence
◆ The stages within the lesson and their purpose
◆ The key questions that will be posed
◆ Anticipated student responses
◆ Planned teacher responses to anticipated students' responses.

In our book, each chapter's 'lesson outline' section presents these elements in summary form.

Live research lesson (*Kenkyu Jugyou*)

Usually in Japan one teacher, from the planning team, teaches the lesson while the rest of the planning team observe alongside other teachers interested in the focus of the lesson. The number of observers varies considerably according to the context of the LS. In some district lessons there could be up to 100 observers watching a lesson happening on a stage while in smaller-scale events the lessons happen in the classroom with a smaller number of observers. Often, each observer focuses on a small group of learners, perhaps so as to cover the whole class, or a representative sample of the class between them, with the intent to understand students' thinking and capture students' reactions to the lesson. This happens also in larger-scale LS where, for practical reasons, the audience is divided into inner and outer circle. The inner circle is given priority in accessing children's working during the lesson, but in all cases participants do this only by observing rather than interacting with the learners. The planning team prepares a number of questions, linked to the research focus, to help guide the observations and these are given to all observers. In our experience of lesson studies for this book, in most cases the lesson and discussions are recorded, observers make copious notes; photos are taken of board work and student work is collected. In each chapter, the 'lesson reflection and analysis' section attempts to capture the experience of the lesson but it also begins to analyse the lesson in a way that would normally occur post-lesson.

Post-lesson discussion (collecting the evidence) *Kenkyu Kyougikai*

Often, the board work is not deleted and is used to initiate the post-LS discussions and reflections; students' work is also brought to the table for the purpose of understanding learners' thinking (Robutti et al., 2016). As stated above the purpose of the discussion is not to refine the lesson but to understand students' responses, by analysing the data (video recording, audio recording of students' discussions, board work, student work) from the lesson. We have provided some examples of pictures of students' work and of work completed at the board, for the purpose of engaging the reader in a vicarious experience of post-lesson reflection.

Summarise learning and identify next steps

The post-lesson discussion usually benefits from the presence of a 'knowledgeable other', the *Koshi* in Japanese, who helps focus the discussion using the data collected during the lesson and the literature they prepared before the event (Takahashi & McDougal, 2016). Such individuals must be experienced in LS and in doing research in education. They usually have the last word and give the team guidance towards next steps, often encouraging the planning team to continue reviewing existing literature (Watanabe, 2002,; Takahashi, 2014). In this book, the 'what have we learned' section of each chapter represents this phase, but also incorporates elements of the post-lesson discussion.

Dissemination

The LS diagram presented in Figure 1.1 reflects the Japanese model by including an essential part of the cycle, the dissemination of findings, which is sometimes less present in the UK. In Japan the dissemination can be through both internal and external publications, through district lessons and through curriculum development.

Dissemination is the aspect of LS we are attempting to achieve with this book, having participated in the LS cycle for each of the lessons described here. We will see that not all lessons were entirely successful in moving the learners forward (although most very much were) but even in such cases they were successful in allowing the LS team and the authors themselves to develop their understanding of the research focus and teaching and learning. It was also observed by the authors that the experience allowed participants to reflect on their own subject content knowledge and pedagogical knowledge.

It is worth noting that in Japan, teachers also consider the after-the-event revelries, which involve all those that took part in the process going out to celebrate, to be an essential part of the LS process, and we would encourage more of this in other contexts, to help develop a sense of community among those engaged in educational practice.

Overcoming obstacles

In Japan, LS is a well-established practice; regular time is often included for LS activities in the school timetable and teachers new to the profession are inducted into existing LS activities within their school and district. LS is, in fact, systematically embedded in the education system. The same cannot be said for other countries where LS is being adapted but where most professional development (PD) is not designed with it in mind (Seleznyov, 2018). Another significant difference with the Japanese context is the lack of teachers and researchers experienced in LS. The lack of expertise often leaves the design of the LS cycle in the hands of enthusiastic individuals who might miss some of the key components of the research lesson.

Some of the possible obstacles that we, and others, have experienced when conducting LS in the UK are outlined below, together with some possible solutions.

- *How to overcome the general lack of time and space to do genuine professional development?*
  Encourage senior leaders and departmental leaders to see the importance and impact of LS. This can be easier if you are enrolled in some form of professional development, which includes LS. Also, parts of team meetings could be used; teachers could take a colleague's class to enable the teacher to meet with other colleagues; some schools even have a day a week with a shorter afternoon and the staff then have time to meet. Sometimes, students in a class can be 'shared out' amongst other classes to free up staff, and holding revision sessions with many classes in one hall can also do this.

- *How do you manage without a Koshi?*
  We have found that collective participation can be enough; when we work collectively we are more than the sum of our parts, and we can view the collective as a more knowledgeable other. The most important aspect is that someone leads the post-lesson reflection, ensuring everyone has a chance to give their thoughts and that discussion remains centred on the research focus.

- *What if there is insufficient time to understand the research?*
  We encourage you to try to read something about the focus and have an initial discussion with your LS team about the issues. Also, you

could find lessons, such as the ones in this book, where some of the background research has been completed for you.

◆ *What to do if there is no time or space for joint planning, or observing the lesson?*
If there is no joint planning and no collaborative observation then this is not genuine LS, but there still will be some advantages if some of the phases are completed collaboratively. The use of video can be helpful too, if some are unable to be in the lesson; however, this could focus too much on the teacher and miss those conversations between students, so we would encourage having audio recorders on desks.

◆ *What if you struggle to find time for post-lesson discussion?*
The post-lesson discussion is a crucial part of the LS cycle, so it is best to plan time in for this from the start. Holding the post-lesson discussion immediately after the lesson has some benefits as everyone is already there and the experience is fresh. There are also advantages to holding it later, when everyone has reviewed the data, including pupil work, video etc. and can come to the discussion more informed. If this is difficult to do, one person could look at the data and feedback on this at the meeting. Meeting immediately after and then again later is of course the ideal, but not always practical.

The Japanese lesson

Japanese lessons, particularly problem-solving lessons, often have a well-defined structure. LS has often focussed on such lessons in the attempt to develop mathematics learning through problem solving approaches. The stages of the lesson can be used as steps for planning the research lesson and therefore we believe it is important to include them here. Considering the different stages of the lesson is helpful in supporting reflection even if a LS cycle, in a country outside of Japan, will not necessarily be expected to have an identical structure.

These different stages are as described by Shimizu (1999):

◆ Presentation of a problem. The problem is presented to students. For example, in Chapter 4 we describe a Japanese lesson. The lesson was aimed at understanding division by decimals and the problem posed at the beginning of the lesson was: 'how much does 1 L of juice cost if 1.6 L cost 320 yen?' Students work independently on the problem for several minutes.

◆ Individual problem solving by students. While students are working independently the teacher moves around to observe their work (this is referred to in Japan as *Kikan-Shido*). At this stage the teachers are looking for ideas they might select to share with the rest of the class. These are not necessarily the best ideas but ideas that will help develop collective understanding of the problem. Having spent a long time reflecting on the lesson plan and expected responses, the teacher will be prepared in looking at and selecting meaningful responses at this stage (e.g. one child uses a calculator to perform a division like 1.6 divided by 320, while another draws a number line). It is, however, our opinion, based on our experience of LS, that it is important to keep an open mind and to allow learners to surprise us with unexpected responses. These should be collected and discussed in the post-lesson discussion. The term *Hatsumon* is used to describe a question that provokes students thinking that is likely to be productive; this question might take the form of a hint aimed at understanding the problem or making a connection between different areas. In the lesson on Chapter 4, for example, the teacher began by asking children to work out the cost of a litre of juice given the cost of 2 litres, which was productive in suggesting division. These questions will have been detailed in the lesson plan.

◆ Whole class discussion about the methods for solving the problem used during the lesson; this is referred in Japan as *Neriage* (pronounced with a hard 'g'). This literally means kneading or polishing up and it is borrowed from the ancient Japanese technique of layering, curving and recombining different colours of clay, creating an intricate pattern. In terms of LS is interpreted as polishing collective ideas. Japanese teachers consider the *Neriage* as an essential part of the lesson.

◆ Summing up. This is described with the term *Matome* in Japan. During this last stage of the lesson the teacher sums up what has been learned. This is different to what would happen in most UK mathematics lessons, where learners would usually be asked to complete some form of assessment task, such as an exit ticket or exam question.

Lesson study in other contexts

Our experiences of LS vary from the Japanese *norm*, as discussed earlier in this chapter, because of our context. Our role, working in university Initial Teacher Education (ITE), is atypical and the forms of LS have necessarily been crafted accordingly. The main advantage as university teachers has been our opportunity to research and subsequently to write up these experiences, which is rare in the UK context where teachers – even those engaged in LS – don't usually get an opportunity to do so, mainly due to workload constraints.

In this section, we explore this further, looking in particular at LS within ITE, PD courses and a UK working group.

Initial teacher education

The authors have successfully adapted LS to meet the needs of pre-service teachers for several years. As discussed above, this is not something our Japanese colleagues would encourage. At best, in Japan pre-service teachers are invited to observe a LS cycle but are rarely involved with the planning team. Despite the disapproval from Japanese colleagues, the authors believe that an adapted version of LS can greatly benefit pre-service teachers in the English context and give them the skills to work reflectively and collaboratively throughout their career. In particular, the authors have researched the impact of a LS experience with Secondary Mathematics trainee teachers and concluded that the experience was significant in mediating the development of reflective practice (Radovic et al., 2014).

In this article, pre-service teachers worked on their own LS in selected schools, working collaboratively with experienced teachers and school-based mentors. We authors, who were also these pre-service teachers' tutors, observed the planning, teaching and acted as *Koshis* during the post-lesson discussions. Here the role of the *Koshi* was in some ways different to the one in the Japanese LS, since the tutors had a vested interest in the pre-service teachers' progress and were also seen as role models by them. The tutors also ensured that the pre-service teachers did not see this as a performative activity and emphasised that the activity would not be graded in any way. The pre-service teachers found the collaborative planning difficult initially (due to disagreements and relationship issues); however, they were aware that as a consequence they had a strong ownership of the lesson, as opposed to the class teacher or school mentors who had little role in the pre-planning; this allowed the participants to analyse the lesson, taking responsibility for bringing together contributions from all involved. Within this experience, imagination had a significant role for reflective practice. Such imagination was facilitated by the focus on improving and 're-teaching' the lesson. The authors also reflected on the importance of the social relations (including power relations) between those working together with the intention to improve their practices. We concluded that engaging all participants on equal terms provided rich opportunities to learn.

Coenders and Verhoef (2018) added to the literature on using LS in ITE. Their paper focuses on the development of teachers and pre-service teachers 'pedagogical content knowledge' (Shulman, 1986). They conclude that the collaborative planning succeeds in creating awareness of such knowledge for all involved. There are also benefits for the experienced teachers. Coenders and Verhoef (2018) also observe that, similarly to the authors' observations, experienced teachers who are initially anxious or reluctant to adopt new practices are encouraged by observing learners' positive reactions in class. Furthermore, experienced teachers involved with LS within ITE have often told the authors that they benefit from observing their classes being taught by a different teacher because they can understand the children better by observing them while they are learning.

Professional development courses involving LS

Two of the authors have been involved with LS through PD courses. The experience there has differed, because the in-service teachers involved with LS were provided with a lesson that, prior to the PD course, had been researched extensively, and was then modelled during the PD course. The participants, usually working in pairs from each school, then adapted the lesson for their own context (and based on their own understanding). The next phases of the LS process: the live research lesson and initial post-lesson discussion, were similar. However, the post-lesson reflection, summarising learning and next steps was enhanced through a collaborative reflection on the PD course where all those teachers that have taught the lesson, in different schools, came back together and began to generalise their experiences. See Chapter 3 for more in depth discussion of this process, and see also Swanson and Morgan (2019).

UK–Japanese differences in LS working group

One of the authors is part of a group of teachers and educators who aim to develop lesson study in the UK. Members of this group have had the opportunity to participate in an intensive training programme on lesson study in mathematics in Japan and have continued to work closely with Japanese mathematics educators (www.collaborative-lesson-research.uk/).

Some of the similarities and differences between LS in the two cultures have become part of the reflection for this group. We observed in previous paragraphs that Japanese educators do not encourage the involvement of pre-service teachers in the LS experience. We have also observed how the tightly sequenced Japanese curriculum allows teachers to have a shared language when discussing lessons. Another observed difference is the way the post-lesson discussion is handled.

It has been argued (Williams et al., 2014) that in the performative culture of the UK, the frequent monitoring of teachers creates an accountability system within which the performance of the teacher is of great importance. Therefore teachers in the UK find it very difficult to discuss possible improvement to the lesson without taking it personally or feeling threatened. This leads to feedback often being kept very vague in order not to upset the teacher who taught the lesson. This significantly and negatively impacts on the quality of the post-lesson discussion and learning outcomes. We would argue conscious effort must be made to overcome this. In our mathematics classrooms we aim for developing students' confidence to share their ideas, to reason, and even argue, and to see misconceptions as opportunities to learn. In the mathematics classroom this takes time to develop in order to overcome the students' own performativity culture, where things are often seen as right or wrong, and individuals fear ridicule. We want teachers to move beyond their own such fears and embrace collective and open reasoning about pedagogy. LS practices, as an alternative to practices aimed at judging performance, can support those teachers in overcoming their fears.

References

Cajkler, W., Wood, P., Norton, J., Pedder, D., & Xu, H. (2015). Teacher perspectives about lesson study in secondary school departments: A collaborative vehicle for professional learning and practice development. *Research Papers in Education*, 30(2), 192–213.

Coenders, F., & Verhoef, N. (2018). Lesson study: Professional development for beginning and experienced teachers. *Professional Development in Education*, 45(2), 217–230.

Fernandez, C., & Yoshida, M. (2004). *Lesson study: A Japanese approach to improving mathematics teaching and learning*. New Jersey: Lawrence Erlbaum Associates.

Fernandez, M. L. (2010). Investigating how and what prospective teachers learn through microteaching lesson study. *Teaching and Teacher Education*, *26*(2), 351–362.

Fujii, T. (2014). Implementing Japanese lesson study in foreign countries: Misconceptions revealed. *Mathematics Teacher Education and Development*, *16*(1), n1.

Hart, L. C., Alston, A., & Murata, A. (Eds.) (2011). *Lesson study research and practice in mathematics education: Learning together*. London: Springer.

Lewis, C., & Tsuchida, I. (1998). A lesson is like a swiftly flowing river. *American Educator*, *22*(4), 12–17.

Norwich, B., & Jones, J. (Eds.) (2014). *Lesson study: Making a difference to teaching pupils with learning difficulties*. London: Bloomsbury.

Radovic, D., Archer, R., Leask, D., Morgan, S., Pope, S., & Williams, J. (2014). Lesson study as a zone of professional development in secondary mathematics ITE: From reflection to reflection-and-imagination. In *Proceedings of the 8th British Congress of Mathematics Education*, 271–278.

Robutti, O., Cusi, A., Clark-Wilson, A., Jaworski, B., Chapman, O., Esteley, C., … Joubert, M. (2016). ICME international survey on teachers working and learning through collaboration: June 2016. *ZDM*, *48*(5), 651–690.

Seleznyov, S. (2018). Lesson study: An exploration of its translation beyond Japan. *International Journal for Lesson and Learning Studies*, *7*(3), 217–229.

Shimizu, Y. (1999). Aspects of mathematics teacher education in Japan: Focusing on teachers' roles. *Journal of Mathematics Teacher Education*, *2*(1), 107–116.

Shulman, L. S. (1986). Those who understand: Knowledge growth in teaching. *Educational Researcher*, *15*(2), 4–14.

Stepanek, J., Appel, G., Leong, M., Mangan, M. T., & Mitchell, M. (2006). *Leading lesson study: A practical guide for teachers and facilitators*. Corwin Press.

Stigler, J. W., & Hiebert, J. (1999) *The teaching gap: Best ideas from the world's teachers for improving education in the classroom*. New York: Free Press.

Swanson, D., & Morgan, S. (2019) *Going beyond lesson study: Professional development courses and the systematic/scientific development of pedagogical understanding*. Manuscript submitted for publication.

Takahashi, A. (2014). The role of the knowledgeable other in lesson study: Examining the final comments of experienced lesson study practitioners. *Mathematics Teacher Education and Development*, *16*(1), n1.

Takahashi, A. (2015). Lesson study: An essential process for improving mathematics teaching and learning. In M. Inprasitha, M. Isoda,

P. Wang-Iverson, & B. H. Yeap (Eds.), *Lesson study: Challenges in mathematics education* (pp. 51–58). London: World Scientific.

Takahashi, A., & McDougal, T. (2016). Collaborative lesson research: Maximizing the impact of lesson study. *ZDM, 48*(4), 513–526.

Watanabe, T. (2002). The role of outside experts in lesson study. In C. Lewis (Ed.), *Lesson study: A handbook of teacher-led instructional improvement* (pp. 85–91). Philadelphia, PA: Research for Better Schools.

Williams, J., Ryan, J., & Morgan, S. (2014). Lesson study in a performative culture. In O. McNamara, J. Murray & M. Jones (Eds.), *Workplace learning in teacher education* (pp. 151–167). Netherlands: Springer.

2

Perimeter and mastery

Introduction

In this chapter we explore an example of 'mastery' teaching focused on the perimeter of compound shapes. We take time in the background of the chapter to clarify the meaning of mastery in this particular context. The head of mathematics at the school where the lesson study was conducted describes the usual processes involved in developing lessons, how lessons are structured, the impact on students and teachers of teaching mathematics this way, and also what has resulted from moving to mixed-attainment teaching (seen by the school as essential to this version of mastery).

The lesson that follows is centred on an 'anchor task', one element of the four-part structure of the mastery lessons in the school. The essential role of anchor tasks is to allow students to start from and build on their existing understanding through tackling a problem, sharing and engaging with each other's approaches, and then writing up what they have learned. Later stages of the lesson attempt to consolidate some of the effective approaches and aspects that have arisen.

The school is a secondary/high school that has been working on mastery for three years having first started with a year 7 intake (age 11–12). Currently, all classes up to year 9 (age 13–14) are now established as mixed attainment classes and are following a mastery approach. The school has a diverse group of students, and given the wide range of student attainment, anchor tasks need to be accessible at many levels so that everyone can make sense of the problem and attempt it. Additionally, they need to be open enough to allow different approaches to arise within the room. The main motivation for designing the lesson in this lesson study was to replace an anchor task that did not sufficiently allow this.

We conducted the lesson study jointly with two teachers at the school who had previously been on our postgraduate teacher training course, both of whom have been recognised as outstanding teachers. The class we worked with was a mixed year 7 (ages 11–12) class. The research focus for the lesson study was on testing a new problem (anchor task) related to perimeter and compound shapes that would be sufficiently accessible and open, allowing a variety of approaches, and to analyse student reasoning that emerges from this problem. Overall, the lesson proved to be effective; this appeared to be linked, in part, to the culture the school has developed through mastery as we will analyse further in this chapter.

Background to the lesson

Currently there is a wide debate in schools and in educational circles in the UK about what mastery is and how a mastery lesson should look. Inspired by the success of East Asian countries such as Singapore in international league tables, the UK Department for Education (2012) conducted a review of the mathematics syllabi and practices in those countries and, based on that review, have since promoted a mastery approach. The mastery agenda has been strongly supported in England by the National Centre for Excellence in Teaching Mathematics (NCETM), the body responsible for continuing professional development of mathematics teachers. It was rolled out first in primary/elementary and then in secondary/high schools. According to the NCETM (2016a) acquiring mastery for learners means

> a deep, long-term, secure and adaptable understanding of the subject … acquiring a solid enough understanding of the maths that's been taught to enable him/her to move on to more advanced material.

This approach to mastery focuses on deep mathematical understanding and rejects learning rules without reason. Fluency on its own does not constitute mastery; however, mastery is achieved when procedural fluency is accompanied by conceptual understanding. Practising rules with the sole intention of committing them to memory is rejected in favour of 'intelligent practice that both reinforces pupils' procedural fluency and develops their conceptual understanding' (NCETM, 2016b, p. 1).

Other features often emphasised in the approach include, in no particular order:

◆ The use of variation (see Watson & Mason, 2006) and using variation to help learners generalise and capture key mathematical ideas
◆ A high level of interaction in lesson, where children are encouraged to work together, discuss mathematical content, express their ideas and learn from each other
◆ The use of manipulatives, imagery and models; the making of connections between different areas of mathematics
◆ Differentiation through using tasks that can be accessed at different levels of depth, rather than acceleration into new content, with scaffolding intervention for those students who might struggle to make sure they don't fall behind.

Although the mastery perspective is based on recent experiences in SE Asia, much of the content of the approach can in turn be seen to be influenced by approaches developed internationally, including in the UK, in the 1970s and 80s.

In the vignette below, the head of mathematics at the school where we conducted this lesson study talks through the department's experiences of introducing mastery in their school.

Motivations for introducing the mastery curriculum

We were keen to develop our KS3 curriculum in light of the challenges of the new GCSE specification. We knew we needed to move to a more problem-based approach to learning maths and what we knew of mastery at the time looked like it would fit the bill. Our GCSE results were good but we are an ambitious school and we want to make sure that all students who come here get the best

(Continued)

grades possible at the end of their time with us. The mastery approach that we have adopted gives students a really deep foundation for them to succeed at GCSE level.

The structure of mastery lessons

We structure our lesson in four parts:

1   Diagnostic question: designed to give an idea of the student's level of prior knowledge
2   Anchor task: a problem that students solve collaboratively. Solutions are shared and students record their favourite solution in a journal
3   Guided learning: a teacher led activity explaining different aspects of a particular topic
4   Independent task: a piece of work that the student completes on their own to show their understanding of the lesson.

The four parts of the lesson usually take 2 hours to complete.

Planning the lessons

Planning is now done in groups; three teachers will plan one unit of work that all teachers then teach. The aim of this is to ensure that lessons are high quality because when teachers are planning lessons, they know that their colleagues will be using them as well.

Mixed attainment grouping and its impact

Mixed attainment groupings go hand in hand with the philosophy that underpins mastery – everybody can do maths. This is a message that we want to give to students who come to our school, no matter what level you are at when you arrive, you can improve and succeed in maths. The mixed attainment groupings have meant that we have a greater flexibility over our groups so we can move students around to get the balance of all the groups right. The mixture of attainment within the group means that discussions can take place between all students.

Surprises

The biggest unexpected impact that we have seen has been from a behaviour point of view. Behaviour incidents in mastery lessons are far fewer than they were when we had set by attainment. We think this is because students don't get into a 'bottom set' mentality. Also, weaker students who previously may have become disengaged now have role models in the classroom so they can see how able mathematicians work whilst they are learning.

Response of staff

Initially, the teachers were very reserved about it as it represented a huge shift in the way we work. They also had particular concerns over mixed attainment groups. Initially, there was a team of six maths teachers planning and delivering mastery in the first year. These teachers were given a lot of time to research, meet, plan and discuss so that all of our initial reservations could be resolved and any problems could be discussed and solved. Now, all teachers plan and teach mastery lessons and feedback from maths staff and other staff in the school has been universally positive.

Impact on student learning, attitudes and engagement

Students' learning and understanding is getting better. Anecdotally, teachers are saying that students understand things better and work harder than previously. The data also confirms this; we carry out Progress Tests annually using GL Assessments Progress Test in maths, which compare our students with other students nationally. The data from these tests show that most of our students who follow a mastery curriculum are working above the national average.

In terms of attitudes and engagement, in the year prior to mastery after one term of school we had 256 behaviour points in year 7. (Behaviour points are given in cases of low level disruption to learning and other incidents where behaviour or engagement in learning is an issue.) In the first year of mastery, we had 123 behaviour points at the same point in the year. We feel this is because our students are in mixed ability groups where there are examples of excellent student behaviour in all groups so all students have role models and can see how to behave in lessons. We also feel that the structure of our lessons mean that students are fully aware of the expectations of them at any point in the lesson. This provides clarity for the students.

The lesson we discuss in this chapter focuses on the anchor task section of the school's four-part lesson structure (with a brief diagnostic task also, at the start). The topic content is perimeter of compound shapes. Anchor tasks are relatively substantial problems, which are meant to be approachable at any level. This allows teaching to be grounded in students' own mathematical productions, which are then further developed through collaborative work and whole class discussion, where connections can be probed and developed between different methods and answers. In the school, the anchor task also includes a reflective task where students write journal entries on their own ideas as they have developed through the problem.

The lesson study was motivated by a need to improve the existing anchor task (Figure 2.1).

This problem has positives to it, as it requires some reasoning and several steps to get to the solution (and, in fact, it wasn't omitted completely but incorporated into the independent task section of the lesson). However, there is unlikely to be much variation in method of solving the problem; there is

The diagram is made up of two different-sized rectangles

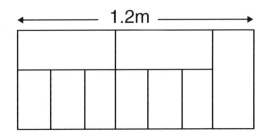

For each large rectangle, the length is double the width.

Work out the perimeter of one of the small rectangles

Figure 2.1 The original anchor task for perimeter of compound shapes

no real range of entry points available, particularly for students who struggle with seeing the initial need to divide 1.2 m by 2.5; and there is little scope to go deeper beyond finding the solution. The teachers who we worked with on the lesson had found that they ended up having to lead students too much through the necessary steps (the opposite of what they aim for in an anchor task), and the resulting student journals were very similar, merely reflecting the teachers' own explanations.

We therefore searched for a task related to perimeter of compound shapes that would have a potential range of starting points, a variety of solutions and methods, and possibilities for greater depth. We found a suitable task 'perimeter expressions' on the NRICH website (see https://nrich.maths.org/7283) and simplified it slightly leading to the problem seen in the next section.

Suggested reading

Jerrim, J., & Vignoles, A. (2016). The link between East Asian 'mastery' teaching methods and English children's mathematics skills. *Economics of Education Review, 50*, 29–44.

NCETM. The relationship between teaching for mastery and 'ability grouping' in secondary school mathematics (2018) https://www.ncetm.org.uk/public/files/95808938/Mastery+and+'ability+grouping'+in+secondary+-schools+Oct+2018.pdf

Lesson outline

Stage 1: diagnostic question
Begin with a diagnostic question, which refreshes perimeter of basic shapes. In the lesson that follows we used a question on finding the perimeter of a triangle with lengths 3 m, 135 cm and 70 cm. A number of different answers are anticipated so time should be allowed for students to write down their answer and thoughts before asking students to share their thinking with the class. First, for the correct answer and then identifying possible mistakes in the incorrect answers.

Stage 2: anchor task
Anchor task for perimeter of compound shapes:

Rosa took a piece of paper that was 18 cm by 24 cm (see Figure 2.2).

She then cut it in half, cut one of those halves in half again and then cut one of those halves in half again.

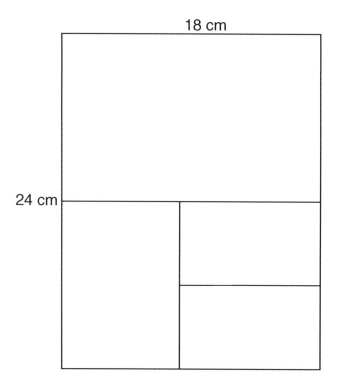

Figure 2.2 Perimeter problem

What is the greatest and what is the smallest perimeter shape she can make from the four pieces?

Rule: When positioning shapes they cannot overhang. The whole length of the smallest touching side must touch the other side, and a corner of each touching side must meet.

Before unveiling the question of biggest/smallest, ensure students understand the diagram by asking the class what else they know. Then discuss the rule, preferably illustrating by moving shapes on an interactive whiteboard, drawing what is and is not allowed, or moving manipulatives. Take questions to securely establish what is and is not possible (e.g. rotation allowed and all shapes must be used).

Provide students with cut-out versions of the shapes to manipulate. These can be laminated shapes to allow writing and rewriting lengths on the shapes, or simply paper versions (but have many extra copies if doing it this way).

Stage 3: pair work

Students work in pairs or in small groups to try and answer the question. There is a wide range of anticipated student responses: working out the perimeter of a shape where all sides fit neatly (e.g. the original); attempting shapes where missing lengths will have to be calculated; approaching the task of biggest/smallest via trial and error; and comparison with others; and developing reasoning about which type of joins will lead to bigger and smaller perimeters; convincing others, or even proving, that they have found the biggest or smallest. It is even possible to attempt to find all possible shapes that can be made (proof by exhaustion through being systematic), however given the many possibilities this is unlikely to be a practical approach here.

Stage 4: discussion and further pair work

After an initial period students share their approaches, and the working out of the lengths of the smaller rectangles. Students return to the task and record their findings.

After another period, students share two examples of finding the greatest perimeter of a particular shape; either by using a visualiser, or through manipulating shapes on an interactive whiteboard (or large cut-out shapes stuck on a whiteboard) or simply drawn. Select interesting examples that give different perimeters, and encourage discussion; why one may be bigger than the other and what strategies may be best (hoping for e.g. larger sides exposed and fewer sides touching). Repeat with examples for smallest, either immediately or after a further pair work depending on time.

Stage 5: journaling

Students write up what they have done and what they have learned (this may happen in the following lesson).

The expected outcomes of the lesson are that students will consolidate and develop their understanding of perimeter. Most students will manage perimeter calculations of simple shapes and move on to compound shapes and some will move further toward reasoning and justifying in relation to the problem, deepening their understanding of perimeter of compound shapes.

Lesson reflection and analysis

The teacher and class were relatively new to the school, a year 7 class (11/12 years old); however, some students had been exposed to the mastery style approach since primary/elementary school.

The lesson starts with the normal classroom routine of a diagnostic question (Figure 2.3). Students have one minute to discuss this question with their partner. Students are keen to discuss with each other and record their answer on their mini whiteboards. When the time is up, all students share their answers by showing the teacher their mini-whiteboards. There is a

Work out the perimeter of the triangle

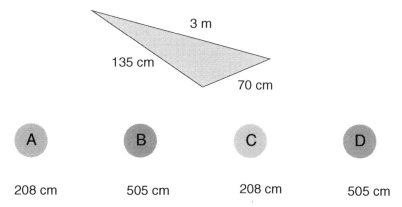

Figure 2.3 Diagnostic question

quick discussion and students share that they cannot add the length around the shape unless the units are the same. All students had correctly chosen D on their mini whiteboards and the teacher briefly asks students what they think the mistakes are in A, B and C. The students are again enthusiastic to share their thoughts. This classroom culture of students wanting to share and not worrying about incorrect solutions has developed over a relatively short period of time and we believe the mastery approach, and particularly their anchor tasks, will have contributed to this. The diagnostic enables the teacher to see that students know how to find the perimeter of a triangle and therefore confidently move on to the anchor task without needing additional intervention.

The rest of the lesson is devoted to the anchor task. The slide (Figure 2.4) is displayed and the teacher uses questioning to clarify the different elements of the diagram; through description but also by physically 'cutting' it in half (using arm actions), then half again and splitting it in half a final time. She demonstrates the rules by moving one of the smaller rectangles to different positions on the diagram on the interactive whiteboard highlighting when it does and does not fit the rule. Students are encouraged to ask further questions before starting to look for the greatest perimeter. Each pair is provided with cut-out shapes (actual dimensions used) representing the four rectangles to support their discussion.

Students work in their pairs for around 6 minutes before the whole class is brought back together for a discussion. During this pair/group work, some initially calculate the dimensions of each rectangle 'the pink one is 6 and 4.5 [partner intervenes] … no it's 6 and 9' and another pair '24 divided by 2 is 12'. Others focus more on the arrangements themselves, some of the discussions/ conversations recorded were; 'squashed it together' [smallest], 'let's make it long from smallest to largest' [greatest]. Also discussions involved looking at adding lengths together to find the total, this involved discussion and confirmation of missing lengths. One student suggested measuring the sides but his partner said 'no, we need to count them up', suggesting that they realised that you could work out missing lengths and just add them all up, without a need for measuring. There was lots of evidence of collaborative work including comments: 'where do you get that from?'; 'oh, OK so you think that's the big one'; 'oh, yeah, that might work'; 'wait no because two corners aren't touching'; 'it's best if we put it here so we don't have to calculate this and this' and 'I'll start adding this one up' showing a sharing of responsibility. One group very quickly thought they had come up with the 'best option' (greatest), but were happy to continue trying different arrangements to see if they could beat it.

Anchor Task

Rosa took a piece of paper which was 18 cm by 24 cm.
Rosa cut the piece of paper in half. She then repeats this twice.

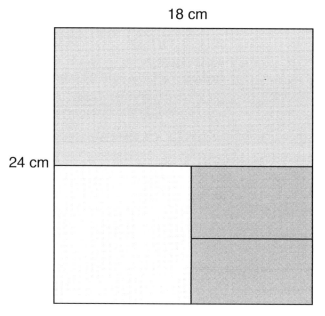

What's the greatest and what's the smallest perimeter that Rosa can make?
Two corners of a rectangle must be touching another rectangle at all times!

Figure 2.4 Anchor task

The teacher brings the class back together to discuss some of the strategies that different groups/pairs used:

Teacher: What was the initial step that you have taken?
Jacob: Tried to make the shape as long as possible, put them all out in a line.
Teacher: So you've tried to get the shape as long as possible. How could Jacob, now he has found his shape, find the perimeter of his shape?

Ebony: Write measurements on his shapes.
Teacher: Yes and you can write with your whiteboard pen on the shapes.

This was followed by general discussion about finding measurements of the new shapes using halving; 24 to 12 and then to 6 (vertical measurements) and then 18 to 9 (horizontal measurements). At this stage of the lesson, the new lengths have been clarified and recorded on the diagram on the board (Figure 2.5). See also the labelled cards created by one pair of pupils (Figure 2.6).

The task is reiterated and the teacher encourages students to prove to her that they have the greatest and least perimeters. Students have a further 10 minutes in pairs, discussing their ideas. One pair that have found what they believe are the biggest and smallest, go on to make a random shape, they discuss how to make it and say 'it might be smaller or bigger', they again support each other with finding missing sides. Some students at this point needed prompting to ensure they remained on task. The teacher asked about the shape arrangements and encouraged the students to find the perimeters. A higher attaining group, when asked by one of the teachers about their work, are very confident with their largest perimeter, believing they have 138 cm (it was actually 126 cm, see later), which was larger than

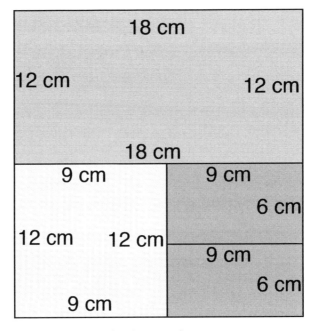

Figure 2.5 Anchor task with dimensions of each rectangle

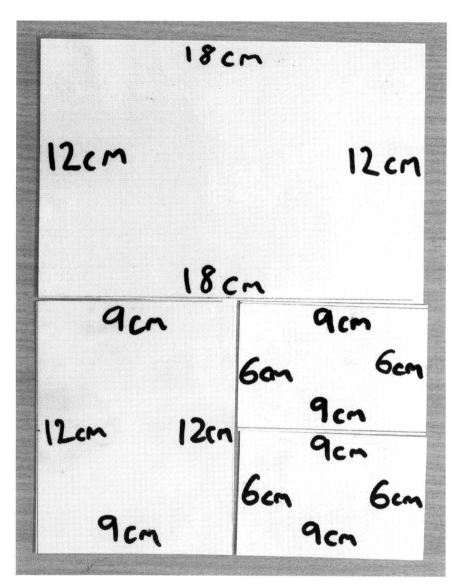

Figure 2.6 Labelled diagram

any others that they heard in the room. 'I need to get all the big shapes with the most space on the outside, so there are like kinda building blocks and stick out' [he then adds] 'I think I can get bigger'. This group are keen to continue working on the smallest perimeter, they keep checking to see if any arrangements will give a smaller perimeter than 84 cm. The group seem to be less convinced with their smallest arrangement than their greatest. This seems counter-intuitive; there are a number of arrangements that will give the greatest perimeter but only one (the arrangement they have) that gives the smallest.

To begin the next whole class interaction, the teacher asked two students to show the class their shapes using the visualiser. Whilst they did this, two students described how they found the greatest perimeters. Zayan said that you needed to 'spread out the shapes to be the longest, so then there's more widths and lengths, so it's a larger perimeter'. Joel explained his shape 'the smallest edges on each rectangle, you can put next to other shapes [then corrects himself] other shapes' smallest edges, so that the smaller numbers are being used up, cause you don't really need them'.

The teacher mentions that she noticed a few groups had this answer and guides the class to check the calculation of the perimeter of Chantelle and Jaya's arrangement (Figure 2.7) by going around the whole shape from the bottom left hand corner, length by length, highlighting the little '3s' on the diagram and concluding that it is 120 cm. This calculation was done mentally and it can be seen that for the lengths 9 and 9, they doubled to get 18 both times.

A second example for the greatest perimeter was discussed (Figure 2.8); this arrangement does give the greatest perimeter, although the calculation was initially incorrect. Matt was invited to share what his group had done at the visualiser. He shared his group's arrangement, which they believed

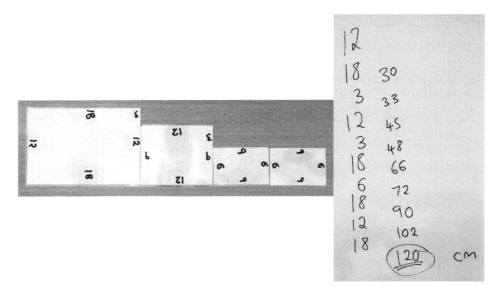

Figure 2.7 Chantelle and Jaya's arrangement and the calculation noted on the board

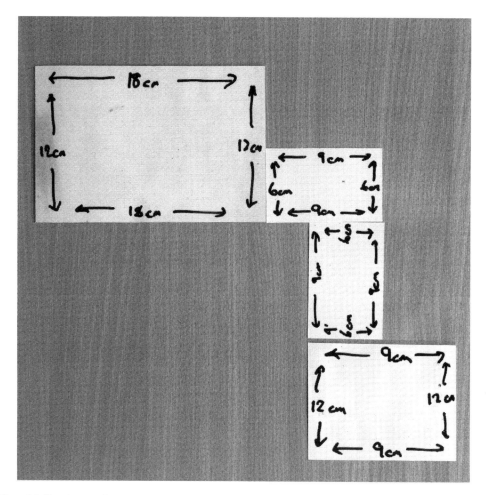

Figure 2.8 Greatest perimeter

to have a perimeter of 138 cm. While Matt explains the arrangement; Omar, from another group, checks the calculation (using a calculator) and states it is 126 cm.

When analysing the lesson, we noticed that the rectangle at the bottom of the arrangement is labelled incorrectly (the 12 cm and 9 cm should be reversed); however, this does not make a difference to its perimeter. There is a brief discussion about why the second arrangement is 6 cm longer, with children responding with 'the way it's set out', and others trying to find an extra 3 cm (twice) in the second diagram to give the extra 6 cm. There is not a discussion about the joins (where the rectangles are touching each other); here the touching edges are 6 cm, 6 cm and 6 cm but in the first arrangement

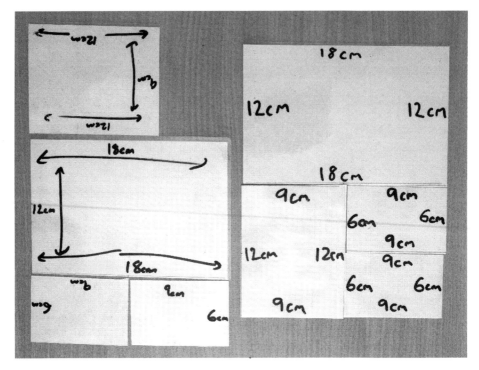

Figure 2.9 Smallest perimeter (Linda and James)

the edges touching are 6 cm, 6 cm and 9 cm, hence the additional 6 cm (3 cm twice) in the second arrangement. Looking at the joins of the shapes may be worth pursuing if we were to teach the lesson again, discussed more in the section 'Anchor task'.

The discussion moves on to look at the smallest perimeter. The teacher asks for two volunteers and the arrangements from Linda's group and James' group are displayed using the visualiser, this time side by side and compared (Figure 2.9). Linda comments that she is not sure if it is the smallest.

When one student comments that they think the arrangement on the right is smallest, the teacher asks 'Why does James's look smaller?' A student responds with 'just from the way it looks, it looks more compact', and another suggests, 'with Linda's, she put a big one on the top of it and that creates more length, whereas James's one is made into a square which creates less space'. There is agreement with this, after the teacher reminds the class it is a rectangle not a square. Another student shares that they did 'adding up' and confirmed that Linda's arrangement is 102 cm [it is actually 90 cm] and 84 cm for James; everyone is happy that the diagram on the right is confirmed as the smallest.

To summarise the task at the end of the lesson, the teacher asks, 'finally, what's the difference when we are trying to find the greatest perimeter and the smallest perimeter?' There are a few responses and one particular student responds, 'for the biggest perimeter try to make more lengths stick out and to make a smaller perimeter you need to make it more compact'. This is a good summary of the conversations that have happened during the lesson. More discussions could come from exploring the task further in different ways; some possibilities are discussed in the next section. However, this was an appropriate place to end this lesson summarising most students' thoughts.

Pause for thought

Consider the above lesson reflection and analysis.

- ★ How was the anchor task accessible and open?
- ★ How were learner's encouraged to share their ideas?
- ★ What were the critical moments?
- ★ How would you have responded in each situation?

What we have learned

Returning to the research focus, we initially reflect on the anchor task and whether it was sufficiently accessible and open, allowing a variety of approaches and then discuss the student reasoning that emerged from it. This is followed by a discussion of the lesson study process and the possible next steps.

Anchor task

One of the teachers commented during the post-lesson discussion that the students were particularly engaged with the anchor task and that having the laminated rectangles supported this immediate engagement with and understanding of what the task involved. Manipulatives, such as these laminated rectangles, can be used successfully, as seen here, to construct meaning and understanding during the concrete phase of the 'Concrete-Pictorial-Abstract' (CPA) approach used by many schools in Singapore (Leong, Ho & Cheng, 2015). CPA is an approach that is beginning to be more widely used within schools in the UK that are involved with mastery teaching.

It was also clear that students knew what to expect from the lesson and shows that they are being taught consistently in a mastery style. The students are all so confident at expressing their ideas; not just in response to teacher questioning but also unprompted they put their hands up to ask questions or just to explain a thought they've just had about the problem. They also speak sufficiently loudly for other students to hear (this differs from many classrooms where students direct their answers to the teacher). This suggests confidence, a high level of engagement and that they want others to hear their suggestions and potentially that they listen to others.

The accessibility of the anchor task was agreed by the lesson study team, as all of the students, including those that sometimes struggle with concepts, found at least one perimeter (84 cm for the original arrangement) and at least one additional perimeter for their 'greatest' arrangement.

The various arrangements discussed, within the previous reflection and analysis section, confirms the openness of the task. There was also potential for some students to develop reasoning and try to convince others of their greatest and least arrangements, with varying degrees of sophistication.

One of the common arrangements thought to give the greatest perimeter was to line the rectangles up from smallest to largest (or vice versa), see image from one pair (Figure 2.10 below). Students did not investigate what happened if the rectangles were in a different order, possibly because they believed that the perimeter would be the same and was not dependent on order. This order A, B, C, D has a perimeter of 120 cm; however, an arrangement with order A, C, B, D has a perimeter of 126 cm. Convincing others of this additional 6 cm could be done by comparing the joins (6,6,9 in the first arrangement and 6,6,6 in the second, as discussed previously).

Through the lesson study analysis, it was also observed that students were not able to translate edges across to help them see the perimeter. For instance, in Figure 2.11, students tended to go around the shape, needing to calculate

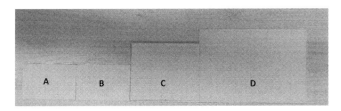

Figure 2.10 Common arrangement for greatest perimeter

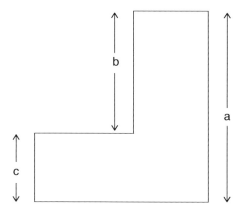

Figure 2.11 Conservation of length

the missing parts by finding the whole length and subtracting another length, rather than noticing that **b+c** is the same as **a** and therefore just doubling **a** (without the need to find the missing side **b** for instance). This could be an area that the teacher focuses on when circulating, is there a different/quicker method to calculate the perimeter?

Lesson study process

The teachers involved with the lesson study had previously experienced lesson study as part of the teacher training course with the authors and were aware of its potential benefits. They were also keen to adapt the anchor task and were therefore involved with the planning stage, developing the lesson, and deciding on the research focus. The post-lesson discussion focused on the research question but also some of the practicalities of the lesson and the lesson study process. The use of the visualiser was discussed; it was felt that this was a useful tool to compare two different diagrams but it was difficult to fit them both on the screen. On reflection it may have been more practical to reduce the size of the laminated rectangles given to pupils using a scale of 1: 0.5 (actual: laminate). However, this would mean that students could not measure missing lengths, so a set of smaller rectangles could be used when sharing with a visualiser, or larger rectangles to use on the whiteboard.

During the lesson study analysis, it would be useful to analyse all arrangements of the shapes, photographs of each arrangement for greatest and each arrangement for least would therefore be needed (we had many but not all). Having laminated shapes to move around supported learning but was more difficult for recording and research purposes. Consideration should also be given to how easy students would find journaling, when the writing up takes place in a subsequent lesson. It may be worthwhile having much smaller paper shapes that they can stick in their books, in addition to the laminates, to aid this part of the mastery lesson structure. This would also continue to support the gathering and recording of student work; an important part of the lesson study process.

Both teachers involved in the lesson study thought that this anchor task was much more effective than the previous one and it is now incorporated in the school's scheme of work. They will also be continuing to do further lesson studies whilst working with a partner primary school.

Next steps

If we were teaching the lesson again, we would encourage some students to explore the order of the rectangles as discussed under 'Anchor task'. Also, to consider why there is one unique arrangement for the smallest perimeter but more than one arrangement for the greatest perimeter.

Linked to the above, we would also focus on what the students noticed when they made changes to their arrangements. For example, the list below gives possible prompts to use when circulating.

- ◆ What happens to the perimeter if you change the orientation of one of the rectangles?
- ◆ What happens to the perimeter if you remove one of the shapes
- ◆ Is this the same if the shape is an 'end shape' or a 'middle shape'?

There is a need for some flexibility with how long you might spend with this anchor task. It could have easily been extended to a further lesson with some useful discussions, as noted above. In some schools this level of flexibility may not be available within mastery; however, the teachers here stated they would extend tasks when they felt it was worthwhile.

Pause for thought

Try the lesson with one of your classes. If you can use it as a research lesson using lesson study with a colleague, even better!

- ★ What would your lesson study focus be?
- ★ How would you develop the use of an anchor task?
- ★ What links can you see with other lessons in the book?

References

Department for Education (DfE). (2012). What can we learn from the English, mathematics and science curricula of high performing jurisdictions? Department for Education Research Report DFE – RR178. London (England): Department for Education. https://www.gov.uk/government/publications/review-of-the-national-curriculum-in-england-what-can-we-learn-from-the-english-mathematics-and-science-curricula-of-high-performing-jurisdictions

Leong, Y. H., Ho, W. K., & Cheng, L. P. (2015). Concrete-pictorial-abstract: Surveying its origins and charting its future. *The Mathematics Educator*, *16*(1), 1–18. http://math.nie.edu.sg/ame/matheduc/tme/tmeV16_1/TME16_1.pdf

NCETM. (2016a). Mastery explained. www.ncetm.org.uk/resources/49450

NCETM. (2016b). The essence of maths teaching for mastery. https://www.ncetm.org.uk/files/37086535/The+Essence+of+Maths+Teaching+for+Mastery+june+2016.pdf

Watson, A., & Mason, J. (2006). Seeing an exercise as a single mathematical object: Using variation to structure sense-making. *Mathematics Thinking and Learning*, *8*(2), 91–111.

Appendix

Lesson plan and resources

Lesson summary

Students combine four rectangles in order to make the greatest and smallest perimeters. They calculate missing edges and justify their answers. Laminated rectangles (manipulatives) are used to support understanding and engagement with the task.

Focus on students learning

a   Calculate perimeters of compound rectilinear shapes.
b   Communicate reasoning effectively to justify greatest and smallest perimeters.

Lesson preparation

Learners will need the laminated rectangles and whiteboard pens. You may wish to use a visualiser or larger rectangles to enable effective whole class discussion and smaller rectangles that could be stuck in the students' books.

The lesson

Stage 1: diagnostic question (optional)

If you wish to refresh perimeter of basic shapes, you could begin with a diagnostic question. In the lesson described we used a question on finding the perimeter of a triangle with lengths 3 m, 135 cm and 70 cm. A number of different answers are anticipated so time should be allowed for students to write down their answer and thoughts before asking students to share their thinking with the class. First, for the correct answer and then identifying possible mistakes in the incorrect answers.

Stage 2: anchor task

Anchor task for perimeter of compound shapes:

Rosa took a piece of paper that was 18 cm by 24 cm.

She then cut it in half, cut one of those halves in half again and then cut one of those halves in half again.

What is the greatest and what is the smallest perimeter shape she can make from the four pieces?

Rule: When positioning shapes they cannot overhang. The whole length of the smallest touching side must touch the other side, and a corner of each touching side must meet.

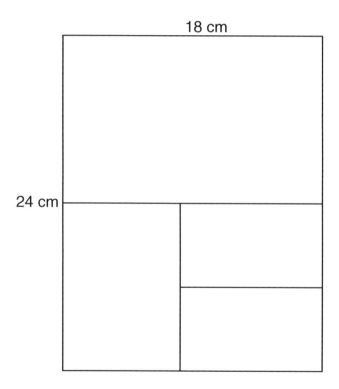

Before unveiling the question of biggest/smallest, ensure students understand the diagram by asking the class what else they know. Then discuss the rule, preferably illustrating by moving shapes on an interactive whiteboard, drawing what is and is not allowed, or moving manipulatives. Take questions to securely establish what is and is not possible (e.g. rotation allowed, all shapes must be used).

Provide students with cut-out versions of the shapes to manipulate. These can be laminated shapes to allow writing and rewriting lengths on the shapes, or simply paper versions (but have many extra copies if doing it this way).

Stage 3: pair work

Students work in pairs or in small groups to try and answer the question. There is a wide range of anticipated student responses: working out the perimeter of a shape where all sides fit neatly (e.g. the original); attempting shapes where missing lengths will have to be calculated; approaching the task of biggest/smallest via trial and error; and comparison with others; and developing reasoning about which type of joins will lead to bigger and smaller perimeters; convincing others, or even proving, that they have found the biggest or smallest. It is even possible to attempt to find all possible shapes that can be made (proof by exhaustion through being systematic), however given the many possibilities this is unlikely to be a practical approach here.

Stage 4: discussion and further pair work

After an initial period students share their approaches, and the working out of the lengths of the smaller rectangles. Students return to the task and record their findings. If anyone thinks they have found the greatest and smallest encourage them to try to convince you and explain their reasoning.

After another period, students share two examples of finding the greatest perimeter of a particular shape; either by using a visualiser, or through manipulating shapes on an interactive whiteboard (or large cut-out shapes stuck on a whiteboard) or simply drawn. Select interesting examples that give different perimeters, and encourage discussion; why one may be bigger than the other and what strategies may be best (hoping for e.g. larger sides exposed, fewer sides touching and length of joins). Repeat with examples for smallest, either immediately or after a further pair work depending on time.

Stage 5: journaling

Students write up what they have done and what they have learned (this may happen in the following lesson).

Possible extension

Is there a unique arrangement to find the greatest perimeter or would other arrangements work? What about the smallest perimeter - is there one unique arrangement or would other arrangements work?

Explain and justify your answer.

Suggestions for lesson study focus

You might want to consider these aspects of students' thinking:

◆ What arrangements do students make?
◆ How do students justify their answers for greatest and smallest?
◆ Is there a hierarchy in their justifications?

Resources

Slides

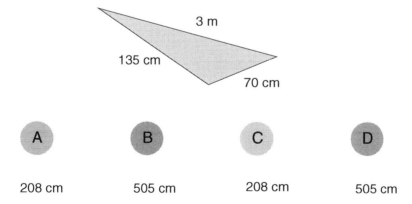

Rosa took a piece of paper which was 18 cm by 24 cm.
Rosa cut the piece of paper in half. She then repeats this twice.

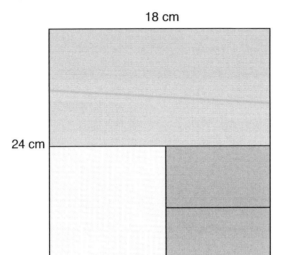

18 cm

24 cm

What's the greatest and what's the smallest perimeter that Rosa can make?
Two corners of a rectangle must be touching another rectangle at all times!

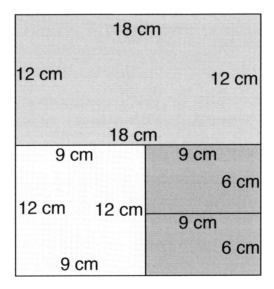

3

Developing understanding of fractions through context

Introduction

Within this chapter, we describe a lesson where pupils were asked to consider a real-life context to explore their understanding of fractions. The context allows the teacher to see what the pupils' concepts of fractions are; in particular about the 'whole'. The main role for the teacher is as facilitator, encouraging exploration of these ideas, provoking contradictions and exploring further.

The school is a relatively new primary/elementary state-funded school in the north of England. It has 60 pupils in each year group and serves a diverse community. The primary academy is on the same site as the secondary/high school and the schools work closely together to develop their mathematics curriculum. The class involved with this lesson study (LS) was a year 5 class (ages 9–10) with a wide range of attainment levels and 24 in attendance for the lesson.

The lesson study group consisted of the year 5 class teacher, their secondary school colleague and two of the authors. There was also a teaching assistant supporting the lesson. Both the year 5 teacher and their secondary school colleague had attended at different times a teacher professional development (PD) course developing multiplicative reasoning through lesson study led by the two authors present. The teachers were familiar with the lesson content and approach through this experience and the lesson study process. The primary teacher was currently attending the course and the secondary school colleague has taught the lesson many times to a variety of classes since she had been on the course two years before.

The lesson study research focus, chosen by the class teacher, was to step back as much as possible and not confirm whether a pupil's ideas are correct, verbally and non-verbally; 'hear it and move on', but value all contributions. His particular focus was on non-verbal communication. This intentional shift in pedagogy was intended to encourage pupils' independent knowledge formation rather than over-reliance on the authority of the teacher. The teacher's role and the observers' roles, in this case, were to focus on this and the contradictions/differences arising from the context of the problem.

Background to the lesson

The lesson discussed in this chapter was developed by Sue Hough and colleagues at the Manchester Metropolitan University[1] and formed part of a PD course facilitated by two of the authors. In this course teachers would be introduced to lessons and the thinking behind them by Sue. They would then adapt the lesson for their own contexts, conduct a lesson study with a colleague around a research focus and then come back as a group to further analyse and generalise from their different experiences (further discussion of the course and the theoretical understanding behind its approach can be found in Swanson & Morgan, 2020). The LS team's understanding of the research background to the lesson and the pedagogy used was, of course, heavily influenced by the perspective of its author, Sue and through our joint experiences on the PD course (for Sue's own 'background to the lesson' see Hough, 2013).

There are three key aspects to the lesson: (1) The use of real-world context to enable the mathematisation of students' own experiences and productions; (2) A focus on a particular conceptual aspect of fractions, the unit or whole; and (3) The use of contradiction to sustain reasoning and aid conceptual development. We look here at each of these aspects in turn.

The lesson was developed from, and within, a Realistic Mathematics Education (RME) perspective. The term 'realistic' in RME does not necessarily mean that the mathematics is connected to real-world experience, only that the problems are somehow real to students, i.e. that they can imagine them meaningfully. But, very often, real-world experience (or, similarly, connecting to the actual problems related to the historical human development of mathematics) can be the best way to make the problem or mathematics imaginable. This lesson focuses on the sharing of sandwiches to connect the formal mathematics of fractions to rich experience. Also, beyond that, it aims to develop a particular model to support understanding of proportional and multiplicative thinking, the bar model, through students' representation of almost rectangular sandwiches.

It is important to understand that concepts are not just formal abstractions that can be transmitted without their experiential content (for a more detailed discussion on this, see the background to the logarithms lesson in Chapter 11). RME has a metaphor of an iceberg with mathematical entities such as $\frac{2}{3}$ (or mathematical models such as the bar model) above the surface, while beneath are all the varied experiences, real world and mathematical, related to $\frac{2}{3}$, which support and infuse the formal mental object.

Sometimes, within schooling, connecting mathematics to experience can feel like sugaring the pill. For example, when dealing with percentage increase, teachers may use examples connected to student interests such as the cost of mobile phones to mask what is essentially a repetitive processing of rules. Sugaring the pill is not a bad thing, and should be much preferred to not doing it, but in this lesson we go beyond that to where experience is actually essential to the development of the mathematics, and there is no pill to be swallowed at all.

Disconnecting fractions from experience can have some negative consequences. It is the one piece of mathematical content frequently mentioned in early experiences of mathematics anxiety (see, for example, Jackson & Leffingwell, 1999). Students bring an almost qualitative understanding of halving, repeated halving and sometimes quarters from their outside school experience, but more complicated fractions are perhaps the first thing they meet that is abstract and detached from their own experience. School fractions can be too superficially connected to the human practices of sharing or measurement, or move too quickly on to abstract operations and manipulations.

One particular aspect of the fraction concept that can be lost is the notion of the whole or unit. Sharing, for example, is a human activity in which there is always *something* that is shared, the 'whole'. If we move from this human, or mathematical, *process* to the resulting mathematical *object*, or worse, try to teach the object detached from the process then we can lose all sense of the whole. This is particularly true if teaching, say, addition of abstract general fractions such as $\frac{1}{2}$ or $\frac{1}{3}$ where there is even less reason to be conscious that they represent $\frac{1}{2}$ or $\frac{1}{3}$ *of* something, i.e. of one. This lesson uses real-world experience in a way that necessitates developing a conscious understanding of the whole when, for example, the sharing of sandwiches can result in different correct answers where individuals get either $\frac{3}{5}$ *or* $\frac{3}{15}$, i.e. $\frac{3}{5}$ of one sandwich *or* $\frac{3}{15}$ of all the sandwiches (for a different problem that also draws out this understanding of the whole, see Swanson & Williams, 2014).

This use of contradiction and comparison is a key part of this lesson, and it appears (potentially) in other forms, particularly including in the potential answers of $\frac{1}{2}+\frac{1}{5}$ or $\frac{1}{2}+\frac{1}{10}$ (this is the key contradiction that emerges and is discussed in the lesson that follows). There is also much potential for discussing whether the many forms of picture students can draw to represent the sharing are the same or different, whether mathematically or in relation to the real life situation, and in whether $\frac{1}{2}+\frac{1}{10}$ is the same as $\frac{3}{5}$.

Such meaningful comparisons can help create a new perspective for students on their own productions and can lead to conscious generalisation (again, see the background of the lesson in Chapter 11 for more on this). The act of comparison can provoke more detailed attention to the particular solutions, and draw out aspects of the concept such as here, the whole. When two different answers emerge in any classroom it provides a great opportunity for further discussion and analysis, but this is even more the case in examples such as this where both answers are, in a sense, correct, as this can sustain attention and dialogue for lengthy periods given a quick resolution is unlikely. We will see something similar in a different form in Chapter 10's coin tossing lesson where an almost irresolvable problem leads to polarised positions that can sustain reasoning for hours or even days.

The essence of this lesson rests on students' own mathematical productions, infused with their own experiences, which are then thrown together through further meaningful problematisation to encourage a developing mathematisation and the deepening of conceptual understanding. Therefore the key focus for the teacher in this lesson is on not explicitly imposing their own understanding, but on encouraging all aspects of this process. The lesson study focus was therefore on this and what student reasoning then emerges. As authors, our initial experience with this lesson on the PD course had been with teachers teaching 11–14-year-olds. We then developed the course to also include those teaching 7–11-year-olds. We were curious, therefore, to see the differences in the impact of this lesson at this earlier stage of conceptual development of fractions and this will also provide a focus for our analysis and reflections.

Suggested reading

Hough, S., & Gough, S. (2007). Realistic mathematics education. *Mathematics Teaching Incorporating Micromath, 203*, 34–38.

Lamon, S. J. (2012). *Teaching fractions and ratios for understanding: Essential content knowledge and instructional strategies for teachers*. Abingdon, Oxon: Routledge.

Nunes, T., & Bryant, P. (2009). *Understanding rational numbers and intensive quantities*. London: Nuffield Foundation. Available at https://www.nuffield foundation.org/wp-content/uploads/2020/03/P3.pdf

Streefland, L. (1991). *Fractions in realistic mathematics education: A paradigm of developmental research*. London: Kluwer Academic Publishers.

Van den Heuvel-panhuizen, M. (2002). Realistic mathematics education as work in progress. Available at www.fisme.science.uu.nl/publicaties/literatu- ur/4966.pdf

Lesson outline

Students are presented with a context involving groups of people and sandwiches from which they develop strategies for sharing the sandwiches fairly (*this was done via a pictorial hand out and PowerPoint slide*).

In doing this they will encounter issues relating to:

◆ The language of fractions
◆ Naming parts of a whole – in relation to the whole
◆ Deciding whether different combinations of sandwich are, in fact, equivalent

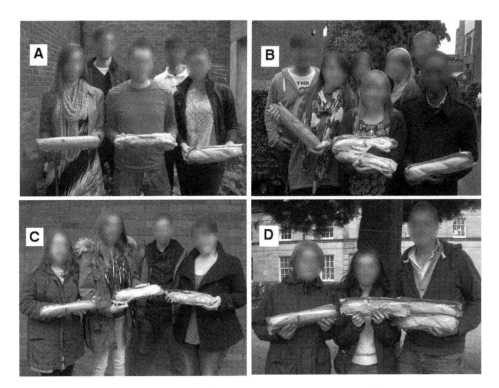

Groups of trainee mathematics teachers are checking some places suitable for a school trip in London. Different groups visit different sites. The university provides the teachers with some large sandwiches for lunch. The sandwiches are handed out as shown in the picture.

1. Which group of teachers get the most to eat? Explain your thinking
2. Which group of teachers get the least to eat? Explain your thinking.

Figure 3.1 The people and sandwiches slide

Potential key moments to consider and expected responses are discussed below.

Stage 1: presenting the context

The class are shown the four different sandwich scenarios (Figure 3.1) and asked to consider when sandwiches are shared out fairly amongst the people, which group gets the most to eat and which group gets the least to eat.

It is anticipated that pupils will find the first question easier, realising that in scenario D there are more sandwiches than people and in all the other scenarios there are more people than sandwiches. For the least they will be able to dismiss C, through comparing A and C, and will then focus their discussion between A and B. At this stage the teacher is looking for informal methods that can persuade other members of the class (the encouragement of informal arguments will require stressing), and would spend a brief amount of time on this to ensure enough time for later parts of the lesson. In particular, it is helpful if the idea of giving each person half a sandwich first, before worrying about the rest, arises here, to later allow a contrast when dividing each sandwich into equal parts.

Stage 2: drawing pictures individually to demonstrate solutions

Students individually draw sandwich-sharing pictures to show how they would share three sandwiches between five people, for situation A. Due to the level that some pupils are working here, some will be given the option of using cut-out sandwich shapes and scissors to support their learning. All students will have plain paper to record their diagrams on. It is anticipated that they will share in one way, either by halving and then looking at what's left or by splitting each sandwich into five equal parts. If these different methods do not occur, then the teacher will prompt students to consider a different way of sharing the sandwiches. They will also be encouraged to write down how much each person gets.

Stage 3: reviewing as a class pupils' pictures and pupils' justifications

At this stage the teacher will choose some of the diagrams to discuss as a class, looking for contradictions to explore (see Figure 3.2 for examples). Students may have $\frac{3}{5}$, some $\frac{3}{15}$ and some $\frac{1}{2}+\frac{1}{5}$ and others $\frac{1}{2}+\frac{1}{10}$.

  If these do not occur then the teacher can draw an example from 'another class' or deliberately write one of the above on the board to spark further discussion. The teacher may also decide to comment on the shape of the sandwiches, some more realistic looking and others more like a model. This stage

Figure 3.2 Types of student output

of the lesson, in particular, is an opportunity for pupils to develop a deeper understanding of fractions; considering 'what is the whole?' and whether fraction calculations are the same.

Stage 4: drawing more pictures and justifying solutions

There is a stage 4 (see lesson plan), where pupils can begin to look at other quantities of teachers and sandwiches, but the class teacher does not expect to move on to this in the lesson.

Pause for thought

Think about teaching this lesson to *your* class.

★ How would you divide the sandwiches in real life, and how many other ways can you think of dividing them?
★ Anticipate the responses that you would get from your students.
★ Considering these anticipated responses, how would you adapt the lesson for your class?

Lesson reflection and analysis

The teacher had been encouraging this class to explain their answers to questions and they were routinely asked 'why?' Early in the lesson, when asked 'what's sir's favourite word?' they all chant back 'because'.

The task is introduced to the class using the context of sharing sandwiches and the two authors present are introduced as the ones that have kindly provided lunch for the trainee teachers in the task. After reinforcing how many people and how many sandwiches are in each situation, the pupils are asked to discuss with the person near them, based on the number of sandwiches and the number of people in each group, which group gets the most to eat and which gets the least.

There is animated discussion between the pupils, and after a few minutes the class are brought back together to discuss their answers. One pupil says group D (with four sandwiches and three people) has the most because there are more sandwiches, the teacher then highlights the importance of both the number of sandwiches and the number of people, then another pupil shares that 'they have more bread than the number of people'. During the group discussion many pupils had commented that D was the only group that had more sandwiches than people. It is agreed by the class that each would have one sandwich and another part, some children saying halves others thirds.

The conversation moves on to looking at the least. One student, describing scenario B (four sandwiches, seven people), states that they would get 'half each, one half left to share'. Another explains that 'there are seven people so divide seven by four and each person would get one half and one seventh. Each person can't get a whole because there are three people left'. The fact that the student has said the division the wrong way round is not picked up by the teacher at this point ('hearing it and moving on' as planned). Most students seem convinced that the teachers in scenario B will get the least. The initial problem sets the tone well for the lesson and the teacher reinforces the context, explaining that sandwiches must be shared equally by saying that just because this person is tall, in scenario D, doesn't mean that he can get two sandwiches and the other two teachers only get one sandwich each.

Pupils move on to the next stage of the lesson, looking at scenario A (three sandwiches, five people) in detail and discuss how these sandwiches can be fairly shared out. Pupils are encouraged to show this using a picture, 'on the paper you have, draw a picture to represent how you would share the three sandwiches amongst the five people'. Any pupils who are not quite sure what to do are encouraged to sit together near the front of the class so the teacher can go through the task again with them. After a minute or so, all pupils are attempting this task, with some supported by cut-out sandwiches that they can split using a pencil or with scissors.

While circulating, it is clear that all the pupils are splitting the sandwiches into halves then trying to deal with the part that is left over. This may be because they were influenced by the description for sharing out B in the previous part of the lesson, or maybe because nine and ten-year-olds are just much more confident using halves. One student when explaining his diagram says 'I have a half and then a tiny piece'. On further questioning he can say it is a fifth but doesn't know how to write a fifth (as $\frac{1}{5}$). Another student explains that they all get a half and then a third and some other students are confident with a half and then another bit, but not sure what to call it.

The class are brought back together and pictures shared on the board. The teacher draws Aalia's method on the board (Figure 3.3), with each sandwich cut into half and each of those halves labelled 1, 2, 3, 4, 5 respectively, with the last one left for now. He asks her to come out to the board and show how she shares the bit left over. She splits the last half in to five parts and gives each person one of these pieces. Simar comes up to the front and says he uses bar

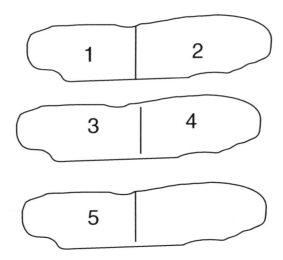

Figure 3.3 An illustration of Aalia's method

models to represent the bread and the people, so each of them gets one half and then he can use the last half; 'I cut it up into five pieces and give each person one piece, like Aalia did'. The class come to an agreement that Aalia's and Simar's approach are the same; each person gets a half and then we deal with the left over half. At this stage there is no discussion about what the pieces in the last half represent.

To encourage pupils to consider other ways of sharing out the sandwiches, the teacher asks the following question 'My question now is what happens if these three sandwiches were ham, tuna and cheese?' He follows with 'Bearing in mind that they have different flavours, how might you go about sharing it in a different way? Can you show me on the paper?' This uses a meaningful aspect of the real-world context to motivate further mathematical activity. Pupils return to working in their groups to try to find a solution to the new task. The teacher continues to support pupils in a group at the front, with the teaching assistant circulating and supporting a number of pupils.

A group of three pupils try initially 'halving it into three' meaning splitting it into three. Using the cut-out sandwiches they realise that not everyone will get an equal amount so then one pupil tries splitting it into five pieces and they can see that they will all get a bit of each sandwich this way. The cut-out sandwiches have helped them realise that they need to split them into five. One pupil in a different group cuts their sandwiches into ten pieces, with 30 pieces altogether. He explains that each person will get six of the ten pieces. This may be because he is more confident working with ten, or perhaps the influence of previous work on decimals. After a few minutes, the teacher interrupts the class and asks pupils to also write down how much each person gets. While circulating, he explains to one student to try to be a bit more mathematical than using the word 'pieces'.

The teacher then shows one student example to the class on the white-board using his tablet. He encourages a different student, Maryam, to share their representation with the class and it is also displayed on the board. When Maryam shares their diagram, she says, 'I gave each person three fives and they all got a taste of everything, so every person gets three fives'. The teacher encourages her to come to the front so she can point at part of their picture as they are explaining to the class. She explains,

> I cutted the three sandwiches into fives. Each person gets three fives … If I didn't cut them into fives it wouldn't be fair … I know my five times tables and counted up in fives and got 15, … and if I made them into one big sandwich, it would be 15 pieces and I would have given everyone three.

The student at this point sees the parts that she is describing clearly as five equal parts but does not yet have the language to describe these parts as fifths.

Speaking to the whole class, the teacher compares the two methods of Aalia (splitting it in halves) and Maryam (splitting in 'fives'). He asks two questions,

> (1) how much does each person get if Aalia shares out the sandwiches and how much sandwich does the person get if Maryam shares out the sandwiches and (2) what impact does that have on the flavours if they choose Aalia or Maryam's method?

Pupils work on this task in pairs/groups with the teacher and teaching assistant supporting for a further 5 minutes or so. The teacher and teaching assistant continue to support, for example, by giving a particular example so a student can see that it does make a difference with respect to flavours.

In one group we hear one student explain that they prefer Aalia's method as they get more that way; they get $\frac{1}{2}$ and $\frac{1}{5}$. In Maryam's method, they only get three fifths which is less than even a half. Another group is thinking about the difference between $\frac{3}{5}$ and $\frac{3}{15}$, as between them they have written both these values down. At first, they assume that they must be the same as the situation of sharing equally implies that they are (and they are, of course, but for different 'wholes'). In justifying this further one student draws comparison with how different methods of multiplication they have seen always end up with the same answer. Another then points out that five goes into 15 three times, using equivalence of fractions to justify that $\frac{3}{5}$ and $\frac{3}{15}$ are therefore the same amount. When asked to draw what $\frac{3}{5}$ and $\frac{3}{15}$ look like, to justify that they are the same, the clear difference in sizes drives them to think further. This leads one student to suddenly explain, that, 'if you're talking about all of them you get $\frac{3}{15}$ and if you're talking about one of them you get $\frac{3}{5}$' and he convinces the others that both values are, in their own way, correct.

The teacher brings the class back together and asks who would like to start. 'How much does each person get and what impact does that have on the flavour?' One student starts to explain Maryam's method stating that they get three fifths each, one bit of ham, one bit of cheese and one bit of tuna; person 1 gets one of each flavour, then person 2 gets one of each flavour … The next student explains Aalia's method and explains that everyone will get one half and one fifth. The teacher focuses on the fifth and asks what is that a fraction of? Is that a fraction of a whole? Pupils say it is a fifth of a half. Another student explains that if that was a whole then it would be tenths, while most are still focusing on a fifth of a half.

The class is asked to focus on the different amounts, in this method they get a half and a fifth and in this one they get three fifths, are they the same? If you think they are try to prove it. Do they get the same amount? One student explains that because we start with three sandwiches and share between five people then it has to be the same value however we split it (i.e. the real-world context is inside the mathematical equivalence). The teacher is trying to get students to focus on this contradiction about what is the part and what is the whole and allows the remaining few minutes for pairs, and a group of eight students working with him, to consider this contradiction.

Some pupils think it must be the same because of the context and others try to show it is or isn't through mathematics. There are a variety of engaged discussions happening in the pairs/groups. One student says to her group that it couldn't be the same because the half part is five fifths and then the extra fifth makes six fifths, which isn't the same as three fifths. Another group decides to try to put five halves and five fifths back together to make the three sandwiches to see if that will work. The group at the front works with the teacher who shows them why the small piece cannot be a fifth. He splits one diagram into tenths and shows that a fifth of a half is actually a tenth. He then asks whether $\frac{6}{10}$ is the same as $\frac{3}{5}$, and uses diagrams to help show that they are the same. Some of the pupils are convinced and others are still unsure.

At the end of the lesson pupils are asked to indicate how confident they are with their work but there is no further time to bring the discussion together. Throughout the lesson students were very engaged with the task and as we have seen all students, with a very wide range of attainment levels, could access the lesson.

Pause for thought

Consider the above lesson reflection and analysis.

★ How was the context used to support the development of understanding of fractions?
★ How was the learning facilitated during the lesson?
★ What were the critical incidents?
★ How would you have responded in each situation?
★ Were there any critical moments that were not anticipated by the lesson plan?

What we have learned

In this section, we begin by reporting what the classroom teacher felt they had learnt from their experience of working with this lesson and being involved with lesson study.

We then add some thoughts of our own on what we have learned from seeing this lesson at an earlier stage of schooling compared to our previous experience. We also share briefly an experience of extending the task further, when working with a year 10 (14/15 years olds) higher attaining class.

Personal reflections from the classroom teacher
He begins by giving his thoughts on the 'Fair Shares' lesson.

The thing that stood out the most was the way that the lesson was really engaging and they were going along with it, you know even those guys who tend to take a lot more motivating to get off the ground and then maintain their effort and their engagement. I think because there was a lot of talk and discussion and freedom, with how they kinda drew things out and … they took to that very well.

His reflections move on to consider what is different to 'normal' lessons.

I think the set-up of that lesson, the structure builds that into it, as opposed to a more traditional lesson that I've seen a lot of, which is this is the process, here's how you deal with the numbers, here's ten examples and then there's a word question to problem solve at the end. You're trying to find ways of weaving problem solving, collaborative work into that set up, as opposed to the sandwich [lesson] where it's there from the beginning, the lesson is set up in that way … the structure of it allows that to happen naturally rather than you trying to find ways … like I've got to remember for them to discuss their answers.

He also focused on differences he saw in the pupils.

I think, one of the main things would be the engagement and the way that it challenges children to have an opinion, cause they'll be asked about it or they'll be listening to other people and if you listen to other people you can copy that opinion or you can, you know, interpret it in your own way. So they are engaged because they are talking about it, they are having to have that deeper understanding rather than just reach the right answer.

He then reflected on the lesson study focus 'hear it and move on'.

Thinking back that's what I had been nervous about before, in my preparation. Sue had done the lesson, discussed it with you guys. I was concerned that, I always like to be very like; oh yes that's great, that's fantastic which alludes to, yes that's right … but actually the 'hear it and move on', I was concerned that that element was going to feel unnatural to the class and it was going to have a negative effect on the lesson, that was my A1 concern before the first lesson. That I was going to change the way that I was doing it, they were going to find that odd and that was going to be negative but actually, I think I found a balance where it was still Mr S_____ who can be really enthusiastic about what I'm doing but without guiding them to; that's good, that's right, I'm not so enthusiastic, therefore that must be wrong. I think that is probably one of the key things that helps keep the conversation going. They're more likely to share if they feel like it's not going to be a 'you're good – you're right', 'you're not good – you're wrong'.

Finally, he reflected on the lesson study process, initially focusing on working with a colleague and then the benefits on this colleague being from the partner secondary school.

That was of benefit. I think, that was really useful and it wouldn't necessarily have to be a secondary colleague … having that ability to bounce off someone is really useful they'll notice things that you might not have noticed or can kind of really give you courage … She [the secondary colleague] understands what goes on in primary and how that is useful and valued in the secondary setting. She's … a maths specialist, so I think as a generalist, as we are in primary, I think that was useful. Whereas, I would hope, that perhaps her benefit would be that more generalist pedagogical primary approach, that she can maybe borrow stuff from us.

Our reflections noted the differences working with primary pupils rather than secondary pupils that we have experienced this lesson with previously. These differences mainly linked to their conceptions of fractions. It was clear that splitting sandwiches in half was preferable to any other split. The challenge for some in sharing equally between five people, when they had to, was seen when some students used the cut-out sandwiches to enable a form of trial and improvement, not cutting into five initially but first three, then four, then realising it had to be five.

The dominance of halving would also be seen in their language with some pupils saying things such as 'halving into threes'. There were other noticeable uses of language, for example, when one student said 'I cutted the three sandwiches into fives'. First of all, we have fives instead of fifths here. But the non-mathematical example in this quote is helpful to look at as it feels there are similar forces at work. In using 'cutted', the student is, arguably quite sensibly, generalising the normal structure of the English past tense to 'cut', it's just unfortunate that the past tense of 'cut' is for some reason still 'cut'. In saying 'halving into threes', they are (rightly) seeing the similarity between the two processes of cutting into equal parts whether two or three, but as they don't yet have the word 'thirds' (similarly fifths in the previous quote), and because there is no word 'thirding' anyway, they use the best words they can in the situation, generalising their usage in a way that isn't technically correct, but still gets the sense across.

In such examples the students have a form of the concept, through their contextual and visual understanding, before they have the correct word for it. But the word will soon follow. In another conversation early in the lesson, where one student was similarly explaining to an observer how they were cutting into 'fives', the student who was sat next to him would pipe up with 'fifths' every time the other said 'fives'. By the end of the lesson the first student was himself confidently using 'fifths'.

There are processes of conceptual generalisation at work in the lesson that have some parallels with the processes of generalising words described above. In the example where one student arrives at an understanding of the whole ($\frac{3}{15}$ of all of them but $\frac{3}{5}$ of one of them), the situation had first driven the students to see that the answers must both be the same and thus equal. One student generalised between the two methods of sharing fairly and the experience of having different methods of multiplication which give the same answer. Another over-generalises one aspect of equivalent fractions (that five goes into 15) to back up that the values must be the same. It is the ongoing contradiction that makes them reach for these connections (whether helpful or unhelpful) to justify their thinking, and the contradiction eventually leads one to an explanation of how both answers can be right and the same, but different, i.e. an understanding of the whole. This understanding remains tied to the particular example, not yet generalised, and without the correct language as yet. This group when exploring the equivalence of the two seemingly correct answers $\frac{3}{5}$ and $\frac{1}{2} + \frac{1}{5}$ can't quickly use their understanding of the whole in this context to solve the contradiction.

Lesson study process

The difference in this lesson study from some others in this book is that the primary colleague who we were working with was more deeply engaged in discussions about both the thinking behind the particular lesson, and about the lesson study process, through the PD course he was currently attending. The secondary colleague had also previously attended this course, had experience of several lesson study cycles through that, and had deepened her understanding of the lesson in her context through her subsequent repeated teaching of it. One impact of this greater engagement was that the primary teacher, rather than the authors, decided on the lesson study focus, 'hear it and move on', as he was keen to work on this for his own development.

There were also differences through the adaption of the lesson for year 5 (ages 9–10) students. This mainly involved providing appropriate scaffolding, through practical and visual aids to support the pupils. We feel it was this age contrast with our previous experiences that led to us noticing, and trying to make sense of, the questions around language and generalisation discussed here.

Next steps

We hope that the nature of the tasks and problems in this book enable their use with a wide range of age groups, often from primary/elementary, through secondary/high school to post-16 students. Sometimes adaptation is required (e.g. the extra scaffolding used here), or some careful thought as to what opportunities exist for conceptual development at different mathematical levels. Sometimes this necessitates extending the central task with a new problem. We briefly outline one such extension to this lesson that we have developed and trialled with a high attaining year 10 (ages 14–15) class. This involves completing stages 1, 2 and 3 but then adding a new stage 4 focusing again on scenario D (Figure 3.4). This time students are asked to consider

Figure 3.4 Scenario D

sharing the four sandwiches equally between three people but only allowing (repeated) cutting in half (with the justification that cutting things accurately in thirds is difficult for some people).

Students can share out one sandwich each but are left with one sandwich to share between three. This sandwich can be cut into quarters, with each getting a quarter, and with a quarter still to share. This can then be cut into quarters, and so on to infinity. This leads students to see that each person gets $1 + \frac{1}{4} + \frac{1}{16} + \frac{1}{64} + \frac{1}{216}$.... as their share (Figure 3.5). They then compare this to sharing equally with any size cuts and therefore the share of $1\frac{1}{3}$.

When we tested this out, some students used a calculator to convince themselves that they were equal, while others were convinced by the situation itself that they must be equal (with strong parallels to the primary lesson above). Through this we can begin to develop an understanding of the sums of infinite series (such as $\frac{1}{4} + \frac{1}{16} + \frac{1}{64} + \frac{1}{216}$.... tending to $\frac{1}{3}$), grounding and infusing the conceptual understanding of that in the same real-world experience that helped bring meaning to the concept of 'the whole'. Students in this extension can then go on to look for other examples with a similar physical representation.

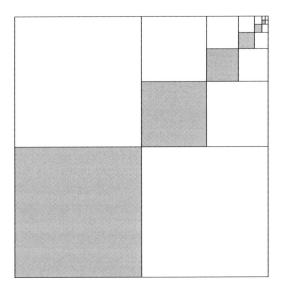

Figure 3.5 Tending to 1/3

Pause for thought

Try the lesson with one of your classes. If you can use it as a research lesson using lesson study with a colleague, even better!

★ What surprised you in the lesson?
★ Look at stage 4 of the lesson in lesson outline, what does this add?
★ How would you develop the use of context further?
★ What links can you see with other lessons in the book?

Note

1   The lesson was based on a 'Fair Shares' lesson from the Mathematics in Context series by 'Holt, Rinehart and Winston, developed by the Wisconsin Center for Education and the Freudenthal Institute.

References

Hough, S. (2013). *NCETM Multiplicative Reasoning – Fair Shares lesson*. Available at: www.ncetm.org.uk/resources/48479

Jackson, C. D., & Leffingwell, R. J. (1999). The role of instructors in creating math anxiety in students from kindergarten through college. *The Mathematics Teacher*, 92(7), 583–586.

Swanson, D., & Morgan, S. (2020). *Going beyond lesson study: Professional development courses and the systematic/scientific development of pedagogical understanding*. Manuscript submitted for publication.

Swanson, D., & Williams, J. (2014). Making abstract mathematics concrete in and out of school. *Educational Studies in Mathematics*, 86(2), 193–209.

Appendix

Lesson plan and resources

A detailed lesson plan, including possible extensions and suggestions for lesson study focus and all resources can be found at

www.ncetm.org.uk/resources/48479

4

Proportional relationships and the double number line

Introduction

Within this chapter, we describe a lesson where the Double Number Line (DNL) was used in order to develop multiplicative and proportional reasoning.

The lesson took place in a Japanese class with children aged 10 and 11. There are significant cultural differences compared with the English classroom. These differences have been analysed in Chapter 1 therefore we will not reflect on them here, as our main focus is in understanding how using the DNL (for example, Figure 4.1) can allow children to develop multiplicative and proportional reasoning.

The lesson took place in an elementary school in Tokyo, Japan with 28 students. An experienced classroom teacher, who had been teaching for over ten years and had taken part in several lesson study (LS) cycles, taught it. The title of this lesson was *Let's Think about Dividing by Decimal Numbers.*

It can be argued that this lesson did not go entirely to plan, as it left many children puzzled about the mathematics. However, the lesson was successful in valuing children's mathematical reflection and helping develop a climate for enquiry in the classroom. We intend to reflect here on the lesson, the role of the DNL and how the lesson could be developed. Within the chapter there are opportunities for you to reflect.

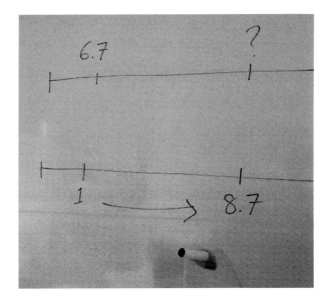

Figure 4.1 A DNL

Unlike most of the lessons in this book, the authors were not involved in the writing of the lesson plan or in the delivery of the lesson. However, the lesson and the lesson briefing were observed by one of the authors.[1]

Background to the lesson

This lesson was chosen because of its links with the DNL and the 'difficult' topic of proportional reasoning. Models such as the DNL can play an important role in the development of mathematical understanding. There are many different models that can help in relation to proportional reasoning: physical objects such as a piece of elastic; the bar model (see Chapter 3); ratio tables; straight-line graphs; and algebraic representations such as $\frac{a}{b} = \frac{c}{d}$.

Different models are useful for different situations, but more than this some models can be particularly good at developing understanding (see Van Den Heuvel-Panhuizen, 2003). The structure of such models must lie close to the structure of the problem and contain key aspects of the structure of more formal mathematical approaches, potentially allowing the classic transition from being a 'model of' to a 'model for' as they are used in an increasing variety of contexts.

There is always a danger, even with such models, that they can become a substitute for understanding, being an easily memorisable method for students this can fit equally well within rote learning. It is also therefore important that students have access to a multiplicity of models, and opportunities for the translation between models that can further deepen understanding (Lesh, Post & Behr, 1987). This can be done, for example, through asking students to explain each other's methods, or looking for a key element or number across different models, or weighing up which is the most effective model for different problems.

The DNL has been used to enhance students' understanding of proportional reasoning (see, for example, Küchemann, Hodgen & Brown, 2011); however, its use is not widespread in UK classrooms. The single number line, however, has been used extensively in UK primary schools; its use was developed following the National Numeracy Strategy (DfEE, 1999). The use of the single number line has been linked to a rise in facility with decimals (see e.g. Hodgen, Küchemann, Brown & Coe, 2009). Kuchemann et al. argue that the DNL could have a similarly dramatic effect. 'By the time students reach secondary school, multiplication is somehow meant to be "understood" and no longer needs to be supported by models'; there is, however, evidence that many secondary students have a shaky understanding of multiplication (Küchemann et al., 2011, p. 2). We argue here that the use of the number line alongside the modelling of the problem into a 'mathematical sentence' can support understanding.

In the example of a DNL (Figure 4.2) we see the illustration of a multiplicative relationship of ×1.5. The variables could easily represent quantities that are either extensive (directly measurable, e.g. distance) or intensive (compound measures, e.g. speed), although the model is particularly useful for illustrating an intensive relationship between two extensive variables. For instance, for speed we can see the relationship between distance and time. It is worth observing that the DNL only works for variables with a non-arbitrary zero and therefore can only support understanding where there is direct proportion. For further reflections on non-arbitrary zeroes the

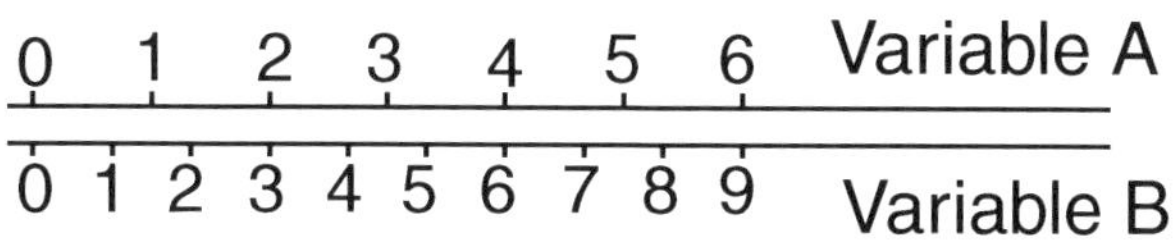

Figure 4.2 A DNL

reader can see Watson, Jones and Pratt (2013). The model implicitly shows the ×1.5 relationship for all values. Each number on scale A is mapped on to its equivalent number on scale B ($x \rightarrow 1.5x$, or $y=1.5x$). The DNL therefore allows building on the lower level proportional understanding within each scale to move toward an understanding of the proportional relationship between the scales.

The DNL has obvious links with the single number line and shares that model's strength in dealing with continuous variables and decimals (although as we will see in the lesson that follows this is not without complications). The DNL also connects well to other models; it can be used in similar ways to a bar model when, for example, numbers for quantity and price are written along the bottom and top of a bar, but can deal more comfortably with extending the relationship in either direction. It is similar to a ratio table but with the added support of ordering and scale, which can assist sense making. The DNL also shows the relationship between two variables as straight line graphs do, but places the two scales in parallel, evoking concrete experience with measurement, rulers and map scales. The DNL loses some of the strengths of linear graphs in doing this – particularly the explicitness of the between-scale proportional relationship and the ability to deal equally well with indirect proportion (i.e. lines that don't go through the origin, for an example see Chapter 8).

Students can have many misconceptions related to multiplicative structures, particularly when multiplying and dividing decimals, where earlier methods often fail. The DNL can assist in the development of multiplicative concepts through its close relationship to measurement and its concrete support toward seeing proportional relationships. When using it with decimals it also helps further develop lower level understanding, for example, in strengthening the sense of density of the number line and the importance of equal partitioning. The lesson below explores some aspects of use of DNLs in more detail. In doing so we hope to deepen understanding of its practicality in the classroom, and encourage a wider adoption of this and the other models of multiplicative reasoning.

Suggested reading

Küchemann, D. E., Hodgen, J., & Brown, M. (2014). The use of alternative double number lines as models of ratio tasks and as models for ratio relations and scaling. In S. Pope (Ed.), *Proceedings of the 8th British Congress of Mathematics Education*, Nottingham. http://eprints.nottingham.ac.uk/32202/1/BCME8-30.pdf

Lesson outline

The expected outcomes of the lesson are:

◆ Students can use the DNL to solve problems involving proportional reasoning.
◆ To develop the learners' skills in discussing mathematics through sharing their strategies and listening to other's ideas.

Potential key moments to consider and expected responses are discussed below.

The problems involve buying juice to share with everyone and working out which is a better buy.

Problem 1

Figure 4.3 The juice problem

1 L bottle costs 216 yen
2 L bottle costs 420 yen

This problem (Figure 4.3) involves whole numbers and it is anticipated that leaners will be able to solve this using a variety of methods – mainly involving halving or doubling numerically or physically, but some may use other models including the DNL.

Problem 2
1.6 L bottle costs 320 yen. Which is the better buy now?
What calculation do we do to find the price of 1 L of juice?

It is anticipated that leaners will find this more difficult to solve, as it can involve dividing by a decimal rather than a whole number. Some of their previous strategies will not work – e.g. making 1.6 equal groups. The use of the DNL and mathematical sentences will be used as a model to support learners' understanding.

Whole class comparison and summary
Ideas will be shared and leaners will summarise strategies used in their own words. This will be used to assess understanding and draw key points together.

Pause for thought

Think about teaching this lesson to *your* class.

★ Anticipate the responses that you would get from your students.
★ Considering these anticipated responses, how would you adapt the lesson for your class?
★ A recipe uses 2 kg of sugar and 3 kg of flour, but we have 3 kg sugar so want to make more cakes! (i) Use only a piece of elastic, a marker and a ruler to work out how much flour we will now need. (ii) Now try the same problem using a DNL.
★ Try and list some of the most common misconceptions encountered when dividing and multiplying decimals. For each misconception, think how the DNL could be used to scaffold understanding.

Lesson reflection and analysis

In discussions with the teacher, it was clear that he values learner contributions and that he also tries to focus on the students who say "I don't get it" during lessons. He encourages those students to clarify what they do understand and what they do not, so that the whole class can share the questions those students have. In this way, he believes, students' sharing has begun to shift from simply explaining their own ideas to making use of their own ideas to answer other students' questions. The teacher informed the observers that students have worked in this way since the beginning of the year; they are therefore comfortable working with each other and are keen to offer solutions.

In order to increase student to student interactions, during the whole class comparison and analysis of strategies, he told the observers that he often encourages students to sit in front of the blackboard with their own notebooks and pencils. He believes that through this students have become much more conscious of others and listen to each other more intently. In his words: 'Some students are now trying to deepen their own ideas and to generate new ideas as they listen to others'.

In the lesson, the first problem was answered in a variety of ways (see Figures 4.5 and 4.6) including some informal doubling methods. After writing the following on the board, the teacher took a number of responses.

One student replied 'A is 216 yen for 1 L, but B is a better buy because if you divide 420 by 2 you only spend 210 yen for 1 L'. Another student commented that B is the correct answer because even though you double the number of litres, you do not double the price. This episode of the lesson therefore was as expected.

Figure 4.4 The initial problem

Figure 4.5 Possible strategies

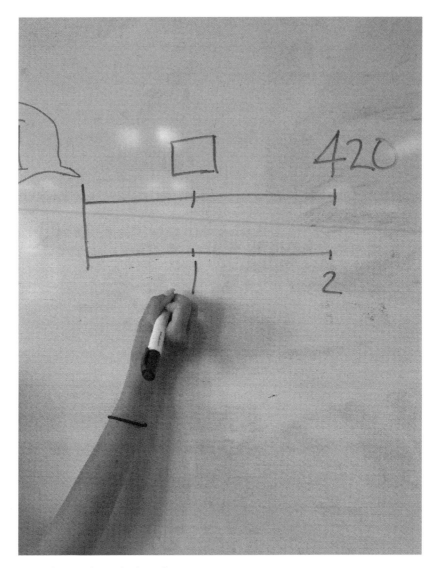

Figure 4.6 A student works on the board

The teacher asked the class how they could show their calculations worked, encouraging the use of a model. A student came up to the board and provided the following DNL example.

The student then annotated the diagram:

□ × 2 = 420
□ = 420 ÷ 2

Note that the DNL drawn has no explicit zero (but the line on the left may represent the zero). Also notice it only has two pairs of values and it does not extend beyond 420 and 2. Most students had drawn a DNL; however, interestingly, one student drew liquid containers to show their method; highlighting the fact that they felt more secure within the real-life situation and hadn't abstracted from this yet (for further examples of this see Chapter 3).

The teacher summarised the different ways of expressing 'divide by 2', including 'one half', 'to halve', 'split into to two equal parts' 'split into two equal groups' before taking another bottle of juice from under the desk and telling the children this was 1.6 L (Problem 2), see Figure 4.7.

Figure 4.7 The 1.6 L bottle

'1.6 L is 320 yen. What should I do?' 'Which bottle should I buy now to get the best value?' 'Can I use the same idea from before to find the per litre price?'

It was noticed that many of the students struggled to use their previous logic from the 2 L problem in this 1.6 L problem.

After a brief time of working independently the teacher asked the students for their thoughts. Most children said $320 \div 1.6$ while two children wanted to divide by 2. One child said he didn't know and the teacher told him, 'You will be a star in the lesson today'.

The teacher wrote the different ideas on the whiteboard (including the 'I don't know' response) and encouraged students to discuss.

1   $320 \div 1.6$
2   $320 \div 2$
3   320×0.4
4   'I don't know'

When asked to vote, many now went for the 'I don't know' option. Further discussion ensued.

One student said that if we divide by two we will know the cost of 0.8 L because the bottle was 1.6 L. However, this was not followed up in class and therefore the opportunity was missed to use the model of the DNL. If the DNL had been used to write this information on, then it could have led to the following diagram (Figure 4.8) and the question 'What else do we know?' This could then lead to 0.4, 0.2 and then therefore 1 (through combining the 0.8 and 0.2, or multiplying 0.2 by 5).

Instead, the teacher attempted to link the previous strategies used in Problem 1 when they divided by two and each time came to the conclusion that none made sense in the context of 1.6 e.g. dividing into 1.6 equal parts. The exception was $\div 2$, which could be replaced with $\div 1.6$ but while students

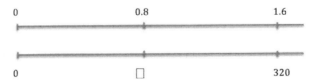

Figure 4.8 DNL for Problem 2

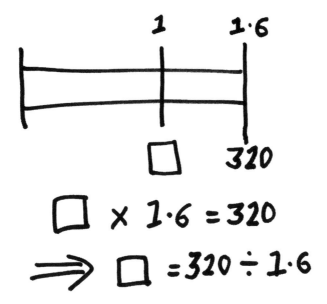

Figure 4.9 Student work

already agreed they should be trying 320 ÷ 1.6 to find the price per litre, they weren't convinced by this logic, and couldn't find a way forward.

One student came to the board and was given space to write their method (see Figure 4.9). The student used the DNL with an empty box to express his understanding. To go any further, division by decimals would have to be used to support drawing the DNL instead of the model supporting division by decimals.

The lesson was concluded with the teacher reassuring the students that dividing by decimals is difficult and they would discuss it further tomorrow.

Pause for thought

Consider the above lesson reflection and analysis.

★ What are the key points for reflection?
★ What were the critical incidents and were there any missed opportunities?
★ How would you have responded in each situation?

What we have learned

We will initially reflect on the use of the double number line as a model, and then discuss the lesson study process and possible next steps.

Use of models

Within this lesson the DNL was being used almost as a ratio table, with students and the teacher focusing on only two pairs of values on the DNL. This has lost many of the strengths of the DNL and limited its ability to support students' understanding. Would allowing more flexibility with the DNL strengthen the students' understanding? Extending the DNL beyond the marked numbers can encourage students to think of values higher than those provided. Would some students then be encouraged to think that 16 L would be 3,200 yen, and if so how would this help their understanding? Would 0.8 L costing 160 yen have led to 0.2 costing 40 yen and therefore 1 L costing 200 yen? Within the lesson the teacher used suggestions from the students but chose not to pursue some and focus on dividing 320 by 1.6. The model, however, as used in this lesson, didn't convince all students.

Lesson study process

It was clearly stated to us, several times, that the planning team had met on numerous occasions to discuss this lesson and the approach to divide by decimals. It was clear that the planning team had gained a lot from this experience and that the lesson was only the tip of the iceberg. In fact, the team had not only gained understanding by observing children learning in the lesson, they also gained a lot from the eight meetings before the lesson. Most of the observers had taught this very same lesson before and therefore could discuss it with insight. Furthermore, the fact that observers had a shared understanding of this lesson allowed the conversations to be deeper and therefore promote deeper understanding.

One of the observers asked why the teacher used 320 yen and 1.6 L instead of 330 yen and 1.5 L. The teacher responded that if the numbers were presenting a solution that was too obvious, the children would not have had a chance to really reflect on the meaning of division.

The planning team chose this research lesson because they believe the topic is difficult to teach. This highlights the importance of the choice of research lesson and that the teachers choose a certain topic because they feel they need to improve their teaching of that particular topic. This really helped the observers from the West to clarify the difference between a demonstration lesson, a master class and LS lesson (see Chapter 1). Observers are part of the process too and are invited to participate, in order to support the planning team and develop the entire profession not just to 'see how to do it'.

At the start of the lesson, when the boy said, 'I don't understand', and the teacher said, 'You're going to be the star of the lesson today', it became apparent that there was a community of respect and trust established. Also evident was that this was a classroom that kept students thinking, and had problem solving at the heart of mathematics instruction. Students in this community shared a responsibility for developing mathematical thinking and mathematical 'self-esteem'. When students engage in productive struggles that succeed, they own the ideas developed and when the mathematical ideas generated come from the students (and not the teacher) the understanding may be deeper.

The *Koshi* or knowledgeable other (as defined in Chapter 1) praised the teacher and the planning team for allowing the children to be involved with productive struggles. He pointed out that children's difficulties when choosing the appropriate calculation is a common problem in Japan and therefore praised the team on choosing this focus for their research lesson and gave suggestions to improve the research further.

In tackling a complex issue the LS process may give rise to a series of connected lesson studies. In this case there are interesting issues that can be researched independently of each other, such as the need for fluency of the DNL, the fluency of choice of operation, the need for a pictorial concrete stage before pictorial abstract. This process exemplifies that the LS approach is an ongoing process of research that often may raise more questions than it answers.

Next steps

If we were going to teach this lesson, we would ensure that the key strengths of the DNL are brought to the fore early on. For example, in the first problem, we would not just stop with the first solution but then have an open question of 'what else do we know?' Students could come to the board to fill in as many different pairs of numbers as they could on the DNL.

This experience would then help the structure of the DNL to support the solution of the second, more difficult problem later in the lesson. The students would have the model to fall back on as a means of calculating the $320 \div 1.6$ that they knew needed to happen.

We have adapted the lesson plan at the end of this chapter to introduce of this strategy, but as with all the lesson plans please feel free to experiment yourself with your own ideas and strategies.

Pause for thought

Try the lesson with one of your classes. If you can use it as a research lesson using LS with a colleague, even better!

★ What surprised you in the lesson?
★ If you were to introduce another different bottle, what size and price would it have? And why?
★ How would you develop the use of the double number line further?
★ What links can you see with other lessons in the book?

Note

1 One of the authors spent two weeks in Japan observing several lesson study cycles as part of the IMPULS Lesson Study Immersion program. The analysis was made based on the Japanese English translation provided by the program. The reader could also refer to Archer (2016) for more reflections on the Japanese model.

References

Archer, R. (2016). Lesson study, a trip to Japan. *Mathematics Teaching, 250,* 36–40.

DfEE. (1999). *Framework for teaching mathematics from reception to year 6.* London: Department for Education and Employment.

Hodgen, J., Küchemann, D., Brown, M., & Coe, R. (2009, September). Secondary students' understanding of mathematics 30 years on. In *British Educational Research Association (BERA) Annual Conference.* University of Manchester.

Küchemann, D., Hodgen, J., & Brown, M. (2011). Using the DNL to model multiplication. In *Proceedings of the Seventh Congress of the European Society for Research in Mathematics Education (CERME7),* 326–335.

Lesh, R., Post, T., & Behr, M. (1987). Representations and translations among representations in mathematics learning and problem solving. In C. Janiver (Ed.), *Problems of representation in the teaching and learning of mathematics* (pp. 33–40). Hillsdale, NJ: Lawrence Erlbaum.

Van Den Heuvel-Panhuizen, M. (2003). The didactical use of models in realistic mathematics education: An example from a longitudinal trajectory on percentage. *Educational Studies in Mathematics*, 54(1), 9–35.

Watson, A., Jones, K., & Pratt, D. (2013). *Key ideas in teaching mathematics: Research-based guidance for ages 9–19*. Oxford: Oxford University Press.

Appendix
Lesson plan and resources

Lesson summary

In this lesson, students work on dividing by decimals. The DNL is used as a representation of the context.

The context used includes comparing prices and finding the unit price.

Students develop the understanding that dividing by decimals is equivalent to dividing by whole numbers when finding the unit price and reflect on a possible algorithm for division.

Focus on students learning

- To use the DNL to represent the mathematical situation and help them explain the mathematical expressions.
- To build students' resilience and help them develop the ability to articulate thinking using mathematical terms by explaining how they extended their prior knowledge of division and multiplication by decimals to solve the given problem.

Lesson preparation

Students are familiar with the use of the DNL. In a previous lesson they should have learned that the positions on a DNL represented the size relationships of quantities and reflected on inverse operations by discovering that as the numbers on the top number line becomes 2, 3, … times as much, the corresponding numbers on the bottom line also became 2, 3, … times as much (proportional relationship).

Mini whiteboards can help students to work collaboratively in pairs or threes (only one pen per pair) and to readily draw their own DNL without having to be neat.

The physical model (bottles shown by the teacher or PowerPoint pictures) can help learners to keep focusing on the real life context.

The lesson plan

Stage 1: setting the problem in context
'We went to buy juice to share with everyone. We saw one package containing 1 L of juice and costing 216 yen. Another package contains 2 L of juice and costs 420 yen'. Question 1: Which package is a better buy? Question 2: Which package would you buy? Students think independently about the problem. Teacher circulates and makes sure students can use words, mathematical expressions and diagrams to explain their ideas. Have students think about the meaning of their expressions).

Stage 2: sharing understanding of the problem
Whole class discussion. Aim to draw the DNL on the board.

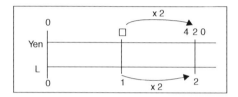

$$\square \times 2 = 420$$
$$\square = 420 \div 2$$
$$\square = 210$$

Encourage the students to relate the mathematical sentences they produce to the real world context.

Extend the problem by asking the students 'what else can you say about price and quantity of juice based on what is on the number line already', i.e. what other pairs of number they could put up on the DNL given what is already there. Possible hints include what if we wanted more or less juice. Try to extend this until a lot of the scale is filled in. If no one has added two pairs of values prompt this at some point, e.g. by saying we know 20 and 30 could we work out what 50 would be? Similarly encourage multiplication or division by numbers that are not 2. In most classes these suggestions won't need prompting if there is sufficient waiting time.

Stage 3: extending the problem
What calculation do we do to find the price of 1 L of juice if 1.6 L of juice is sold for 320 yen? Show this new bottle of juice (or picture of it). Learners

should work independently as the teacher circulates. Make sure students think about the meaning of the expression.

Expected responses: 'We are doing (price) ÷ L'; 'When we want to calculate the per unit quantity, we use division'. Encourage using models that they have used including the DNL. Encourage learners to help each other. Instruct those students who came up with their own idea to give hint to other students who may be struggling.

Stage 4: sharing of ideas

Encourage learners to relate their mathematical sentence to the context. If $320 ÷ 1.6$ emerges that is good, but try to keep the focus on using the DNL to find this, through proportional reasoning within scales. If students are struggling, have the students explain why they could not come up with their own ideas through questions such as 'Where are you stuck?' Make sure other students understand their questions. On the board draw arrows to highlight the common ideas between whole number and decimal number situations so that we can leave an explicit record of expansion of the meaning of division.

Expected responses:

> When we had whole numbers, we did (Price) ÷ L. For example, when the package had 2 L, we did $420 ÷ 2$. Even when the package contained 1 L, we can do $216 ÷ 1$. So, even though we have a decimal number, to find the price for 1 L will be $320 ÷ 1.6$.

> To find the per unit quantity, we used division. So, even when we have a decimal number, I think we can use division to find the per unit quantity. So, $320 ÷ 1.6$.

> I looked at the DNL diagram. When we had 2 L, arrows indicated × 2. So, if we have 1.6 L, they should be × 1.6. Since nothing else has changed, I think this must be correct.

> Because 320 is 1.6 times as much of the unknown quantity, $\square × 1.6 = 320$ So, $\square = 320 ÷ 1.6$.

> We could find 0.8 by halving.

> We could halve again to get 0.4 and again to get 0.2.

We could multiply 0.2 by 5.

We could add the 0.8 to the 0.2.

16 would be 3200.

If one solution emerges, encourage the students to find a different way of getting the same answer.

Stage 5: summary

♦ If there is time, introduce one or more new examples to consolidate the students' understanding. Try to summarise the student productions in the lesson and the development of the solution, linking what they did with whole numbers to what they did with decimal.

Possible extension

Based on an example, write problems that will be solved by multiplication or division of decimal numbers. They will solve the problems created by each other.

Suggestions for lesson study focus

♦ How does using context influence students' responses?
♦ How does using context help build students' resilience?
♦ What evidence can we gather that using the DNL enhances understanding?
♦ How can the teacher develop the students' ability to articulate what they do not understand?

5

Communicating mathematically about shape

Introduction

The task at the centre of the lesson in this chapter is a simple one. Pairs of students sit back-to-back and one student describes an image that only they can see while the other student attempts to draw what is being described. The amount of communication the students are allowed is increased over the task, with the student who draws going from not being allowed to speak at all at first, to being allowed to answer yes or no to questions, to being able to fully participate in dialogue.

Pause for thought

★ Look at the first two figures in Appendix B at the end of this chapter. How would you describe these shapes so that someone else could then draw them accurately?

The lesson took place in a special needs school, in Trafford. The school caters for students aged 11 to 19 who have statements of special education for moderate learning difficulties. Students have a range of additional complex needs including autism spectrum conditions, speech, language and communication difficulties, and physical disabilities. A significant number of learners have additional social, emotional and behavioural difficulties. At the time the lesson took place the students were working at entry level 3 in the UK. (For international comparisons this is the expected level in schools at age 9–11, equal to level 2 in international numeracy comparisons including IALS, ALL and PIAAC).

An experienced classroom teacher, who is also the Head of Department, taught the lesson. Two of our pre-service teachers, on placement at the school, were involved in the lesson study cycle along with two of the authors; and they all assisted the teacher in the delivery of the lesson.

The research focus of the lesson study was to look at ways to support learners in communicating mathematically and bringing to their conscious awareness how communicating together can also help them develop their understanding (a meta-dialogue about communicating mathematically). The class teacher felt that her students demonstrated skills well beyond her expectations during this lesson.

We will also reflect on the impact the lesson had upon the planning team and the student teachers in particular.

Background to the lesson

The precise origins of this lesson are impossible to ascertain. Like the original writers of *traditional* songs, whoever came up with the idea first has long been forgotten. Versions of the central task have been used in many domains, but particularly within teacher education. We authors have ourselves used this lesson many times, including participating in a lesson study group around this lesson in higher education, and we begin here with some of those experiences. That lesson study group included teachers of a range of classes, whose students were at a variety of stages on the path to (potentially) becoming teachers, from undergraduate education courses (likely to lead to primary/ elementary/middle school teaching), to subject knowledge enhancement courses (in preparation for a teacher training course in secondary/high school mathematics), and to our one-year post-graduate teacher training course (for secondary/high school mathematics).

For such university students, the key discussions we hope to elicit through engaging in the task are around the differences between monologue and dialogue, and how that relates to monologue and dialogue within the mathematics classroom more generally. Two key points tend to emerge from student discussions. The first is about how important it is for the describer to be as precise and clear with their instructions as possible. We found that the closer the students are to engaging in classroom practice the more frequently and strongly this will be expressed, no doubt due to the impending sense of responsibility to explain mathematics to their future students. The second point that arises is that dialogue makes things easier, more engaging (and more pleasant), than when only one person can speak. Here again, there are potential parallels to draw with the mathematics classroom. The first point could be argued to fit more with a traditional approach to mathematics teaching, with the teacher as expert passing knowledge on to students through the clarity of their explanations. The second seems to fit with different approaches, which emphasise problem solving, collaboration and an active role for students. Within the lesson we try to develop discussion around the possible contradiction between these two perspectives.

The type of conversation that pre-service teachers can have when engaged in the task would seem less likely to arise in a school mathematics classroom. Elements of this type of discussion might appear, however, such as awareness of the need for expressing thoughts clearly when engaged in dialogue. Alongside this, awareness of the relative clarity and efficiency of mathematical language can also emerge. In schools, it is also possible to develop discussions from the drawing task around a broader range of questions, for example, what counts as the same or different in the drawings; what makes some drawings easier or more difficult to describe or draw; and, what different strategies are possible such as giving, or not giving, an initial overview description before sequentially describing individual parts. At a basic level, the central task of back-to-back describing and drawing can simply provide opportunity to use and develop mathematical language within an engaging game-like task.

The importance of using dialogue in the mathematics classroom to help develop understanding has been a well-established element of the common sense of the mathematics education community since (at least[1]) the emergence of *social constructivism*. Social constructivism built upon *constructivism*, which asserted (and argued for recognition of) the importance of an active role for students in constructing their own knowledge. Social constructivism adds to this that individuals usually do not, and cannot, do this on their own, but do so as part of, and through, engagement in social activity. Where constructivism was influenced by thinkers such as Piaget, and had a generally individualistic, child-centred philosophy, social constructivism was influenced particularly by Vygotsky (and other authors such as Volosinov and Bakhtin), and had a philosophy whose starting point was the social rather than the individual.

Vygotsky's basic idea (put very crudely) is that everything 'inside' an individual's head arises first between that individual and other people within some social activity. If you think about all the words that you have used or read and understood today, it is extremely unlikely that you as an individual invented any of them. We have generally picked up all our words, and their meaning, from others while engaged in activity related to those words. Sometimes, such as in schooling, words and their meaning are deliberately introduced and explained by others in relation to other words we know. Also, when we use words ourselves, most of the time our choice of words is profoundly shaped by the social activity we are engaged in, and the individuals we are talking to. This dominance of the social, in our words and therefore our verbal thinking, doesn't mean we lose our individuality and uniqueness though. We are an active and creative part of the social experiences that shape us.

Grasping this basic understanding of how we are all fundamentally social is, however, far from understanding in a more detailed way how mathematical dialogue acts to develop the understanding of individuals. There are many interacting complex elements within any particular dialogue in a classroom including the immediate context, the nature of the activity engaged in, the history and understanding of the individuals involved, the structural elements such as the general nature of schooling, power relationships and so on. If we want to understand how understanding develops through dialogue then these complexities present within any dialogue can feel overwhelming.

The drawing task described here simplifies many of those elements, present in most dialogue, to an extent. There is a clear and simple activity, which, if students are engaged in it, can perhaps let us ignore much that lies beyond it; although the individuals involved in the task will be as rich and complex as ever, their vocabulary within the dialogue will usually be restricted to that which is relevant to the task at hand. Such restrictions can make the task of analysing some real-life mathematical dialogue easier, and may lead to insights. So, just as the task gives a way in to begin discussing the role of dialogue within the classroom for teacher educators, within schools it also provides a way in to exploring in a more detailed way how dialogue actually works in the classroom.

This lesson study explores these questions further. We worked with a class in a special needs school hoping that this particular perspective, less typical in our experience, may lead to general insight.

Visualisation is seen as an important and powerful aspect of mathematical thinking, particularly when integrated with social dialogue. Johnston-Wilder and Mason (2005) describe how simply describing what is seen, or making judgements on what is seen, can make attention more specific and more conscious and deliberate. In this lesson, we see those processes in relation to simple and clear examples of shapes, the words used to describe them and the thinking behind the words.

As Tasova and Delice state 'visualisation can play a significant role in the development of thinking or understanding mathematical concepts' (Tasova & Delice, 2012, p. 297).

Suggested reading

Johnston-Wilder, S., & Mason, J. (Eds.). (2005). *Developing thinking in geometry*. London: Sage.

Palmer, S., & Dolya, G. (2004). Freedom of thought. *Times Educational Supplement*, 30. Available online: www.tes.com/news/freedom-thought

Ryan, J., & Williams, J. (2007). *Children's mathematics 4–15: Learning from errors and misconceptions*. London: McGraw-Hill Education.

Stewart, T. T. (2010). A dialogic pedagogy: Looking to Mikhail Bakhtin for alternatives to standards period teaching practices. *Critical Education*, *1*(6), 1–20.

Tasova, H. I., & Delice, A. (2012). An analysis of pre-service mathematics teachers' performance in modelling tasks in terms of spatial visualisation ability. *Research in Mathematics Education*, *14*(3), 297–298.

Lesson outline

The expected outcomes of this lesson are that the students will develop their communication skills and strategies through describing mathematical shapes. Potential key moments to consider and expected responses are discussed below.

The tasks involve students, in pairs, sitting back-to-back trying to describe and draw a mathematical diagram. The task is initially modelled for the class. In what follows, students describing the diagram are called 'describers' and those listening and trying to draw the diagram as 'drawers'. A variety of diagrams were used, see resource sheet in Appendix B.

Stage 1: describer allowed to talk but drawer not allowed to talk

One student from the pair starts by describing the diagram they have been given to their partner (the drawer). They are sitting back-to-back so that the drawer cannot see the diagram and the describer cannot see what is being drawn. During this first stage the drawer cannot talk. After this first example, the students can swap over their roles and try another diagram before moving on to the next stage. It is anticipated that students will find this first stage more difficult and possibly frustrating and will not be able to replicate the actual diagrams.

Before stage 2 the class is brought back together for a whole class discussion on how they have got on so far, focusing on what is the same and different between the original drawing and the end result. It can also be useful at this stage to discuss how the experience felt, for both describers and drawers, and why.

Stage 2: both describer and drawer allowed to talk

This stage is modelled prior to the students engaging with the task (although modelling is not necessary for higher attaining groups). Again, the students sit in pairs, back-to-back, but this time the describer can ask questions and expect a reply, 'Do you understand?', 'Are you ready to move on?', etc. Also the drawer can ask questions and clarify any of the instructions that are unclear to them. During this stage, we anticipate that students will develop their strategies and questions to enable them to get a diagram that more closely replicates the original. It is possible to also use an intermediate stage before this one, where describers are allowed to ask yes or no questions, and drawers are allowed to speak, but only to say yes or no.

Stage 3: whole class discussion

This will be used to summarise key points related to strategies used during both stages and highlight the development of language both mathematical and instructional. We anticipate that attention will become more specific and conscious through the task and that language use will develop.

Pause for thought

- ★ Think about teaching this lesson to *your* class.
- ★ What mathematical thinking, language use, or metacognitive awareness would be a useful focus for your students?
- ★ Anticipate the responses that you would get from your students.
- ★ Considering these anticipated responses, and your focus, how would you adapt the lesson for your class?
- ★ Try and list some of the most common misconceptions encountered when describing shapes. For each misconception, consider how visualisation could help dealing with them.
- ★ Consider key words used when describing shape, how can these cause misconceptions?

Lesson analysis and reflection

The class teacher had been teaching this group for the past five years; therefore, she knew them extremely well and had established a very strong working relationship with them. She told us that she often has mathematical discussions with them and that there is a strong sense of trust and respect in the class. There were only 8 students, aged 15 to 16, in the class, with a teaching assistant who supports the class every lesson. The teacher was confident in their dexterity and did not envisage any problems caused by the act of drawing. There was a student in the class who is a selective mute; however, at the time of the lesson she was starting to feel more comfortable and occasionally spoke.

Before starting the first activity, the teacher told the learners she expected them to communicate with each other during the lesson. Then, the two pre-service teachers, 'Miss and Sir', modelled the activity for the students. Before starting, the teacher asked them if they believed 'Sir' would be able to draw (Figure 5.1) what 'Miss' described and they all said no. We believe, at this point the students were already imagining doing the activity themselves and perhaps feeling they did not have the mathematical language to complete the task.

Miss and Sir had not seen the shape they were going to draw in advance but still managed to produce a picture that was almost identical to the original (this doesn't happen often in this lesson), with Sir having stayed silent throughout the task. The students were shown the result and they all cheered.

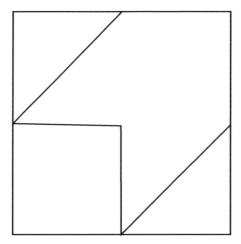

Figure 5.1 Miss and Sir draw this shape

To help focus the students on thinking about the activity, the teacher asked, 'did Miss explain it well or was it Sir that did a good drawing?' Worried about having sufficient time to complete the lesson, the teacher let the students think about that for a moment before moving on to attempting the task themselves. The students were reminded once again that drawers were not allowed to talk or ask questions, and describers were not allowed to look at their partner's attempted drawing until the end of the task. One of the students asked: 'What if they are doing it wrong?' and the teacher replied: 'It doesn't matter, there is no right or wrong', which visibly relaxed many of the students.

Different pairs of students were given different shapes, with the set of pictures colour-coded so the teacher could decide which shape was appropriate to give to each pair. In the planning stages we decided to give students different sets since we were concerned their descriptions might be affected by overhearing what other pairs were doing. We observed, however, that all pairs were engrossed in the task and almost forgot that other groups around them were also completing the activity. In the planning meeting, we also discussed which shapes to give the students and decided to stick to simpler shapes such as squares, rectangles, triangles, and circles. There was an adult observing the interactions of each pair; however, they all (including the teaching assistant) had been told not to intervene with the activity unless they were off task or breaking the rules, and to allow the students to work independently. We had worried that the two pre-service teachers modelling the activity so effectively might have hindered reflection on the activity or influenced the students too directly causing the class to imitate the language that they had used; however, this didn't happen.

The opening lines of the describers were[2]: 'On the right-hand side of the paper there's a square'; 'There's a square and there's another square diagonal'; 'There's four squares'; and 'Draw a medium square'. Only one of the pairs had therefore given any indication of size before moving on to describe the next part of the shape, none had given any sort of advanced overview of the drawing, but most had broken the drawing down sufficiently to give their partner one clear thing to draw.

Once the drawing had been completed each adult working with the pairs asked them to decide if the resulting drawing was close to the original and to explain their answers. The intention was to allow the learners to observe what was similar and what was different. They also asked both the describer and drawer what they would have said differently if they were asked to do it again. The main issue that students noticed were discrepancies in size, with the pair where the describer had used the word medium being the exception. During the rest of the lesson, using the words small, medium, or large to represent size, the most common strategy used to indicate size, seemed to work sufficiently for students to see the resulting drawing as the same.

Now the teacher brought the class back together and asked them: 'What did we get right?' Some learners observed that they had got the shapes right, and the teacher congratulated them for recognising mathematical shapes. The learners suggested that they did not get the size quite right and at this point it was agreed that asking questions would have helped.

The students in this class are said to have significant difficulties with long-term and working memory so the teacher felt they would benefit from a quick reminder of key words, and displayed some on the whiteboard (Figure 5.2). We wondered whether sharing these words might restrict the students' creativity and shape their language too directly, and we return to this question at later points in the discussion.

Now Miss and Sir demonstrated the activity again, this time with roles reversed and with both being allowed to talk freely. The class teacher asked the students to listen in for good communication. The students had been working on measuring and estimating lengths in the week previous to the

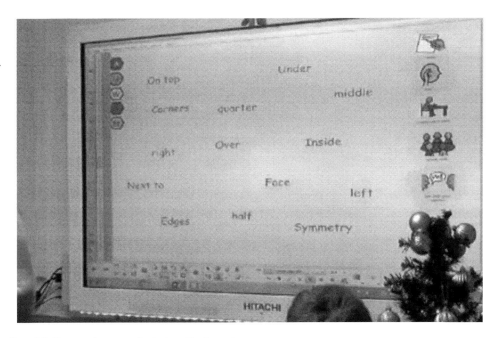

Figure 5.2 Key words are projected on the board

lesson and had practised using their bodies to estimate lengths. The teacher reminded them that their index finger was roughly one centimetre wide, which would lead some of the describers to use their finger to estimate the length of the sides. The teacher also reminded them again to talk to each other and to look at the key words on the board for inspiration.

Now that the drawers were allowed to ask questions, the selective mute was initially not confident to speak up so she whispered her instructions to Sir who repeated them for the describer. Eventually, though, she became so engrossed in the activity that she began to speak to the drawer directly.

There was clear evidence that their work improved once they were allowed to ask questions and ask the describer to clarify instructions. Students also became attentive to aspects that had led to errors in previous drawings. For example, in their first attempt, when describing Figure 5.3, one pair had described and drawn a square with a diagonal line. The describer then simply said 'and draw the circle on the left-hand side and then you're done'. This led to the drawer drawing a much smaller circle near the left-hand corner that didn't touch the sides of the square, and was far from touching the diagonal line (Figure 5.4). In their second attempt (trying Figure 5.5), having drawn 'a diamond' and being asked to draw a square 'over it', the drawer (in the same role as last time) asked, 'touching the sides?'

The adults working with the pairs again asked the learners to reflect on what was similar and what was different between the original and the drawing. One pair reflected on the main difficulty in Figure 5.5 being how much the inscribed square had been rotated, 'because it was turned but it wasn't

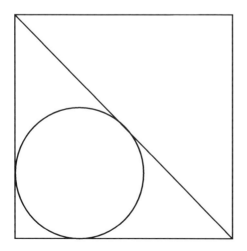

Figure 5.3 Shape with square and circle

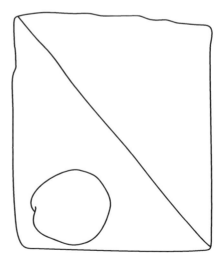

Figure 5.4 Student's drawing

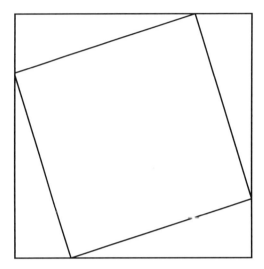

Figure 5.5 Inscribed square

a diamond exactly'. Her partner agreeing that 'if it was a diamond I would have gotten that!'

Once the class was brought together the idea of measuring was mentioned again. The learners also suggested measuring angles. Different drawings were shown to the class and learners explained how they managed to communicate certain features of the shapes, like size of lines and angles. The teacher asked the learners about 90°, 180° angles in terms of turns. Learners volunteered answers and the teacher used her body to visualise such angles. When questioned, at this stage, the learners were aware that their work had improved.

Learners now went back to working in pairs, swapping roles if they hadn't already. At this point we observed that, once they had completed the task, learners were independently commenting on what was similar and what was different between the original and the drawing and some of them suggested questions they could have used.

Language use continued to evolve through the task for individual students. Earlier, when the teacher had shown possible words they might use, she had checked whether the class knew what *quarter* meant. At that point most seemed to, but the teacher had explained to one student who looked confused by drawing a shape and describing cutting it into halves, and then cutting it in 'four pieces that are the same'. A little later, a pair on their third drawing encountered a square cut into quarters (Figure 5.7). But on being told to 'do quarters in it', the drawer asks 'what's a quarter?' The describer

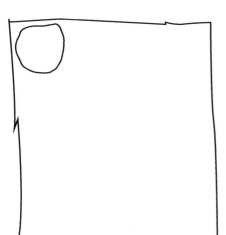

Figure 5.6 Student's drawing

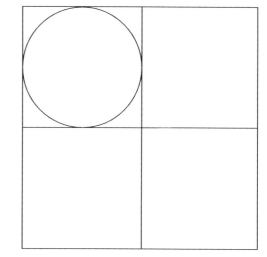

Figure 5.7 A square divided into quarters

struggles to explain: 'basically it's a line down and a line … how do you explain it now?' The drawer then (confidently) guesses wrongly what it might be (see the diagonal line at the top corner of Figure 5.6). However, seeing the original drawing (Figure 5.7) at the end of the task is sufficient for her to learn (or presumably re-learn) what quarters mean in practice. When that same student, now in the role of describer, attempts Figure 5.8 as the pairs' fifth drawing she says, 'Draw a medium-sized circle … inside middle do a little circle', and then, confidently, 'then do quarters'.

The class came together again at the end of the lesson. The teacher asked: 'were any shapes easier than others?'

Learners agreed that they did not do so well when drawing the shape in Figure 5.5 but did a lot better when drawing the shape in Figure 5.8. One of the learners observed that this was because the shape in Figure 5.8 was symmetrical, and another that when the shapes were rotated from their usual perspective the drawings were more difficult (students are sometimes exclusively shown squares, for example, which have a base parallel to the horizontal). The teachers went through a few shapes on the board and asked the learners to think about which words made the description easier. One of the boys remembered that they learned in art about an artist who drew circles and squares and connected this with a shape from the lesson. We believe he was referring to the painting *Squares with concentric circles* by Kandinsky.

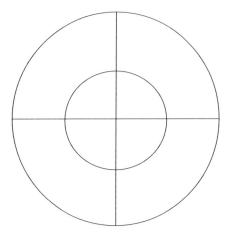

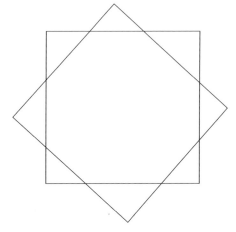

Figure 5.8 Concentric circles

Figure 5.9 Two squares

One of the learners told the class how it had been helpful to imagine the shape before beginning the description. He said that before describing the shape in Figure 5.9 he had told the drawer to imagine the Star of David but with squares instead of triangles. This was, we believe, a significant critical moment in the lesson where some learners had begun to use their previous experience outside the mathematics classroom to think mathematically, could bring this process to conscious awareness, and explain what they had done to the rest of the class. The class teacher and the planning team agreed during the post-lesson discussion that a few of the learners, but not all of them, had used this type of strategy to complete the task, something the planning team had not anticipated for these students. With hindsight, this student's strategy perhaps could have been shared within the class earlier to see if this kind of strategy would be developed by others.

At the end, all learners agreed that they liked this lesson. One of them told the teacher it helped them understand the importance of paying attention to detail while the boy who mentioned the Star of David said that the lesson helped him expand his imagination.

Pause for thought

Consider the above lesson reflection and analysis.
- ★ How was the mathematical language developed?
- ★ What were the advantages and disadvantages of providing key words?
- ★ How was language brought to consciousness for the learners?
- ★ How would you have responded in each situation?

What we have learned

We will initially reflect on the importance of dialogue within the lesson, then our thoughts on the lesson study process, followed by possible next steps.

Dialogue within activity

We all judged this task as very engaging for these learners, and given we have seen similar engagement with the task at university level, perhaps for all learners. This was noticeable for all students in the class but was exemplified by the student who was described as the selective mute in the class. She started off by whispering in a trainee teacher's ear when she had to describe, who would then amplify her words to her partner. She became more audible when they enthusiastically discussed their first results and mistakes. She still avoided being the describer for most of the lesson, but near the end the pair of students described a shape together for one of the trainee teachers to draw. At first she took a back seat in this, but as she disagreed with some of the descriptions being given she became animated and even loud, taking over the describing from the other student.

Such engagement is, of course, useful in any learning experience, and much effort should be made therefore to find and design mathematical tasks that are engaging, but it is the specifics of how the task engaged that is particularly relevant for us here. Students had the freedom to describe shapes how they wanted, with few, if any, negative consequences for any mistakes, as mistakes were very much expected and valued. Having concentrated on describing or drawing they then received instant feedback in visual form when comparing the drawing they produced with the original, and motivated to try another, they would then act upon the things they had noticed, through asking questions or developing their use of language.

As we have seen, what was noticed and acted on early on were simple factors such as the size of the shape, and whether, and where, shapes were touching. As the lesson developed, words that students had little or no prior grasp on began to be used with confidence. The example of this above where students developed their use of 'quarter' offers more general points. The word and its meaning had previously been introduced by the teacher to no effect for one of the students. This may be because the student hadn't been paying attention, or because of the limitations of attempts to directly transmit concepts. Either way, the engagement with this task with its necessity for communication, combined with the visualisation aspect, enabled this student to go on to use the concept in a confident and meaningful way.

The power of visualisation as part of this process is also seen in her partner's behaviour. She could quite confidently use 'quarter' in practice much earlier, but yet struggled to put what the concept meant into other words that would help. In general, it is a big shift from being able to use a concept to being able to describe that concept.

This task provides opportunities for making that shift, particularly when students discuss their results. It partly does so because students can experience and use concepts first, so they have something to build on and then make sense of. When looking to help students develop mathematical concepts it can be useful to begin with the experiential, concrete side of concepts, and then to provide space and motivation for students to reflect, verbalise and so make that experience more conscious.

Omitting the experiential side makes learning harder than it needs to be for students.

As the lesson progressed, students began noticing, communicating and acting on more complicated aspects of the task. This included mathematical aspects such as rotation and angles, but also more meta-aspects such as developing and communicating strategies and reasoning about what made some shapes harder than others (what some call 'higher order thinking').

These expressions of meta-awareness in relation to the immediate task were surprising for some of us involved in this lesson study. Particularly since it was also observed that they were little, if at all, influenced by their perception of how their partner would imagine the shape. In discussions, the students were able to reflect on how and why they did not get the right shape when drawing, or how they could have described it differently when describing, but they rarely articulated what may have gone wrong from the other person's perspective. This contrasts with our experience of university students, particularly those training to be teachers who are driven by the task and their context to see things more from the other person's perspective. As one university student described the task in a previous lesson study within university:

> It made me think a lot about my use of mathematical language and context so that the drawer would understand me … It made me reflect what it would be like as a teacher to explain to others and also what I could improve with my own perception of myself.

Without the additional motivation that pre-service teachers may have, it is still useful for students to be able to distance themselves from their own immediate perspective. For the students discussed in this chapter the development of some forms of meta-perspective and distance from the immediate, through comparing shapes or discussing strategies perhaps provides some useful steps towards this. It would be interesting to explore this question in other contexts too.

The lesson study process

Involving two pre-service teachers and their mentor in the lesson study was different to some of our other LS experiences. The two pre-service teachers had also been involved with the lesson when it was modelled and discussed as part of their university teacher training course, so were familiar with it. We share some of their reflections below.

During the post-lesson discussion the teacher (mentor) told the team that she felt the learners initially struggled to ask questions because they were not sure what to ask but with prompting from the adults they developed their questioning. She said this lesson had helped her realise that we, as teachers, don't often take time to allow learners to develop the skill of asking questions and how important that was. Students can answer questions but rarely have opportunities to use questioning to challenge their own understanding.

One of the pre-service teachers involved shared their thoughts on the experience:

What I found interesting about the lesson study experience was having the freedom to focus on one particular aspect of teaching. At that time when I was teaching I was trying to do 500 different things at once, and behaviour is always a dominating focus in lessons. Having that stripped away and being able to focus on pedagogy instead was helpful for me. And observing learners and their dialogue in the lesson was really helpful for me and it gave me insight into what goes on in a classroom from the students' perspective rather than just looking at what the teacher is doing. The main parallel I see between learning to teach and learning maths is that neither is a spectator sport. Students gain very little from watching mathematics being done, as trainees gain limited amounts from just learning about teaching without any practice. And I partly realised this from the lesson studies where the focus was shifted from what the teacher was doing, to analysing what was going on with the learners. And in general I think that it's good to be reminded during your time as a trainee when you are so conscious and aware of yourself that what is going on in the students' heads is far more important than what you are doing.

Finally, we observed that all those involved gained insight through the experience. The extent of the insights gained varied partially on the basis of the extent of their involvement in the elements of the lesson study process and their previous experiences of the lesson and lesson study. We authors are arguably the only ones who get the full lesson study experience here, from conscious design of the lesson through to the generalisations made through writing up what we have learned. We have often been surprised, and have learned much from those who have shared part of the journey with us. We discuss these questions further and in particular what role writing up can play in the lesson study process in Chapter 12.

Next steps

One of the ways we would develop our thinking further would be by conducting a more in-depth analysis into the changes in dialogue through the different stages of the lesson. One way of having more conscious discussion about dialogue with students in the classroom would be to have an observer (as well as a drawer and a describer) who has the task of capturing the processes involved. A group of pre-service teachers tried this approach in their own lesson study. After reflecting on an initial lesson they devised an observer recording sheet; the aim of this sheet was to stop the observer being drawn into the activity too much and to focus their reflection, see Appendix C.

Pause for thought

Try the lesson with one of your classes. If you can use it as a research lesson using lesson study with a colleague, even better!

- ★ Could you think of new rules for the game?
- ★ Could you let the students come up with their own rules?
- ★ What links can you see with other lessons in the book?
- ★ Could you investigate the influence of students typically seeing shapes with a particular orientation?

Notes

1   See, for example Freudenthal (1971) on early examples of dialogic mathematics teaching by Socrates in the fifth-century BC.
2   These opening lines were referring to Figures 5.3, 5.5, 5.7 and 5.3 (again) respectively.

References

Freudenthal, H. (1971). Geometry between the devil and the deep sea. In H. G. Steiner (Eds.), *The teaching of geometry at the pre-college level* (pp. 137–159). Dordrecht, The Netherlands: Springer.

Johnston-Wilder, S., & Mason, J. (Eds.). (2005). *Developing thinking in geometry.* London: Sage.

Tasova, H. I., & Delice, A. (2012). An analysis of pre-service mathematics teachers' performance in modelling tasks in terms of spatial visualisation ability. *Research in Mathematics Education, 14*(3), 297–298.

Appendix A
Lesson plan and resources

Lesson summary

Students describe to each other some compound geometrical shapes with the intent of drawing them. Students take it in turn to be a drawer and a describer. In between each episode learners have an opportunity to reflect on the process. The reflection is a meta-dialogue about their own developing understanding of shape.

Focus on students learning

a   Communicate instructions effectively to draw a two-dimensional compound shapes (describer)
b   Follow instructions to draw a two-dimensional shape (drawer)
c   Record any dialogue, what works, mathematical terms, effective mathematical language (both)

Lesson preparation

Learners will need the mathematical shapes and mini whiteboards to draw these shapes on. You may wish to use the observers sheet too, if you decide to have groups of three and include an observer role.

The lesson

Starter: Model the activity.

Stage 1: describer allowed to talk but drawer not allowed to talk
One student from the pair starts by describing the diagram they have been given to their partner (the drawer). They are sitting back-to-back so that the drawer cannot see the diagram and the describer cannot see what is being

drawn. During this first stage the drawer cannot talk. After this first example, the students can swap over their roles and try another diagram before moving on to the next stage. It is anticipated that students may find this first stage difficult, and possibly frustrating, and will not be able to replicate the actual diagrams.

Before stage 2 the class is brought back together for a whole class discussion on how they have got on so far. Focusing on what is the same and different between the original drawing and the end result. It can also be useful at this stage to discuss how the experience felt, for both describers and drawers, and why.

Stage 2: both describer and drawer allowed to talk

This stage is also modelled prior to the students engaging with the task (although modelling this stage is not always necessary for higher attaining groups). Again, the students sit in pairs, back-to-back, but this time the describer can ask questions and expect a reply, 'Do you understand?', 'Are you ready to move on?' et cetera. Also, the drawer can ask questions and clarify any of the instructions that are unclear to them. During this stage, we anticipate that students will develop their strategies and questions to enable them to get a diagram that more closely replicates the original. It is possible to also use an intermediate stage before this one, where describers are allowed to ask yes or no questions, and drawers are allowed to speak, but only to say yes or no.

Stage 3: whole class discussion

This will be used to summarise key points related to strategies used during both stages and highlight the development of language both mathematical and instructional. We anticipate that attention will become more specific and conscious through the task and that language use will develop.

Suggestions for lesson study focus

You might want to consider these aspects of students' thinking:

◆ How do students describe their shape? In parts or sequentially?
◆ What changes when both students can speak?
◆ How do students discuss ideas about dialogue?

Appendix B

Possible shapes for the task

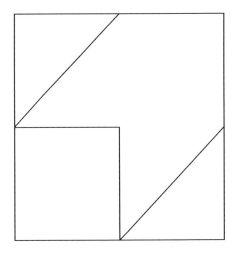

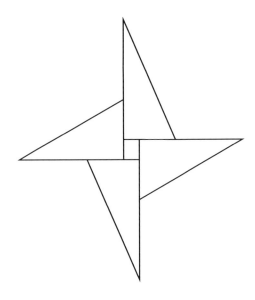

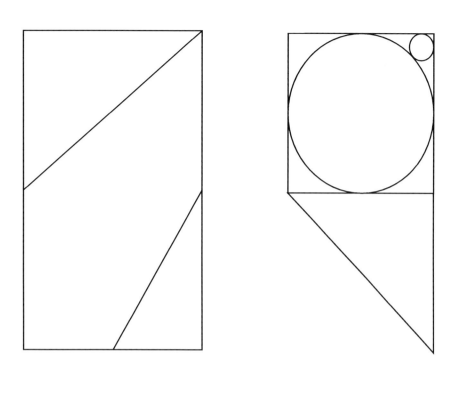

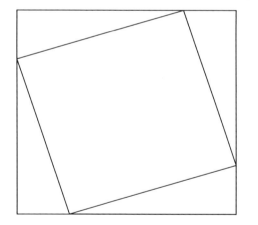

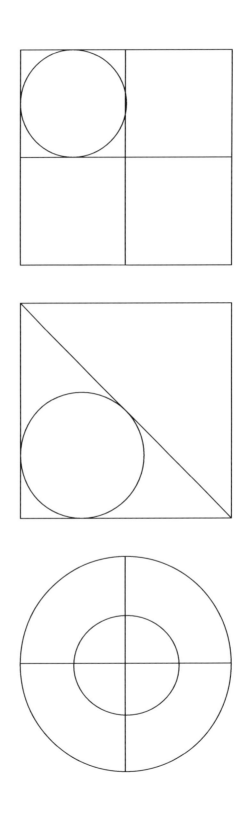

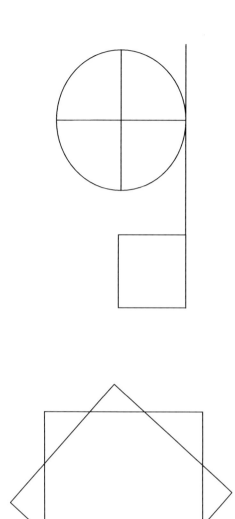

Appendix C

Observer's sheet

Turn 1	No questioning
Mark out of 10 for drawing (Drawing used)	
Maths language used	
Did it look easy/medium/hard	
Turn 2	YES/NO questioning
Mark out of 10 for drawing (Drawing used)	
Maths language used	
Questions asked	
Did it look easy/medium/hard	
Turn 3	Open questioning
Mark out of 10 for drawing (Drawing used)	
Maths language used	
Questions asked	
Did it look easy/medium/hard	

6

Constructing deep geometrical understanding

Introduction

The focus for this chapter is a lesson on enlargement. It was taught to two classes within the same school, both as part of a lesson study (LS). The task was used to deepen understanding of enlargement.

The lessons took place in a high school in a disadvantaged area of Greater Manchester with students aged 13 to 14. The authors planned the lesson with the Head of Department (HoD) and a Newly Qualified Teacher (NQT). The HoD taught the first lesson and the NQT taught the second lesson.

The lesson was based around one of Foster's mathematical études (2013a). Foster describes these mathematical études as 'mathematical tasks that embed extensive practice of a well-defined mathematical technique within a richer, more aesthetically pleasing mathematical context' (Foster, 2013a, p. 766). This particular étude was designed to develop understanding of the key aspects of enlargement and work creatively while identifying patterns. The lesson involves students deciding where to position centres of enlargement (COEs) for a given shape, with a particular scale factor of enlargement, so the image stays on the page (the grid is provided in Appendix B).

The research focus for this LS was to observe how embedding practice of centre of enlargement (COE) within a wider problem helps develop a deeper relational understanding of COE. Relational understanding (Skemp, 1976) means knowing what to do and why, rather than using rules without reason. We will use the van Hiele framework to support our analysis of learners' responses.

Scale factor was new to most learners, although some had encountered it before. The idea of reversing the task, finding the COE instead of finding the image or the scale factor, would help them to reason mathematically and to develop a deeper understanding of enlargement, in particular of the importance of the COE. We also felt that the activity is open and therefore would work well with mixed attaining students, providing opportunities for using the sharing of different learners' approaches to move forward the learning of the whole class. This was a particular interest at the time, since although the classes we worked with were divided according to attainment, the school was moving towards teaching in mixed attainment classes and the teachers were interested in developing such tasks.

Both lessons were successful in continuing to encourage the learners to think independently and construct understanding as we will describe in the lesson analysis.

We intend to reflect here on the lesson, how the lesson could be developed and if the chosen activities allowed learners to construct deep understanding of enlargement through this mathematical étude.

Background to the lesson

In order to better understand how learners develop their geometrical thinking we consider the van Hiele model for geometry and situate the lesson analysed here within this framework. The van Hieles, husband and wife Dutch educators, developed their model by observing the difficulties encountered by their students while learning geometry. The model describes five levels pertaining to how children learn to reason in geometry (Mason, 2009). These levels (numbered originally 0 to 4) describe how learners' reasoning develops in stages, leading to the highest level; geometrical proof.

0   **Visualisation**: Learners are able to compare geometric shapes by appearance alone to each other and to everyday objects; they may name them but cannot articulate their properties.

1   **Analysis**: Learners are able to name and recognise properties of shapes but they cannot see their relationships and establish the

importance of each property (Vojkuvkova, 2012). The van Hieles believed that it is not possible to move to a higher level unless enough time and energy is spent investigating the properties of shapes at this stage. They stated that memorisation of properties does not lead to effective learning. Learning only happens when teachers provide experiences designed at the appropriate level of learning.

Foster (2014) recognises that memorising through repetition does not support understanding but also that learners need to be fluent in mathematics in the sense that they need to be able to recall with ease a mathematical technique when they recognise that this is needed. Therefore he designed the activity we used for this lesson, amongst others, to demonstrate that fluency can be achieved by more open-ended problem-solving approaches. The authors propose that the lesson discussed in this chapter begins at this stage, when learners are encouraged to briefly consider enlargement before being given, or agreeing upon, a formal definition. This is done by asking learners 'what is the same, and what is different' about the examples, a question that can draw attention to what is mathematically significant (Brown & Coles, 2000, p. 118). According to the van Hieles, a successful lesson allows learners through reflection and discussion to move to the next level, in our case abstraction, which is described below.

2   **Abstraction**: Learners can make sense of definitions and can understand relationships between properties. They are able to use simple arguments to justify their reasoning and can draw logical maps, sketches and diagrams. The Van Hieles believed that many students get stuck at this level and therefore struggle with formal deduction later on. We believe that the experience provided by the lesson would help learners to make sense of definitions and therefore move to this level.

There are two further levels, deduction and rigor. These are not part of the analysis of this lesson but are important in order to fully understand the framework.

3   **Deduction**: Learners understand the meaning of definitions, theorems and proofs. They can understand which properties are deduced from others and can give deductive geometric proof.

4   **Rigor**: Learners can use all types of proof and understand the difference between Euclidean and non Euclidean geometry.

Following observations of their learners, the van Hieles theorised that learning happens when students actively experience the objects of study and are actively engaged in discussion and reflection (Vojkuvkova, 2012). It is therefore the teacher's responsibility to provide opportunities for students to experience shapes in different ways and to reflect and discuss their developing understanding.

Children's knowledge about spatial relations, level 0 (van Hiele levels), is developed from a very young age through school mathematics but also from observations of real-life situations. At level 0, children can compare shapes with everyday prototypes, for example 'this looks like a door' (Vojkuvkova, 2012, p. 73). Enlargement, in particular, is an idea that is often encountered by children in their everyday life and in the study of natural science (Friedlander & Lappan, 1987). For example, they can recognise a photograph of a person or of a place and understand that a map represents a much bigger area than the one it depicts.

Van Hiele theory suggests that levels cannot be skipped and that each level has its own linguistic symbols and its own relationships (Vojkuvkova, 2012). However, they also recognise that learners might be sitting at different levels in different areas of geometry depending on experience. What we experienced in the classroom is possibly more complicated than this, as students can often operate at multiple levels, even within one problem (see e.g. Burger & Shaughnessy, 1986). Despite these complications this empirical theory is still very useful in analysing how learners construct geometrical meaning.

One of the most important challenges in mathematical education is how best to harness the implicit knowledge in lessons about space (Nunes, Bryant & Watson, 2009). In terms of van Hiele levels, when learning about transformations an important task in order to move from level 1, analysis, to level 2, abstraction, is to understand which variables remain unchanged after the transformation. This can pose significant difficulties since children are used to classifying transformed shapes as equivalent. Another difficulty that arises is linking the idea of enlargement with that of the ratio between sides. While enlargement can be intuitively understood, the idea of ratio might pose more difficulties and therefore get in the way of solving problems with enlargement (Johnston-Wilder & Mason, 2005). The concept of enlargement is also associated with multiplication and division; children are able to apply multiplicative reasoning to abstract concepts related to number but might struggle when applying these ideas to continuous quantities and geometric relationships (Nunes et al., 2009).

For this lesson, we were primarily concerned with guiding learners to form a mental image of enlargement, recognising what changes and what stays the same when enlarging shapes using a COE. The étude also encourages a degree of freedom and creativity as well as making sure learners become procedurally fluent in enlargement. We will see in the analysis how the activity helps to develop relational understanding, as well as becoming fluent as described in the national curriculum in England (Department for Education, 2014). We will also return to the van Hieles levels both in the analysis and the 'what have we learned' sections.

Suggested reading

Foster, C. (2014). Mathematical fluency *without* drill and practice. *Mathematics Teaching*, *240*, 5–7.
Foster, C. (2017). Mathematical etudes. NRICH article available at: https://nrich.maths.org/13206
Jones, K. (1998). Geometry working group. *Proceedings of the British Society for Research into Learning Mathematics*, *18*, 29–34.

Lesson outline

The expected outcomes of the lesson are that students can visualise enlargement and appreciate how the enlargement changes when the COE is changed. The intention is to develop the learners' skills in visualising mathematics through repetitive practice within a more open task, to enable students to focus on the importance of the centre of enlargement (COE) through sharing their reasoning and listening to other's ideas.

Potential key moments to consider and expected responses are discussed below.

This problem involves enlargement and it is anticipated that some leaners will initially struggle to draw the enlargement and may not move beyond particular examples. We intend to use dialogue, questioning and sharing learners' examples to help learners develop their reasoning around how changing the COE changes the position of the shape.

Problem 1

Two similar shapes are projected, see Figure 6.2. Learners observe the diagram and write what they can see. We don't expect them to see immediately that the COE has not been defined; however, this is important to discuss.

Problem 2

The problem is introduced (Figure 6.1): a triangle is given on a grid and learners are asked to find a COE that will enable the image of that triangle to 'stay on the page' (be on the grid) given a particular scale factor. A COE that does work (stays on the page) and/or doesn't work (the enlarged shape does not stay on the page) is then shared.

The learners try the COE and are encouraged to explain why it does/ doesn't work. We expect learners to struggle to find the right language to

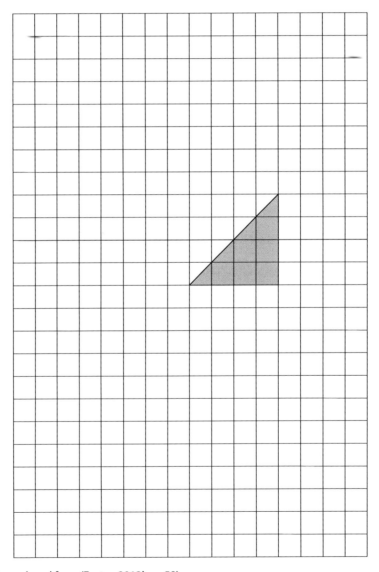

Figure 6.1 Reproduced from (Foster, 2013b, p. 58)

express their findings. At this point learners will practice enlarging the triangle. This testing of different points can be seen as level 1 (analysis) in terms of van Hiele levels. Some learners might start to appreciate that there are some critical points on the grid and move towards level 2 (abstraction).

Problem 3

Learners are then asked to find all COEs that work, so that the enlarged shape fits on the page. We expect to see a variety of strategies: systematic or not; trial and error approaches; noting COEs that don't work, seeing the CEOs that work as a region; and/or looking for edges of a region. Tracing paper and cut-out shapes can be provided to support students to master level 1 before moving to level 2.

Mid-lesson reflection

After a few minutes working on the task, once they have found one or two examples, the class will share strategies and their reasoning at that point. The teacher will model one enlargement for those learners who are not sure about the formal procedure. Key questions, such as 'what is the same?', 'what is different?' will be used to help learners to reflect on what happens for different points. At this stage, we anticipate that they will start to see that there are a few different points that work and may begin to see a region. Learners then continue to work on finding more points, COEs that work and the region.

Whole class comparison and summary

Ideas will be shared as a class and learners will summarise their reasoning, their strategies used and discoveries made. At this point the teacher will guide the learners towards the abstraction level by asking questions such as 'why does this point not work?', 'why does this work', 'will this work if I mover the COE on to the right'. These questions will allow learners to generalise, observe similarities and difference and move from The van Hieles level 1 to level 2.

Pause for thought

Think about teaching this lesson to *your* class.

- ★ Anticipate the responses that you would get from your students. Do you think learners will appreciate the need to have a COE?
- ★ Consider how you would support students in finding the region. What questions might you ask?

Lesson reflection and analysis

We will report here on two lessons that happened within a few months of each other in the same secondary school, with two year 9 (ages 13–14) top set classes. At the time year 7 and 8 were taught in mixed attainment classes but this had not yet filtered through to year 9. The HoD taught the first lesson to a class nearing the end of year 9, while a beginning teacher, NQT taught the second one to a class nearer the start of year 9. Both teachers believe strongly that mathematical discovery and using dialogue supports learners developing deep mathematical understanding and mathematical reasoning. Their commitment to creating cognitive conflict in order to construct understanding and encouraging learners to support each other and share ideas was known to us and evident throughout the LS process.

The sharing of the experiences of the LS team and analysis of students' responses to both lessons will allow us to compare and contrast and develop a stronger understanding of how this activity can support learners' mathematical development. We will initially discuss the first lesson taught by the HoD with the NQT in a supporting role before discussing the second lesson, taught by the NQT.

Lesson 1: This LS involved one of the authors with both the HoD and NQT. The lesson itself was observed by approximately 40 pre-service teachers and so is similar in some ways to the 'district lessons' held in Japan (see Chapter 1).

After having agreed on the activity, all of the members of LS team tried the activity before meeting to discuss their reflections. The team felt it would be important for learners to reflect on the importance of the COE. The first part of the lesson therefore included two diagrams; diagram 1 had a scale drawing of two shapes drawn on squared paper, and diagram 2 was a set of Cartesian axes with an enlargement (Figure 6.2). The teacher asked students to write in their books what is the same and what is different and to write whatever they notice.

After the learners discussed this in pairs, the teacher asked them to share their responses. The first student to respond replied 'enlarged shapes' and the next 'similar shapes'. When then asked what it means for two shapes to be similar, one student noted that they have the same angles, showing this on the board. The teacher adds that in mathematics we say 'the corresponding angles are equal'. Another student discusses the scale factor and sides of the shapes and this is followed by a comment from another student that the distances from the centre doubles as well, using the diagram on the board to

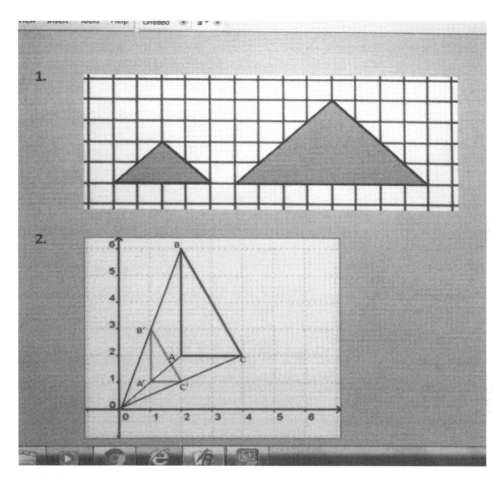

Figure 6.2 Starter task

help, but thinks this doesn't work for diagram 1. The teacher agreed that it doesn't work for the first diagram and asks what's missing. Students reply that the COE is missing and the teacher emphasises the need for a COE. The COE for the first diagram, and its possible position, is not discussed further. Looking at what is the same and what is different has helped the class to take note of the COE – initially, through considering similarity, then scale/size, then distances and, finally, the COE. This process shows an emergence of concepts, which the teacher provides the mathematical terms for.

The 'staying on the page' task is introduced and we note here that the LS team decided to use a scale factor 2 instead of the suggested scale factor 3. This was initially decided in order to give learners more opportunities to practice and to use scale factor 3 as an extension; however, it was agreed in the post-lesson discussion, having observed learners' responses, that the increased repetition did not necessarily enhance the experience.

After the students attempt the task for a few minutes, the teacher shows one of the learner's examples with a COE to the class. This reassures any students in the class who were unsure of how to start and begins a discussion about the fact that there is more than one solution. This is followed by further work where learners support each other with the task and are encouraged to move around the classroom to do this. At this point learners are working at level 1. During the next whole class discussion, in order to move learners to level 2, the teacher asks one learner to share their conjecture; 'all of my centres make a four by four square', and encourages the learner to also share with the class how she had realised it was false by testing a few more points. As observed before, the Van Hiele levels here are not as clear-cut as stated in the theory; in fact, the presence of a conjecture would suggest that some learners are working at level 3. This encouraged others in the class to consider/ create their own conjectures about the possible region. Another learner shares with the class their process of using a COE to find the image using a counting squares across and up strategy. When asked to explain their next COE, they explained that 'I moved down the centre of enlargement, so the shape moves down'. Another learner intervenes at this point, saying that 'if the centre of enlargement moves down then the shape is going up'. There is further discussion around this point and learners are given further time to try to find the region. In this phase of the lesson, some of the students are beginning to move away from pure trial and improvement to beginning to generalise and notice patterns. This is developed further by the sharing of these examples with the whole class and this can be seen as another example of 'the same' and 'different' but here we have students each working on the same task in slightly different ways so they can make sense of each other's work and generalise between them.

It is useful to analyse some learners' responses to finding this region. Figure 6.3 shows a learner working systematically trying several points but it is unclear which were successful and which were not, while Figure 6.4 shows a learner beginning to reason on the allowed region by generalising from a couple of possible COEs.

Figure 6.5 shows a learner trying three different COEs but it is unclear whether they had a strategy. This learner did not find the region but practiced a number of enlargements correctly and arguably gained some insight of the expected region through the class reflection and discussion.

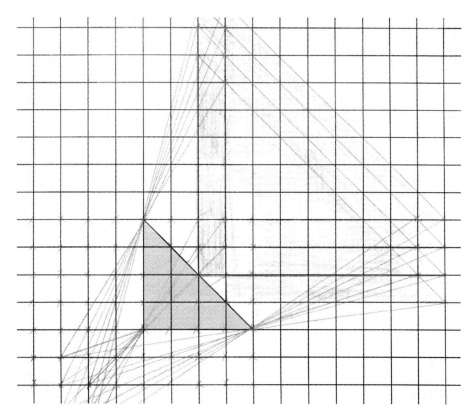

Figure 6.3 Student work 1

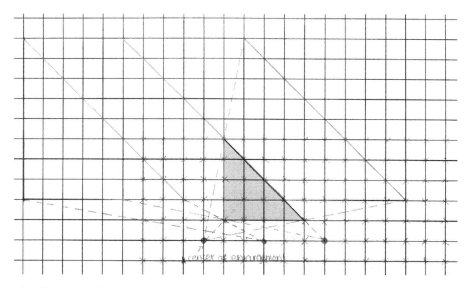

center of enlargement

Figure 6.4 Student work 2

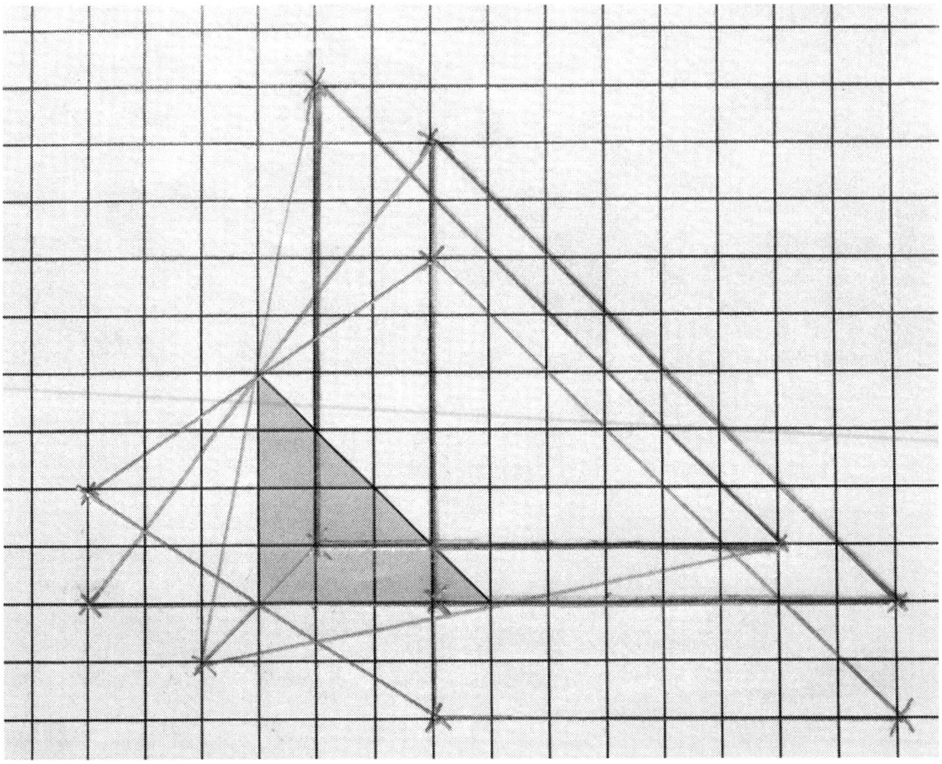

Figure 6.5 Student work 3

More than half of the class identified the correct region for this problem by the end of the lesson. This shows that they were able to start movement towards level 2 where they were seeing relationships between shapes and points. In fact, some movement toward level 3 was also observed with some learners making conjectures on the region of allowed COE. Their homework was to continue the task and consider how using a scale factor 3 and 4 might change the region. It was noted that none of the learners proceeded by finding COEs/regions that didn't work, but focused their pattern spotting/reasoning on the ones that did. It was also observed that having critical values (the boundary of the allowed region) on the edge of the paper could have caused the learners some confusion. In fact, some learners assumed the points on the edge of the paper would not be in the allowed region and therefore did not investigate them. The grid used was changed for the second lesson, a scale factor 3 was agreed and the co-ordinate grid was changed to a grid with edges within the paper (see Appendix B).

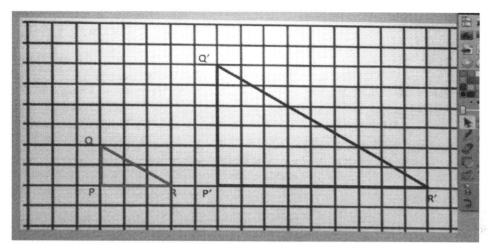

Figure 6.6 First activity

Lesson 2: This LS involved two of the authors and the NQT that had been part of the first LS cycle, described previously. During the first activity, the teacher wanted the learners to explore what enlargement meant without providing any definitions or models, so changed the diagram so there was a pair of similar triangles but no diagram with a COE (see Figure 6.6). Learners were encouraged to comment on the projected image in order to construct the idea of enlargement (not yet COE).

The learners observed that one triangle had been obtained from enlarging the other. Responses at this stage were as expected. One student says: 'line PR is three squares long and the bigger one nine squares long. I think the smaller triangle has been enlarged by three to get bigger triangle'. The teacher replied 'so that one is same as that one but multiplied by three'.

At this point, following the lesson plan, the teacher was trying to allow learners to observe how the enlargement changes position if the COE is moved; however, this was not asked explicitly. The teacher asked 'what if this point is moved up?' while pointing at point Q'.

One student drew a ray between the top vertices of the triangles and was convinced that there was a unique point, see label A (Figure 6.7), (the COE, he didn't have this terminology at this point) and argued that if it (the COE) was moved one place to the left that it wouldn't work (i.e. would no longer be a COE for those shapes). In Figure 6.7 he was trying to demonstrate to the class his point. Despite not having the language, he is beginning to analyse the situation and can share what he has noticed with a logical diagram.

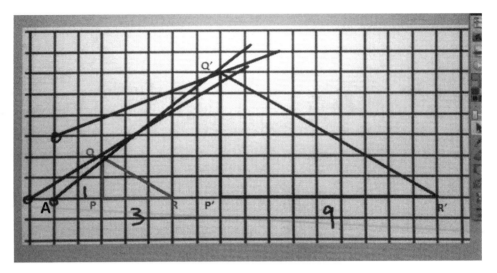

Another student said 'what if the shape was put somewhere else?' This comment could have been used to draw the class's attention to the special case; the bases of both triangles were on the same horizontal line. Maybe drawing the original triangles in different places would have given learners an opportunity to develop a firmer understanding.

At this point a student says she thinks it would be called a point of enlargement. She observed that if the COE was in a different position the enlarged triangle would be somewhere else. The teacher said that it was called the COE and the terminology was agreed for the rest of the lesson. Another learner observed that if triangle P'Q'R' was lower, then the COE would move up. This was a useful observation, showing that understanding was developing and definitions being formed.

Having agreed on the role of the COE and having constructed the concept of enlargement the class began the 'staying on the page' activity. At this point we were 35 minutes into the lesson with only 25 minutes left. During the post-lesson discussion the class teacher explained that she was surprised that the class had less prior knowledge of enlargement than expected and therefore decided it was necessary to spend more time constructing the idea.

After a brief class discussion, it was agreed that the task was asking students to find all the COEs so that the shape stays on the page after an enlargement of scale factor 3. At this point many learners were not sure of what

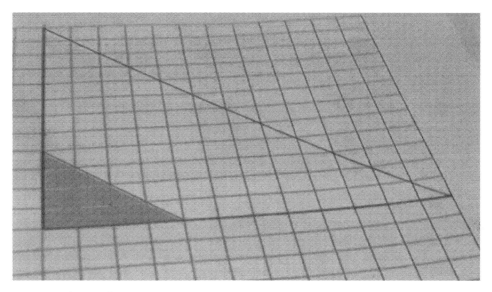

Figure 6.8 Student work

they were supposed to do. Having only taught the class for four months, the teacher was keen to develop their ability to work independently and support each other and therefore decided not to model an example. If you wanted to move students on quicker, at this point, it would be helpful to model one enlargement with the class, or an example that didn't work.

At this stage, several drew one triangle within the other (Figure 6.8). When the class teacher questioned the students who had done this, they were not able to tell her where the COE was on their diagram. Students often struggle with these special cases where the object is on the edge or within the image; the COE is within the object. Students are developing an understanding of enlargement, but the complexities of COE are still to be developed for some.

By the end of the lesson there is a range of outcomes present in the room, including those grappling with the basics of COE and others that were making steps towards solving the task. For example, one learner comes up to demonstrate how they could always find a COE regardless of where the enlarged shape is on the grid. He used rays to support him in doing this (Figure 6.9).

During this lesson students had not progressed sufficiently to begin a whole class discussion on potential regions (see Appendix C for a solution). However, the teacher continued with the activity in the subsequent lesson.

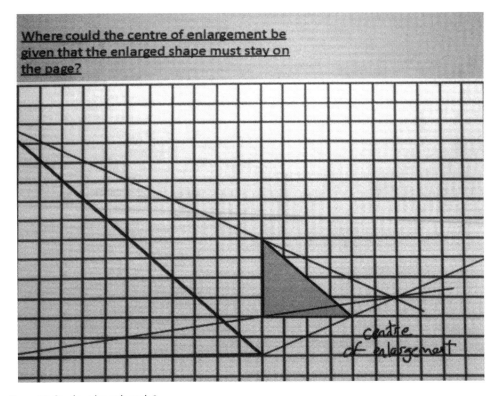

Figure 6.9 Student board work 2

Pause for thought

Consider the above lesson reflection and analysis.

★ What are the key points for reflection?
★ What were the critical incidents and were there any missed opportunities?
★ How would you have responded in each situation?

Consider the above learners responses.

★ Can you anticipate how your class will respond to this task?

What we have learned

We focus here initially on the van Hiele model, then the role of the teacher as facilitator in whole class discussion and the dilemmas within that, followed by the LS process, and then possible next steps. The research focus for this

LS was to observe how embedding practice of COE within a wider problem helps develop a deeper relational understanding of COE.

The van Hiele model

During the early part of lesson 1, the teacher posed a question of what is the same and what is different. This encourages generalisation by the students where they move towards ideas of similarity and COE. This is part of the process of moving from level 1 (analysis) to level 2 (abstraction) and at this stage the teacher provides them with the words/terms to use for the concepts that are emerging.

At level 0 learners might be able to recognise enlargement as shadows of spaces, while at level 1 they can start to recognise which properties are preserved when enlarging shapes. When the students, in lesson 1, are encouraged to share their strategies their thinking can be mapped to van Hieles level 2 as they are beginning to confidently use their COEs within a wider problem and are starting to generalise relational aspects of COE, such as moving the COE down moves the image up.

In lesson 2, we see examples of where levels are not as linear and distinct but they, in fact, co-exist and interrelate. For example, see Figure 6.7, where a student cannot name the COE (van Hieles level 0) but can show an understanding of the relationships involved, and can also draw a diagram to justify and illustrate the logical relationships (van Hieles level 2). We believe the process of generalisation can create a structured connection between lower and higher level concepts which then becomes part of the lower level concept, qualitatively changing it.

Teacher as facilitator

The role of the teacher as facilitator within this lesson is key, as we have seen in many of our other chapters. There are a number of decisions to consider during the discussion parts of the lesson: when is an appropriate point to bring the class together; which example of learners work to share; which learners to question; whether to affirm or not learners' reasoning and how much to intervene within these whole class discussions. As Stein, Engle, Smith and Hughes, (2008, p. 319) state, 'conducting "show and tell" discussions cannot be counted on to move an entire class forward mathematically'. What is needed is careful selection of work, based on the mathematics, and an emphasis on drawing learners' attention to the connections between learners' reasoning. We see this within the first lesson, where the teacher ensures there is some modelling of certain aspects: COE; more than one solution.

Also, through asking questions like 'what is the same?' 'what is different?' or through getting students to probe each other's work in order to encourage the shifts in levels of thinking discussed above.

Some teachers believe that for whole class teaching to be focused on student thinking, they must not provide any kind of guidance (Stein et al., 2008). Within the first lesson, there are a number of useful interventions by the teacher, linked to specific mathematical language, strategies used and conjectures made. Within the second lesson, with the teacher wanting the learners to build resilience and construct their own learning, there were fewer interventions. This approach helps to build learner independence but may mean that perceived progress within an activity can seem slower.

Lesson study process

As discussed in the introduction, the LS team decided to teach this lesson for their research lesson because of the more open nature of the task and the opportunity to develop reasoning through repeated practice, noticing patterns and sharing of ideas. This is another lesson that we discuss with our pre-service teachers during their course and so the authors and NQT were familiar with it prior to the start of the LS.

The lesson studies took on a different form for each LS cycle, both being planned and discussed within the LS team. However, the first experience, where there was an experienced HoD teaching the lesson with many pre-service teachers observing, became more like a demonstration lesson rather than LS. This was particularly evident during the lesson with observers removed from the students at the back of the room and during the post-lesson discussion. The second was slightly different. The learner started from a different point, with very little or no previous experience of enlargement, and therefore a lot of time was spent to understand about the process of enlargement. As we saw in the lesson analysis, the time spent investigating enlargement and discussing it allow learners to develop understanding of the process. In this lesson we saw the understating beginning to be formed that was continued in following lessons.

Next steps

Possible next steps would be to work with the lesson again, possibly over two lessons, and focus on the reasoning around the region of COEs and how that would change with different scale factors and different original shapes. Using the same grid would be helpful, however a discussion about what happens if the grid is changed would also be worth further investigation.

Pause for thought

Try the lesson with one of your classes. If you can use it as a research lesson using LS with a colleague, even better!

- ★ What surprised you in the lesson?
- ★ If you were to use a different scale factor what would you use and why?
- ★ How would you develop the lesson further?
- ★ What links can you see with other areas of the mathematics curriculum?

References

Brown, L., & Coles, A. (2000). Same/Different: A 'natural' way of learning mathematics. In T. Nakahara & M. Koyama (Eds.) *Proceedings of the 24th Conference of the International Group for the Psychology of Mathematics Education, Vol 2*, pp. 113–120, Hiroshima, Japan.

Burger, W. F., & Shaughnessy, J. M. (1986). Characterizing the van Hiele levels of development in geometry. *Journal for Research in Mathematics Education*, 17, 31–48.

Department for Education. (2014). *National curriculum in England: Framework for key stages 1 to 4*. London: Author.

Foster, C. (2013a). Mathematical études: Embedding opportunities for developing procedural fluency within rich mathematical contexts. *International Journal of Mathematical Education in Science and Technology*, 44(5), 765–774.

Foster, C. (2013b). Staying on the page. *Teach Secondary*, 3(1), 57–59.

Foster, C. (2014). Mathematical fluency without drill and practice. *Mathematics Teaching*, 240, 5–7.

Friedlander, A., & Lappan, G. (1987). Similarity: Investigations at the middle grade level. *Learning and Teaching Geometry, K-12, the national council of Teachers of Mathematics, Virginia, USA*, 136–143.

Johnston-Wilder, S., & Mason, J. (Eds.) (2005). *Developing thinking in geometry*. London: Sage.

Mason, M. (2009). The van Hiele levels of geometric understanding. *Colección Digital Eudoxus*, 1(2).

Nunes, T., Bryant, P., & Watson, A. (2009). Key understandings in mathematics learning. *London: Nuffield Foundation*, 22, 276.

Skemp, R. R. (1976). Relational understanding and instrumental understanding. *Mathematics Teaching*, 77(1), 20–26.

Stein, M. K., Engle, R. A., Smith, M. S., & Hughes, E. K. (2008). Orchestrating productive mathematical discussions: Five practices for helping teachers move beyond show and tell. *Mathematical Thinking and Learning, 10*(4), 313–340.

Vojkuvkova, I. (2012). The van Hiele model of geometric thinking. *WDS'12 Proceedings of Contributed Papers, 1,* 72–75.

Appendix A

Lesson plan and resources

In this lesson students practice enlargement and use reasoning to find a region of all possible centres of enlargement (COEs) that allow the image to 'stay on the page'. They are given a grid with an object drawn on and a scale factor. Students develop their understanding of enlargement and reasoning through dialogue. You may find that this could be extended over two lessons.

Focus on students learning

a   Understand the importance of both the centre of enlargement and scale factor
b   Draw correct images from centres of enlargement that they trial
c   Look for a region of centres of enlargement that fulfil the task.
d   Share their strategies and reasoning with others in the class.

Lesson preparation

Learners will need the grid and a pencil, ruler and rubber. A different coloured pencil might be useful too. You may wish to use tracing paper and cut out shapes to move round the page.

The lesson

Setting the problem

Learners observe the image and write what they see. This initial episode is independent work. Learners are encouraged to say what they can see.

The teacher, through discussion, encourages them to identify which information is needed to get from one shape to the enlarged one. They are expected to observe how much bigger the image is. They will also be encouraged to appreciate the fact that the centre of enlargement is important to determine the location of the image. If the learners are struggling to see this the teacher can show them a different enlarged shape (same scale factor) and ask them to describe what is the same and what is different. Through discussion also get the learners to observe that the angles on the enlarged triangle stay the same.

Stage 1
Task sheet (see Appendix B) is given out. Learners are asked to enlarge by scale factor 3 given a centre on enlargement (as marked on the sheet). Learners observe that it is not possible to do so without some of the image being off the page. Learners are asked, initially in pairs and then as a class to explain why this centre of enlargement doesn't work.

Stage 2
Learners suggest one centre that is possible, one example is modelled and copied on to their grid and left visible on the board. Ensure learners mark possible centres with a different colour/symbol than those that don't work. Some learners might ask if we should consider centres of enlargement that are not on grid points (Foster, 2013b). To start with, learners can focus on centres that are on grid points but can generalise to regions later on.

Stage 3
Learners work independently on the sheet. The teacher walks round and encourages learners to explain why it is or isn't possible. Encourage leaners to explain what is different and what is the same for different examples. Make a note of possible strategies followed. Look for learners looking for critical points; the edge or corner of the region. These could possibly be shared with the class.

Stage 4
Class discussion. If possible, use a visualiser to project some examples. Encourage students that have worked systematically (as observed by the teacher in stage 3) to present their ideas. Expected responses include: some leaners working from the edge of the sheet and working backwards to where the centre should be and work from all edges; others start seeing patterns from the trial and error; some start from the image while others work with the centres and look for patterns. Others work with several points but because they are not systematic they may fail to see patterns.

Stage 5
Learners continue to work on the task and are encouraged to write down their reasoning. See 'deeper understanding' below for possible extension.

Plenary
Findings are shared; the visualiser is used to model the work. Learners describe their reasoning and how they visualised the task. The teacher draws ideas together and makes connections.

Deeper understanding
The task can be extended by asking: 'what happens to the region if we change the scale factor to 2, 4?' Is it possible to do this extension task without doing the task again but by generalising the findings from the first task? Move the position of the original triangle. Change the shape or size of the grid on the paper. Change the shape or size of the original object (triangle, rectangle).

Suggestions for LS focus

You might want to consider these aspects of student thinking:

◆ How do students tackle the task: systematically, looking for extreme points, spotting a pattern?
◆ Which examples are useful to share with the class?
◆ How can the teacher facilitate dialogue around reasoning?

Appendix B

The task

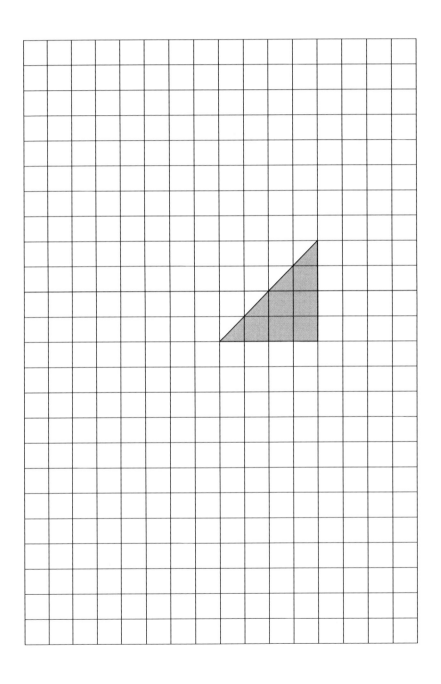

Appendix C

Solution

Region of possible COEs with scale factor 3

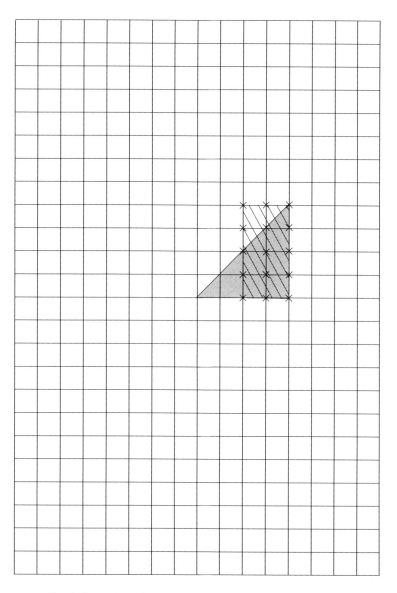

7

Modelling through open-ended tasks

Introduction

Within this chapter, we describe a lesson where a hypothetical real-life scenario is introduced to develop mathematical modelling. The scenario involves a virus breaking out in a city. The learners are given a budget to spend on the vaccine and there are three vaccines available at different costs. The lesson was designed by Bowland (2008a), to be done on the computer using a spreadsheet; however, we felt it would be interesting to do it in the classroom allowing learners to use calculators. The planning team was, in fact, interested to see if working in the classroom would facilitate group work and discussion. The room was set up with groups of tables so learners could work in groups of 4 to 6 learners each.

The lesson took place in an 11–16 school in an area of socio-economic disadvantage in the north on England with a year 10 class (learners aged 14 to 15). This was a class of high attainers who had worked with the same teacher for the past two years. The teacher spoke about having a lot of fun talking about mathematics with this class and developing deep mathematical understanding. The learners are used to questioning their own understanding and constructing new ideas by working in groups. A group of five pre-service teachers, who were half way through their initial teacher education (ITE), and their tutor (one of the authors) were part of the planning team and had spent considerable time doing the task themselves, in order to predict learners' responses, and plan the lesson. They had met the class earlier in the school year and had observed them learning. Two of the pre-service teachers taught the lesson. The class teacher was part of the LS study team in a peripheral way. She had been sent the plans in advance but was not involved in the planning or delivery of the lesson.

Our research focus was to reflect on how teachers can support learners in embracing an open-ended task. In particular, we reflected on how the teacher can support the development of open-ended tasks without taking away from the openness of the activity.

In the opinion of the lesson study (LS) participants, this lesson was successful in engaging learners in using mathematical modelling in order to solve a real-life problem. It was, however, less successful in encouraging learners to reflect on the effectiveness of their strategies. The task was purposefully kept very open but it was felt a more structured approach would have given learners more time to critically evaluate their strategies.

Background to the lesson

For the context of this lesson we will use Blum's definition of mathematical modelling. Mathematical modelling involves simplifying a real-life situation then mathematising it, i.e. choosing suitable mathematical methods to produce a solution; the mathematical solutions are then interpreted with respect to the real scenario Blum (1993).

Modelling allows learners to make use of the mathematics they learn in order to solve real-life problems giving the learning of school mathematics a purpose and helping to dispel the widespread view that mathematics is abstract and divorced from reality (Maaß, 2006). Furthermore, Blum (1993) observes how working with real-life examples can contribute towards a deep understanding of mathematics and long-term retention. Boaler (2001), drawing on large empirical study, confirms that mathematical modelling and problem solving are essential components of the mathematics curriculum and argues that mathematics is not the only subject of learning in school. In mathematics lessons young people should not only acquire the ability to interpret cues that would help them pass exams but also a more flexible type of knowledge, which is useful in a range of situations, including passing exams, and allows them to see how mathematics is relevant to their everyday life. In the

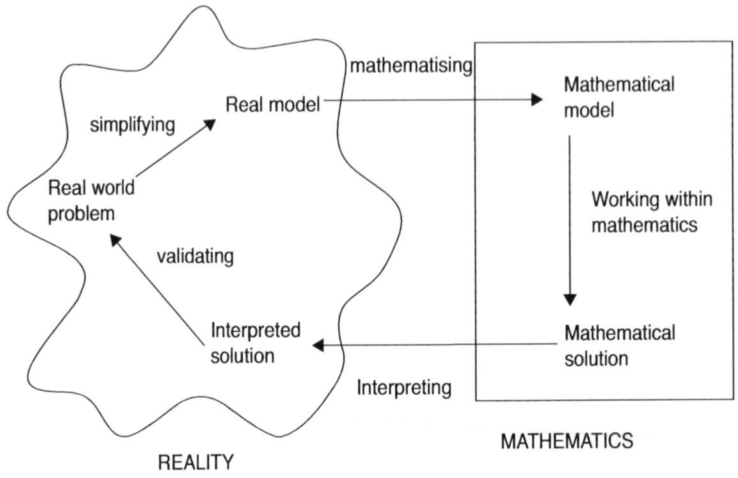

Figure 7.1 Reproduced from Maaß (2006)

fictional scenario of this lesson, imagining being scientists, who are tasked with saving people lives, motivates learners.

Maaß (2006) developed the diagram above (Figure 7.1) to exemplify the mathematical modelling process.

At the simplifying stages the model has not yet been mathematised but the situation has been simplified. The version of reality created in this first stage is crafted according to the questions the person/people doing the modelling wish or need to answer. At the mathematising stage different mathematical models can be developed. Maaß (2006) observes that a common misconception is the belief that all models are valid. It is, on the contrary, essential to choose a model that is suitable for the task; the fact that the model is not unique does not mean that any model will do. The choice of model is a very important conversation to have with learners. For this lesson the simplest model would involve giving everybody the second cheapest. After observing this fact, learners can be guided to refine their model in order to save more people from catching the disease. After the mathematising the mathematical problem is solved by choosing appropriate mathematical techniques (working with mathematics). At this stage mathematical errors could lead to an invalid solution. The mathematical solution is then interpreted back into the real world. Finally, the solution is validated or the whole cycle can start again if there are any discrepancies (Blum, 1993).

Maaß (2006) lists the competencies necessary to be successful in mathematical modelling. These are divided into competencies:

◆ To understand the problem (simplify the real-life scenario, identify key variables, recognise which ones are significant for the situation and develop relationships between variables)
◆ To set up the model (mathematise and simplify the relevant quantities and their relationship as well as choosing mathematical notations and representations)
◆ To solve the mathematical question within the mathematical model (recognise similar situations, in order to adopt similar strategies and observe how varying the quantities affects the situation)
◆ To interpret the mathematical result (communicate and critically reflect on the proposed solution as well as generalise solutions developed for special cases).

Maaß (2006) observes that in order for the students to want to solve a problem the context needs to be chosen appropriately for the chosen audience. The debate on how strictly realistic the problem needs to be is unresolved. Certainly, it needs to capture the learner's interest; this doesn't always mean that it needs to represent a lived situation. A task that is achievable and plausible can capture young people's imagination even if does not refer to their lived everyday experience. For this lesson learners can draw from their everyday experiences to make mathematical decisions about their model.

If mathematical modelling is such a vital part of learning mathematics, why is it difficult to embed it in the curriculum? Certainly, an exam focused education is not ideally positioned to encourage mathematical modelling. Modelling is, in fact, very difficult to assess with a rigid mark scheme and therefore rarely included in formal examinations. Learners need time to refine their strategies; often, their explanations are messy (because life is messy) and difficult to follow. The resulting mathematics, representing an idea that is being formed, is not always 'elegant' and clear. We believe that this interim messy stage when ideas are being formed and discussed is essential in learners' development. It is, however, very difficult and time consuming for teachers and other learners to understand an idea that is being formed in a very short space of time. Blum (1993) also observes that modelling makes teaching more demanding; however, we believe it is not necessarily more demanding but the demands are different; if teachers are new to using modelling in their lessons they will find adapting to the change initially challenging. Teachers might also struggle to find time for modelling in an already very packed curriculum.

Pre-service teachers are at an advantage when trying less traditional and more risky approaches to teaching since they are, in a sense, expected to make mistakes and are less accountable to the school community. Furthermore, they don't know any different, have had no time to become set in their ways and almost everything they do they are trying for the first time. If the lesson doesn't go to plan they don't have to face a class the next day and have to restore relationships after having made a negative impression. However, not knowing the class and not being able to predict how they would respond could be a threat for pre-service teachers who might also lack confidence and classroom management skills. Pre-service teachers are still developing the skills to facilitate problem-solving lessons and might lack the confidence and experience to manage the class discussion; the lesson study process and the re-teaching of the lesson gives them a way into imagination of improvements (Radovic et al., 2014).

The open nature of mathematical modelling, even if difficult to handle, is an essential component of the experience. If we tell learners to try a particular approach, opportunities for decision-making are taken away from them; the lesson therefore becomes an exercise in imitating a method (Mason, Burton & Stacey, 1982). Being trained in the use of mathematical tools does not imply being able to think mathematically. According to Schoenfeld

> Learning to think mathematically means (a) developing a mathematical point of view – valuing the processes of mathematization and abstraction and having the predilection to apply them, and (b) developing competence with the tools of the trade …
>
> (1992, p. 3)

For this lesson we analyse how teachers can give learners space and time to develop a 'mathematical point of view' while also providing some structure for the lesson.

It is also important for the learners to accept messy solutions and to consider being stuck as part of the modelling process. Mason et al. (1982) reflect on the importance of 'being stuck' when working on thinking mathematically and focus on the importance of capitalising on the observation of feelings and the psychological state associated with wrestling with a difficult problem. Mathematical thinking can be improved once 'being stuck' is accepted as a part of it and therefore does not provoke feelings of panic and questioning of self-worth and self-confidence. Mathematical thinking can be improved if learners accept that a lot can be learned from unsuccessful attempts. Teachers should give learners plenty of time to familiarise themselves with the problem, and not demand a quick solution, since this might hinder the willingness to work independently and push them to ask for help too soon. When learners are 'stuck' instead of over simplifying the problem or breaking it down for them, providing hints in the form of questions can be helpful, for example:

> How could you get started on this problem? What have you tried so far? Can you try a specific example? How can you be systematic here? Can you think of a helpful representation?
>
> (Bowland, 2008b, p. 1)

Teachers will be able to ask effective questions only if they have spent time doing the modelling activity themselves and can therefore reflect on the difficulties they have encountered. This is how LS can be significant in allowing teachers to reflect on possible approaches and difficulties by exchanging ideas with colleagues and by observing learners at work.

Learners should also be encouraged to articulate their understanding by explaining their results to others and by comparing different strategies. The ability to reflect on their learning can, in fact, be achieved by classroom discussion. Galbraith and Clatworthy (1990) assert that discussion in small groups, in which the work of others is analysed and critically appraised, can be productive.

This lesson explores further how to support learners in developing their mathematical modelling skills. In particular, our research focus is to reflect on how teachers can support learners in embracing an open-ended task.

Suggested reading

Bowland Maths. Imaginative resources for rich problem solving in secondary school maths. www.bowlandmaths.org.uk/index.html

Compass. The site contains some ideas for modelling of real life scenarios that connect science and mathematics. Support materials are provided as well as resources. www.compass-project.eu/resources_detail.php?UG_hodnota_id=2

Freudenthal Repository. Teaching materials for STEM. www.fi.uu.nl/publicaties/subsets/en/

Mason, J., Burton, L., & Stacey, K. (1982). *Thinking mathematically*. London: Addison-Wesley contains many ideas (open ended tasks, investigations and mathematical modelling) to help develop mathematical thinking.

Mathematics Assessment Project. Some mathematical modelling activities can also be found here. Not all tasks are open. Resources as well as support materials are available on the site. http://map.mathshell.org

Lesson outline

The lesson was designed by Bowland Maths (2008a) for students to explore the use of mathematics in a disease management context. In the fictional scenario the students are scientists who try and contain the spread of a dangerous virus. The scenario involves a virus breaking out in a city of 945,550 people. The learners are given a £5,000,000 budget to buy a vaccine. There are three vaccines available: vaccine A costs £8 and is 95% effective, vaccine B costs £3.50 and is 70% effective while vaccine C costs £1.25 and is 55% effective. The learners are also given a breakdown of the population (medical workers, key service workers, school-aged children, children under 5, etc.) and are tasked with the decision of who to give which vaccine. The series of lessons (of which this is one) has been designed to support learners' mathematical modelling, reasoning, thinking and problem-solving skills. The lesson, originally designed to be supported by ICT, can also be used in the classroom with the support of calculators. The LS team felt it would be interesting to carry it out in the classroom, giving learners more time to deal with the calculations in order to allow discussion around problem solving and encourage group work.

The aim of the lesson was to allow learners to design a strategy and extract key information to model and solve a problem related to a real-life scenario.

Stage 1
A starter is used to check if learners are comfortable with finding a percentage of an amount and expressing an amount as a percentage of another amount.

Stage 2
The problem is introduced and learners work in groups to discuss it. Only one sheet per table is handed out in order to facilitate group work. At this stage the task is kept very open and learners are expected to observe that they have enough money to give everybody vaccine B and therefore save 70% of the population. This option will not, however, give them a choice on who they save.

Stage 3
Proposed strategies are shared with the teacher facilitating the discussion at the front. The teacher will make sure that they all agree they can save 70% of the population by giving vaccine B and ask the learners to check if they can save more people. The moral dilemma is introduced by discussion – who should they save?

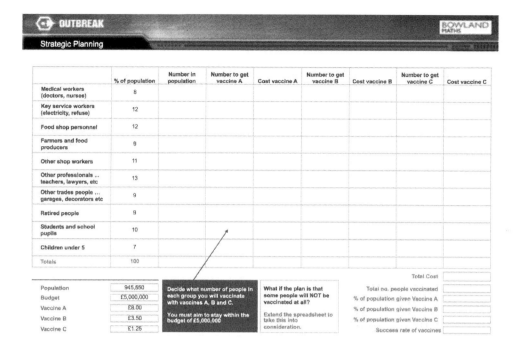

Figure 7.2 Reproduced from Bowland (2008a)

Stage 4

The table with the breakdown of figures is given out (see Figure 7.2). Learners work in groups to design a mathematical model for the situation. At this stage the learners are expected to mathematise the problem.

Stage 5

The teacher will lead learners in evaluating and comparing their strategies based on the initial question, e.g. comparing how many people were saved in different models or justifying why saving one group might result in a better outcome.

> **Pause for thought**
>
> Think about teaching this lesson to *your* class.
>
> ★ What difficulties do you think you will encounter?
> ★ Do you think the learners will try to resist this type of activity and why?
> ★ How could you encourage the learners to share their modelling strategy?

Lesson reflection and analysis

Before presenting the problem to the class, the LS team wanted to assess how confident the class was with percentages and therefore the lesson starts with the learners working out what percentage of the UK population lives in Manchester. The learners respond confidently and therefore the teacher moves on to the main activity.

The students are handed out the introductory sheet that describes the task[1] and are asked to consider a strategy they want to employ. As we observed earlier, in Background to the lesson, at this stage the learners are simplifying the problem and drawing on the competency to understand the problem and recognise the variables involved. The task is kept purposefully very open at this stage and the only instruction learners are given is to discuss the task in groups.

Most groups quickly realise that one of the main variables involved is the amount of money they decide to spend and that there is enough money to give the entire population vaccine B and start talking about what they could do with the money left over. The LS team, having worked on the task, were expecting this response. The class teacher had told us that the class would engage with the problem quickly since they are used to working in groups to solve problems and that their mathematical reasoning would be supported by strong calculation skills. One group observes that by giving everybody vaccine B they would be able to save 70% of the population. They think that giving everybody the same vaccine would be fair and observe that saving 70% is a success since this is more than half. Learners are already starting to critically reflect on their strategies even if they have not fully solved the problem. Another group realises that they needed to consider other variables and check if it was possible to save more people by giving different vaccines to different people. A third group suggests giving vaccine A to those people for whom vaccine B didn't work.

After 10 minutes the class is brought back together. In order to help the class reflect on key information the teacher asks the following questions:

Can you give everybody vaccine A?
Can you give everybody vaccine B?
How many would you save if you gave everybody vaccine B?
How much money would you have left over?

Having made sure the whole class understood the problem and identified some of the variables before moving on the teacher asks: 'if it was guaranteed that everybody would get the virus would you change how you managed this problem?' This question was meant to raise a moral dilemma and compare this scenario with what would actually happen in real life. At this stage the learners are reluctant to participate in discussion beyond their own groups. This is possibly due to the fact that the learners are intimidated by having so many observers in the room and by being guided by somebody who is not their usual teacher. During feedback, we discussed how it would have been helpful to give learners time to discuss the moral dilemma in groups before sharing with the whole class.

At this point the learners are given a table, which provides a breakdown of the population by category (Figure 7.2). Having taught the lesson before, the LS team felt that if this sheet was given too early, learners would concentrate on filling in the blanks instead of devising a modelling strategy for this problem. For this reason the sheet is handed out at this phase of the lesson so the mathematising would not happen before the problem is fully understood.

During this phase of the lesson most groups start setting up their model by filling in the provided table and calculating costs (Figure 7.3).

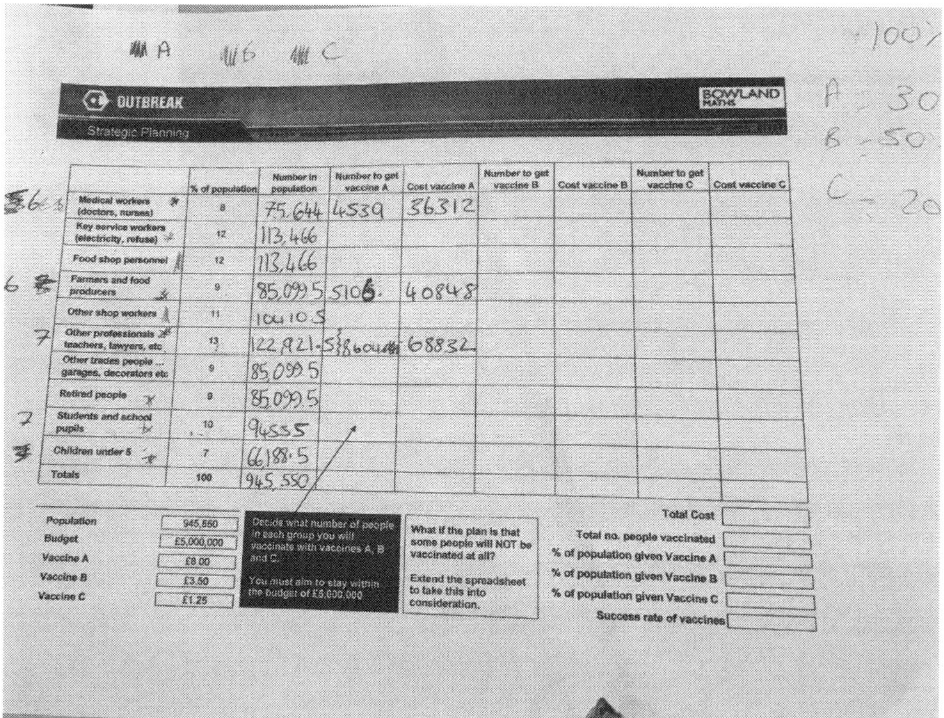

Figure 7.3 Example of pupil work

One of the groups starts considering which categories are more likely to spread the virus. One group observes that retired people, service workers and young children are less likely to spread the virus so they would need the cheaper vaccine. However, one of the boys suggested that retired people have families and therefore are likely to spread the virus within their household. Not all learners in the group agree with him. Another group is busy discussing which groups of people have stronger immune systems. One group suggests that doctors need vaccine A since they are most likely to spread the virus. One of the learners, who, we learnt, has a strong interest in biology, is really inspired by this lesson and keen to share his knowledge of antibodies with his group. Maaß (2006) warns that context can motivate but can also provide a distraction from the mathematics, which might have been the case in this instance.

The two teachers facilitating the lesson are walking around the classroom, while the class is working, trying to capture ideas that could be shared with the class later on. After another 10 minutes one of the teachers interrupts the learners in order to assess strategies and share ideas.

The questions in Figure 7.4 are written on the whiteboard while the learners are working independently. One of the teachers reads the questions to the class but holds back from sharing strategies until the last stage of the lesson.

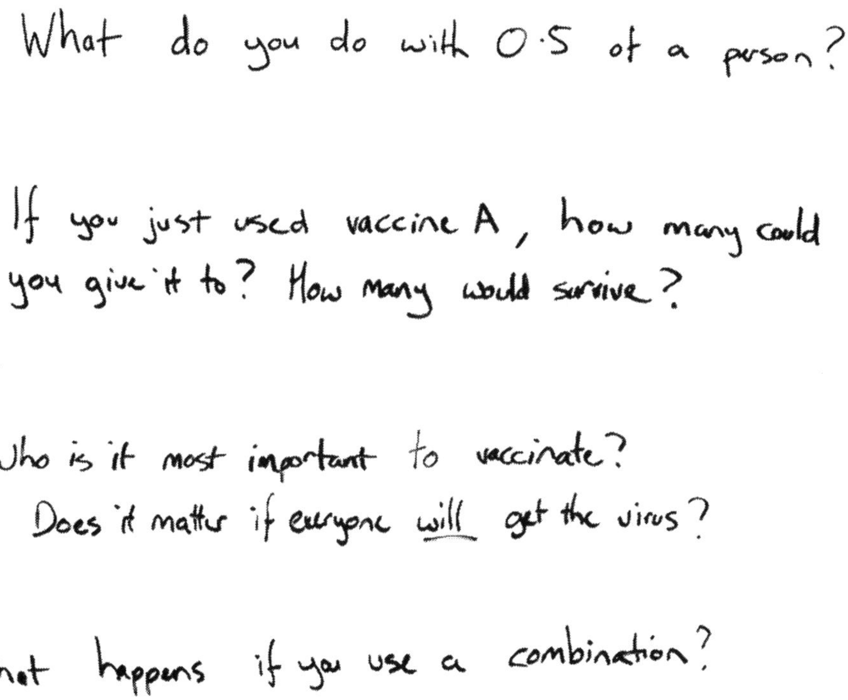

What do you do with 0.5 of a person?

If you just used vaccine A, how many could you give it to? How many would survive?

Who is it most important to vaccinate?
Does it matter if everyone will get the virus?

What happens if you use a combination?

Figure 7.4 Questions

During the planning stage it was decided against having a solution ready for the class to look at/analyse/criticise. While this technique would have helped the teacher to guide learners towards a desired solution, the planning team felt this would have closed the task too much and taken decisions away from the learners. The planning team was aiming to pick up significant strategies while walking round to share during the whole class episodes. Those teaching the lesson didn't want to interrupt the flow of the lesson as the students were very engaged and the task perhaps remained too open. At this point there is an opportunity to structure the task more, in order to allow learners to move forward with their mathematical model. The teachers could facilitate the mathematising by asking learners to observe what would happen if they decided to give a certain vaccine to another group of people. Questions such as, 'Can you save more people by changing your priorities?' and 'What will happen if we change this?'

At this stage of the lesson all learners have worked out how much it would cost to give the whole population vaccine B and how many people this would save, and most learners are using trial and error to test different strategies. Learners use mathematical calculations to analyse their decisions, for example one group writes: '26% of the population gets A, which costs £1,966,744'. However, at this stage most learners are not working systematically. Another group ranked the different categories to help decide how many people to save from each category. One group shares that they had saved 62% of the population (having made a calculation mistake). They feel this is a good result since they had saved more than half of the population; however, they have not critically analysed their results and observed that by giving everybody vaccine B they could have saved more people. Another group, however, spots their mistake. Another group has given everybody vaccine B and then shared the remaining money to give some people vaccine A; however, they make a mistake and divide the left over money by £8 forgetting that these people had already been counted for receiving vaccine B.

At this point the teachers could have facilitated the reflection by asking questions such as: do we have enough money to give all medical workers vaccine A? How many people can we save if we do that? We believe that at this stage it would be more efficient if learners were working with a spreadsheet or if a spreadsheet had been used to model the activity on the board so the effect of changing some of the variables could have been observed quickly.

Certainly, the learners had gained an insight by discussing the task and trying to make decisions but needed more time to mathematise the task and structure their thinking by considering, what would happen if variables and parameters were changed? This could be done in a following lesson using spreadsheets to record costs. Not using the spreadsheet for this lesson allowed students to discuss the real-life situation in groups and fully understand the task.

While leaving the room one of the learners told the teachers: 'I loved this lesson'. When asked why, he told them that that he was planning to study economics and felt that the skills he acquired today would be very useful. He also told them: 'I like to use mathematics to put my point across'.

Pause for thought

Consider the above lesson reflection and analysis.

★ How would giving a prompt sheet to record strategies affect learners in their choice of model?

What we have learned

We will initially reflect on the research question of how teachers can support learners in embracing an open-ended task. We will then share our thoughts on the LS process within Initial Teacher Education (ITE) and finally discuss possible next steps.

Teachers facilitating an open task

The task was kept very open on purpose to allow learners to think mathematically instead of imitating a method or using mathematical tools without reasoning.

However, it was observed that adding some structure to the task, midway through the lesson would have helped in focusing mathematical conversations. Learners could have been guided on reflecting on their model by asking them to observe what happened if some of the parameters and variables were changed. The planning team decided that they wanted to encourage group work and allow learners to work in groups in order to support each other in analysing their strategies and discuss the moral dilemma related to this task. Working on a PC can, in fact, be isolating because of the physical position of the screen. However, the use of a spreadsheet would have allowed learners to quickly establish what happened if one of the parameters was changed. We therefore believe that after having spent enough time allowing the learners to work in groups in order understand the problem and recognise the variables, working on a spreadsheet would have allowed them to quickly and efficiently investigate relationship between variables. Finally, learners should communicate their results and critically reflect on their strategies by discussing (with the teacher, in small groups, or as a class) and by analysing their own and other people's work.

An issue raised by some of the LS team was that of impact. It was difficult to establish from this lesson how much progress learners had made. As discussed in Background to the lesson, learning is not always 'elegantly' presented but, as a human endeavour, is often messy and complicated. The value associated with such activities is related to one's philosophy of education. If the purpose of mathematics education is identified as a way to encourage learners to develop independent thinking strategies, such activities become of paramount importance as observed in the learners' feedback described below.

The planning team felt that learners enjoyed developing their mathematical modelling skills. In particular, two of the learners were vocal about having enjoyed applying mathematics to real-life scenarios, with one of them suggesting how real-life application of mathematics helps him to develop his understanding.

Lesson study process within (ITE)

This LS cycle is different from the others discussed in this book since the pre-service teachers are more actively involved in the process. As described in Chapter 1, some of the Japanese educators who theorise LS would disagree in involving pre-service teachers in a LS cycle. However, this experience was important since pre-service teachers were able to experience a difficult to teach lesson in a safe environment and were able to stop and reflect on the importance of mathematical modelling as well as on its associated difficulties. For new and pre-service teachers, it can be difficult to find time and confidence to approach such open tasks. The school management and their mentors might not trust them with a difficult to teach lesson and prefer them to play safe in order to be able to evidence leaners' progress. This lesson allowed pre-service teachers to try to analyse a difficult to teach lesson and therefore improve their practice.

The class teacher had not been part of the planning team and was present in the lesson only as an observer. It was therefore important to all involved to understand that she was there to learn and not to judge the lesson. Fortunately, the class teacher was very open to learning and discussion. She was not tempted to turn the post-lesson discussion into an evaluation session and supported the reflection and analysis throughout, bringing some very helpful conversations to the table. She told the planning team that she would probably not have used this lesson before but having seen the value of it, she was now keen to try it again with other classes.

Next steps

The LS team would have liked learners to be more deliberate in their choice of model and come forward with more enthusiasm when sharing strategies. Their reticence to share strategies during the whole class episode was in our opinion due to (apart from the presence of so many strangers in the room) the fact that the task had insufficient structure. During the post-lesson discussion the possibility of having a way to record modelling strategies was discussed, possibly a recording sheet or a mind map. It was also suggested that one hour might not be enough to give learners enough time to articulate and share their strategies and that a follow-up lesson would have evidenced more progress.

We have adapted the lesson plan at the end of this chapter to reflect our analysis.

Note

1   A copy of the sheet is provided in Appendix B.

References

Boaler, J. (2001). Mathematical modelling and new theories of learning. *Teaching Mathematics and Its Applications: International Journal of the IMA*, 20(3), 121–128.

Bowland. (2008a). Classroom projects – Outbreak. www.bowlandmaths.org.uk/projects/outbreak.html

Bowland. (2008b). Tackling unstructured problems. *Handout 4*. www.bowlandmaths.org.uk/materials/pd/online/pd_01/pdf/pd_01_handbook_full.pdf

Blum, W. (1993). Mathematical modelling in mathematics education and instruction. In T. Breiteig, I. Huntley & G. Daiser-Messmer (Eds.), *Teaching and Learning Mathematics in Context* (pp. 3–14). London: Ellis Horwood.

Galbraith, P. L., & Clatworthy, N. J. (1990). Beyond standard models—meeting the challenge of modelling. *Educational Studies in Mathematics, 21*(2), 137–163.

Maaß, K. (2006). What are modelling competencies? *ZDM –Mathematics Education, 38*(2), 113–142.

Mason, J., Burton, L., & Stacey, K. (1982) *Thinking mathematically*. London: Addison-Wesley.

Radovic, D., Archer, R., Leask, D., Morgan, S., Pope, S., & Williams, J. (2014). Lesson study as a Zone of Professional Development in secondary mathematics ITE: From reflection to reflection-and-imagination. In *Proceedings of the 8th British congress of mathematics education*, 271–278.

Schoenfeld, A. H. (1992). Learning to think mathematically: Problem solving, metacognition, and sense making in mathematics. *Handbook of research on mathematics teaching and learning*, 334–370.

Appendix A
Lesson plan

Lesson summary

In this lesson students work on a real-life scenario.

The context used includes comparing the cost effectiveness of administering three different vaccines to the inhabitants of a fictional city.

Students develop strategies to administer three different vaccines and compare the cost effectiveness. They use their calculations and mathematical arguments to justify their choices.

Focus on students learning

- ◆ To use percentages to represent the mathematical situation.
- ◆ To build students' ability to use mathematical modelling and help them develop the ability to articulate thinking using mathematical language by explaining how they used mathematics to make decisions and to solve the given real-life problem.
- ◆ To be able to explain and reflect on how changing one of the parameters in their model would change the solution.

Lesson preparation

Students need some familiarity with the use of percentages.

The learners are given the 'outbreak' problem on the board while the sheet with the breakdown of the figures will be given out later. They will be given 5 minutes to initially look at the problem and process the information. This should stop them from becoming bogged down in the calculations before engaging with the mathematical modelling.

PowerPoint slides and worksheets are available from the Bowland (2008a) website.

The lesson plan

Stage 1: presupposed knowledge

What percentage of the UK population lives in your area? This will help the teacher assesses previous knowledge and tackle possible misconceptions or gaps.

Stage 2: understanding the problem

The introductory sheet is given out. At this stage no figures are given to prevent the learners from getting bogged down in calculations without reasoning. Learners work in small groups to devise a strategy. At this stage not many calculations are expected. Learners are expected to observe that they have enough money to give the whole population vaccine B.

Stage 3: Sharing of ideas

Strategies are shared. The teachers will insist on asking for strategies to tackle the problems and not on calculations. Calculations will be discussed only if misconceptions or errors are identified. The teacher will still focus on the real-life scenario, leaving the mathematising until later. Questioning will encourage learners to identify the variables significant for this problem. 'How many people can they save and why?' 'Can you give everybody vaccine A'; 'Can you give everybody vaccine B'; 'How many people do you save if you do that?' 'Will you have any money left over?' 'If everybody got the virus would you change your strategy?' 'Which is the maximum number of people you can save?' 'Do you think this is an effective strategy and why?' Teachers will emphasise that there isn't a unique strategy but that some strategies are more efficient than others. Learners are expected to understand that by giving everybody vaccine B they will save 70% of the population (assuming everybody is going to be exposed to the virus)

Stage 4: Group work

The table with the breakdown of figures is given out. Several questions can be written on the board while the learners work independently. The questions are related to observation of learners' work and are aimed at picking up on good ideas and significant strategies. At this stage the learners are expected to mathematise the problem and work with mathematical tools. The teachers can guide different groups by asking questions like, how much will it cost to give the health workers vaccine A? How much money do we have left over?

What happens if we give key service workers vaccine C instead? What percentage of the population will we save in this case?

Stage 5: Sharing of results

The teacher will lead learners to evaluate their strategies and compare results based on the initial question. A spreadsheet is used on the projector so that the effect of changing some of the parameters and variables can be evaluated quickly. Questions like: 'How many people did you save?'; 'What percentage of the population did you save?' 'How could have you saved more?' 'Why did you decide to save …?' 'Have you spent all your money?' 'Do you think the strategy was efficient and why?' 'Who saved the most people?' Learners will also be encouraged to critically evaluate each other's strategies by using questions like: 'Do we all agree with this group?', 'Who thinks it is more important to save students and school pupils and why?'

Suggestions for lesson study focus

- ◆ How does working in a computer room enhance reasoning?
- ◆ How does working in groups enhance reasoning?
- ◆ How do learners respond to dealing with a moral dilemma when working with mathematics?
- ◆ How can we help learners embrace messy solutions and build resilience through a real-life situation?

Appendix B
The task

Work is underway to try and prevent more people from being infected with the virus.

You have been put in charge of vaccinating people across a number of London Boroughs.

You have been given three different types of vaccines. Each one will not work 100% of the time but they have different levels of success.

Each vaccine costs a different amount of money per person.
You have a budget of **£5,000,000** and you have **945,550** people to vaccinate.

Your three vaccines are:

	Success rate	Cost of vaccine per person
Vaccine A	95%	£8.00
Vaccine B	70%	£3.50
Vaccine C	55%	£1.25

It's up to you to decide how best to vaccinate the population of your city. Go to the 'Planning' worksheet to start allocating vaccines.

Good luck!

 **OUTBREAK**

Strategic Planning

BOWLAND MATHS

	% of population	Number in population	Number to get vaccine A	Cost vaccine A	Number to get vaccine B	Cost vaccine B	Number to get vaccine C	Cost vaccine C
Medical workers (doctors, nurses)	8							
Key service workers (electricity, refuse)	12							
Food shop personnel	12							
Farmers and food producers	9							
Other shop workers	11							
Other professionals ... teachers, lawyers, etc	13							
Other trades people ... garages, decorators etc	9							
Retired people	9							
Students and school pupils	10							
Children under 5	7							
Totals	100							

Population	945,550
Budget	£5,000,000
Vaccine A	£8.00
Vaccine B	£3.50
Vaccine C	£1.25

Decide what number of people in each group you will vaccinate with vaccines A, B and C.

You must aim to stay within the budget of £5,000,000

What if the plan is that some people will NOT be vaccinated at all?

Extend the spreadsheet to take this into consideration.

Total Cost

Total no. people vaccinated
% of population given Vaccine A
% of population given Vaccine B
% of population given Vaccine C
Success rate of vaccines

Early algebra using real-life scenarios

Introduction

Within this chapter, we describe a lesson where learners are encouraged to investigate the relationship between two variables. In the fictional scenario a class is spending a day at the lake and the learners are tasked with a choice of hiring a boat from two different outlets. Billy's Brilliant Boat charges £27 up front plus £10 per hour while Sally's Super Sails charges £16 an hour with no extra cost. This lesson was adapted from a lesson developed as part of the Increasing Student Competence and Confidence in Algebra and Multiplicative Structures project (ICCAMS); see (Hodgen, Küchemann & Brown, 2014) for the original problem and more on ICCAMS generally. Within ICCAMS the activity encourages learners to make connections between different algebraic representations. The lesson discussed here is loosely based on the original but we decided to use different numbers (see reasons below), and was used as an introduction to algebra rather than dealing with multiple representations.

The lesson took place in a school in Manchester. The planning team consisted of a pre-service teacher and two of the authors, who were also the pre-service teacher's university tutors. The team met twice before the lesson to spend time on planning and the pre-service teacher taught the lesson while the two university tutors observed the learners' responses. All three participants were present during the post-lesson discussion. The pre-service teacher had previously been involved in a lesson study (LS) cycle that researched this particular lesson within our initial teacher education (ITE) course. This was particularly helpful for the planning team since the pre-service teacher could comment on what happened previously when justifying choices she wanted to make concerning this lesson. The learners, aged 11 to 12, were in their first year of secondary school and the lesson took place towards the end of the academic year as part of the introduction to an algebra unit. Class sizes are quite small at the school and there were only nine learners in this class, seven girls and two boys, but their attainment range was quite wide. Some learners were already familiar with algebra and were expected to be confident writing algebraic expressions while others were complete beginners. The pre-service teacher told the planning team that the children were all interested in mathematics and willing to engage with problems but despite their willingness to try, they were not confident discussing their mathematical ideas and she felt that some prompting and encouragement would be needed. She purposefully avoided writing the learning objectives on the board at the beginning of the lesson since she was concerned that the learners might switch off when they saw the word algebra.

The research focus for this lesson was: how does the use of a real-life scenario support the development of early algebraic understanding? We were not looking for young learners to move freely between different representations at this stage of their mathematical development, but we believed that it was important to give them a choice of representation to help them articulate their mathematical understanding. During planning, time was spent thinking about how to prompt learners to use algebraic representations to deal with a real-life problem.

Background to the lesson

Algebra is a very important part of the mathematics curriculum and at the heart of understanding mathematical structure. But many young learners see algebra as a system of arbitrary rules and the teaching of algebra often emphasises the procedural manipulation of symbols (Hodgen et al., 2014)

Algebraic *reasoning* is, however, a lot more than manipulating numbers and figures and, as in the lesson which follows, can be used within wider reasoning about real world contexts.

Learners have consistently had significant difficulties when learning the topic (see, for example, Hodgen, Küchemann, Brown & Coe, 2009). with the shift to abstract thinking being something that learners find most difficult. We are analysing here how using abstract ideas applied to real-life scenarios allows the development of mathematical understanding. For our analysis of the lesson, we will use the work on street mathematics developed by Nunes, Schliemann and Carraher (1993). Street mathematics is defined as the mathematical activity that is learned and undertaken outside school. Mathematical activity in street mathematics, in the marketplace in particular, is guided both by social and logical rules. It is mathematics that is useful and therefore involves the development of mathematical concepts as opposed to learning procedures by rote, without thinking. Nunes et al. (1993) find that people can more successfully solve equivalent mathematical problems to those found in school outside school, when assisted by the situational context. They, therefore, claim that addressing the disconnect between school mathematics and street mathematics has the potential to make mathematics learning accessible to a large number of people who traditionally would be considered unable to learn mathematics.

In their work, Nunes et al. (1993) reject the idea that street mathematics and school mathematics are polar opposites, one dealing with the general and the other one dealing with the particular. They develop a third way of thinking about mathematics learning, that of pragmatic schemas. Pragmatic schemas blur the boundaries between the general and particular. These schemas are ways of understanding new ideas that are developed through lived experience that are neither general nor particular but context sensitive. The context is not seen as a loss of generality but as an opportunity for learners to analyse the meaning and reasonableness of their answers. Street mathematics knowledge can therefore be translated into new situations that involve logico-mathematical relationships. They therefore advocate encouraging children to build their school mathematics on the foundation of their already available knowledge of street mathematics.

As observed in Chapter 7, teachers can experience difficulties in working with problem solving and mathematical modelling or in helping learners develop relational understanding (Skemp, 1976) since they can be preoccupied with getting their students through examinations and therefore find it quicker to present them with algorithms without a context. For example, the authors have observed that it is still common practice in many schools to focus on memorising rules such as 'taking to the other side' when solving equations rather than focusing on the comprehension of the meaning of the symbol '=' and of inverse operations. Although a minority of learners are able to make sense independently of algebraic rules through repetitive practice, the majority are left behind (Watson, Jones & Pratt, 2013).

This lesson deals mainly with understanding the idea of a variable, a concept that learners often find challenging. Variables are used in different ways in school algebra, for example:

- In their abstract manipulation, e.g. $2x + 3x = 5x$
- As a variable for which we want to find one (e.g. by solving linear equations) or more values (e.g. by solving linear inequalities or in studying more complex functions)
- As a parameter that can take a range of values but is temporarily fixed.

If young learners do not see the difference between these representations they can have problems.

The English language also causes confusion for learners (Mason & Sutherland, 2002). The words 'a', 'any', 'all' and 'everybody' can be used to indicate both the general and the particular ('consider *a* number', 'the sum of the angles of *a* triangle', 'take *any* number between 1 and 10'). Often, learners assume that the answer to a problem must necessarily be a number and transform the expression $3x + 4$ into the equation $3x + 4 = 0$ to achieve a numerical solution. Similarly, they might simplify 3a + 2b to 5ab.

Some learners might ignore a letter if they cannot comprehend its meaning (e.g. 3n becomes 3), others might believe that different letters must assume different values and would reject the solution $x = y = 1$. It is also important to observe that some of the writing rules in algebra contradict the arithmetic rules, for example 2a in algebra means $2 \times a$, while 27 is not 2×7 (Hart et al., 1981).

In this lesson, we attempt to encourage learners to construct their own understanding of algebra through a real-life scenario and build understanding upon their own experience of street (or outside-school) mathematics. Keeping in mind the situation in which the problem is represented allows learners to build their knowledge of school mathematics. We will also observe how learners develop their understanding while working in groups. The constructivist theory (based on work by Piaget) tells us that people have to construct their own knowledge but we must not forget that we are also social animals and that in real life we rarely solve a problem on our own. Nunes et al. (1993) also observed that oral explanations allow learners to use pragmatic schemas better than written explanations.

Suggested reading

Blum, W., Galbraith, P. L., Henn, H. W., & Niss, M. (2007). *Modelling and applications in mathematics education* (pp. 3–33). New York: Springer.

Chapman, O. (2007). Mathematical modelling in high school mathematics: Teachers' thinking and practice. In W. Blum, P. Galbraith, H. Henn, and M. Niss (Eds.), *Modelling and applications in mathematics education: The 14th ICMI study* (pp. 325–332). New York: Springer.

Shell Centre – The language of functions and graphs. www.mathshell.com/publications/tss/lfg/lfg_teacher.pdf. This resource contains classroom materials that support the use of different mathematical representations to describe and analyse the real world.

Lesson outline

The task involves deciding which boat hire outlet is the best choice, Billy's Brilliant Boat, which charges £27 up front plus £10 per hour or Sally's Super Sails which charges £16 an hour. In order to continue relating to the real-life scenario and prompt discussion other factors are introduced to the task, such as opening times and opportunities to provide lunch. The introduction of these extra pieces of information aims to allow learners to remain focused on the real-life scenario and get used to considering several factors, mathematical and not, when modelling real-life scenarios with algebra. The planning team believed that introducing other factors would encourage learners to discuss the task using everyday language and use their own knowledge of street mathematics.

The cost for each outlet had been carefully chosen so that it would be realistic, since the planning team felt it would be important for the learners to imagine themselves in the fictional scenario. Nunes et al. (1993) when reporting on some case studies observed that people refuse to engage with mathematical problems if they contradict their lived experience. Another important factor in deciding the cost was not to make it too easy to notice the point where hiring either would cost the same. If this was too obvious at first sight (with the solution being a whole number, for example) it might have trivialised the task. Often learners can (quite justifiably) not see the point of using algebra to solve a problem if said problem is easily solved at first sight using only common sense.

Boat hire task

Stage 1

Begin by presenting the scenario and probing whether the learners under-stand the problem as described. Then ask the learners to write down indi-vidually their own views and reasons related to which boat to hire. This is followed by a class discussion to share and reflect on their ideas. At this point, it may or may not arise that the different options will be cheaper depending on the length of time they are hired for. If this idea is introduced by students, it can be explored further. Contextual factors will arise and will be acknowl-edged by the teacher.

Stage 2

The next step is to break the learners into groups to agree an option and pre-pare a presentation and arguments to justify their choice. The relationship between the cost and the number of hours might be in the room at this stage, but we anticipate only a few learners will be able to fully articulate this. This next step aims to sustain discussion around the question in order to spread that understanding further.

Stage 3

In the final phase of the lesson, when they are presenting their group's ideas, many other factors unconnected with price may arise, e.g. how the boat looks. This is fine as this is the nature of street mathematics: other factors genuinely play a role in our decision-making. To refocus on mathematics, however, the teacher can ask questions such as what happens if the boat is being hired for 4.5 hours, if that hasn't arisen (again real-world factors may arise here, as often they will be hired only for full hours): which boat is best if we think we may be enjoying ourselves and want to extend another hour?; what happens at 0 hours?; and, how often do the costs cross over?

Lesson reflection and analysis

The LS lesson begins with a task (see Figure 8.1), pictures of boats were pro-jected alongside the task, and learners being asked to explain what they see. At this point the teacher is not focusing on the mathematics but is encourag-ing them to think about social and logical rules, as one would consider when

Sally Super Sails	Billy's Brilliant Boat
Only £16 per hour	£27 initial cost + £10 per hour
No hidden costs	Open weekdays and weekends
7 days a week	
We can provide lunch on request	

Figure 8.1 The task

using street mathematics. Nunes et al. (1993) observed that people engaging with mathematics are more likely to succeed if they engage in an activity they can imagine. This can refer to their lived experience but can also mean allowing them to imagine the situation and mentally represent the situation.

The learners comment on the task, including on the opening hours. They are then given a printout of the task and are asked to work independently. They have a blank piece of paper to record their thoughts. Some learners ask if they are allowed to choose one boat because they prefer how it looks and the teacher answers yes but also reminds them to use mathematics to justify their choice. In writing down their thoughts most learners produce a mix of contextual and mathematical reasons (see Figure 8.2)

In the discussion that follows, Zara says 'I don't need to do any mathematics. I can see that Sally is cheaper because I am not going to spend more than 4 hours on the boat'. Nina announces she has worked out the cost for each outlet for 1 hour and Lauren replies: 'but what if you want to stay longer?' Nina says: 'If you go for a long time one price will overlap the other one. So we need to work it out for a bit longer, but I worked it out for 3 hours and Sally is still cheaper'.

Another learner, Nadia, comments, 'I worked it out for 1 h, 2 h, 3 h, 6 h, 10 h but nobody would hire the boat for so long'. There is a discussion on how

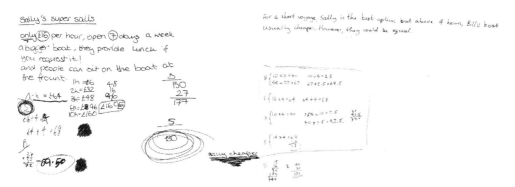

Figure 8.2 Examples of learners' work

long it is reasonable to spend on a boat at the lake. The teacher asks if it is reasonable to calculate the cost for 100 h and they all agree that there would be no point. This shows that the real-life scenario has engaged the learners and they are using the mathematics to make sense of it.

Nadia comments, 'in Billy's you need to pay nearly £30 [before even starting] that is worth nearly 3 hours on the boat [Billy's]'. There is a class discussion here. Some learners believe you need to add £27 each time. At this point it might have been helpful to construct a formula, or a table, so everybody could analyse how the £27 affected the cost.

Nina says, 'I checked for 5 hours, Sally is £80 and Billy is £77'. At this point the teacher intervenes and says, 'Zara you said Sally is always cheaper, is this true?' Zara responds, 'it depends on how many hours you want to spend on the boat'. At this point many in the class seem to agree that the answer to the question is: 'it depends'.

For the next episode the teacher splits the class into two groups. One group is asked to imagine they want to spend 5 hours on the boat and the other group imagine that they want to spend 4 hours on the boat. The two groups are asked to persuade the teacher, and the other group, on which plan is best to take and they are given blank paper to write out their sales pitch. This required choice for each group perhaps could have limited the possible discussions around which boat is cheaper. Learners might have been more engaged with the discussion if they had to come up with their own joint position. On the other hand, asking them to imagine a specific position can make learners engage more easily with a problem, and it does ensure there is discussion either side of the crossover point of 4.5 hours.

In the '4 hour' group, Nadia says, 'for 4 hours Sally is cheaper, only by £3 but you can buy sandwiches with that'. Omar observes that 'for 5 hours it changes'. Zara says:' I think Billy was cheaper' and the group respond in one voice, 'it depends!' The learners then start discussing how for 5 hours with Billy you would need to bring your own lunch and this leads the group away from the mathematics (which they feel they already agree on) and back into the contextual factors. Partly this is still cost-related such as how much lunch costs, but then also includes wider factors such as what they will get for lunch and how big and comfortable each of the boats would be.

As discussed earlier, the learners are using their pragmatic schemas, being able to make generalisations about this task but remaining focused on the context. 'Keeping the situation in perspective seems to help not only with carrying out arithmetic but also with using situational schemas for solving

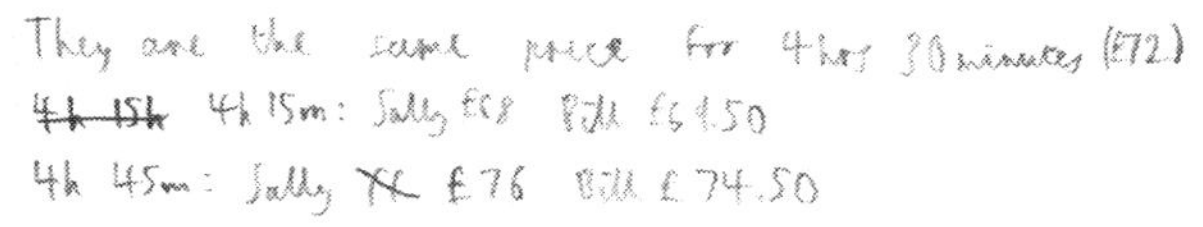

They are the same price for that 30 minutes (£72)
~~4h 15h~~ 4h 15m: Sally £68 Bill £69.50
4h 45m: Sally ~~£~~ £76 Bill £74.50

Figure 8.3 Example of learner's work

more complex problems' (Nunes et al., 1993. p. 145). After a few minutes, the learners present their argument to the teacher. While the development of mathematical thinking is evident in what the learners have come up with, the cost of hire is generally assumed and a lot more attention is given to other factors such as how a boat looks, and comfort and lunch. This shows that the learners feel confident with their understanding; which will be cheapest 'depends' and, while taking that for granted, see that the other factors matter more now.

The teacher then wants to bring the focus back to the mathematical questions and try to develop understanding further. She asks the class when both groups have finished presenting, 'Can we check what happens if we want the boat for 4.5 hours?'

Omar says, 'You cost it for 4 hours and then add £5 for Billy'. David says, '[For Sally] 16 times 4 plus 8'. See Figure 8.3 for a written example from one pupil.

The teacher then asks, 'What happens if I want to hire for 4 h and 15 minutes?' Lauren says, 'Just half again'. It is evident at this point that learners are using substitution correctly. The teacher was, however, very surprised that nobody observed that after 4.5 hours Billy is always cheaper but that they would go back to the substitution each time. Could they have been encouraged to observe that after 4.5 hours Sally is always more expensive through a question such as, 'can you predict what happens after 10 hours'? It may also have been useful here to bring in an alternative presentation (i.e. a graph as in the original ICCAMS lesson), but here the choice of numbers, chosen to seem more realistic, was not particularly conducive to that.

Five minutes before the end of the lesson a brief assessment task is given out (see Figure 8.4) and learners work independently in silence. All learners apart from two answered that $3n$ is bigger than $n + 3$. They seem not to have made a link between the lesson activity and the assessment problem. This difficulty could also link back to the street mathematics discussed in 8.2 and the fact that the assessment task has no context. Maybe they would have made the connection if the boat hire activity had ended having agreed on algebraic formulae to work out the cost.

In particular, the work below shows that Omar (Figures 8.4 and 8.5) has fully understood how to use algebra in the context of the boat hire task but has not linked it with the final activity.

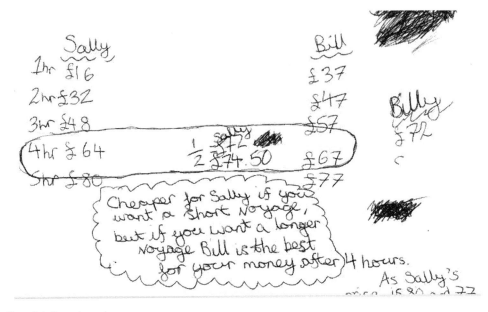

Figure 8.4 Omar's work

Exit ticket:

Which one is bigger and why?

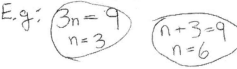

Figure 8.5 Omar's assessment task

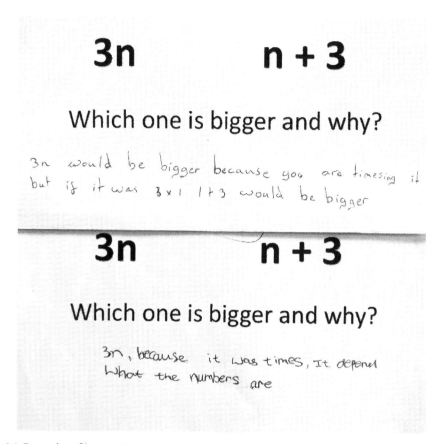

3n   **n + 3**

Which one is bigger and why?

3n would be bigger because you are timesing it but if it was 3×1 1+3 would be bigger

3n   **n + 3**

Which one is bigger and why?

3n, because it was times, It depend What the numbers are

Figure 8.6 Examples of learners' assessment tasks

Looking at learners' work from the pictures above (Figure 8.6) they have certainly developed some understanding of algebra within this particular context. They have not yet generalised their understating and are still very interested in the context of this particular problem. We believe, however, that this lesson has prepared the groundwork for them to generalise and move more comfortably into algebra in the very near future.

> **Pause for thought**
>
> Consider the above lesson reflection and analysis.
> - ★ Were there any critical moments that were not anticipated by the lesson plan?
> - ★ If you were going to teach this lesson to one of your classes when would you introduce a formula and why?

What we have learned

Within this section, we initially return to the research focus 'how does the use of a real-life scenario support the development of early algebraic understanding?' We then discuss the lesson study process and how this differs from other chapters and finally discuss possible next steps.

Real-life scenario

As expected at the beginning of the lesson all learners believed that Sally's boat hire was cheaper; however, their understanding developed throughout the lesson within the context of the scenario. After a while they could competently substitute values in order to calculate the cost, even if many did not generalise what they were doing to a more abstract scenario. The learners' understanding developed significantly within a meaningful context and mathematics and the real world were connected throughout the lesson, but learners were using their pragmatic schemas, keeping their reasoning in the context of the boat hire situation. They were able to test the impact of different mathematical models within the lived (or make-believe lived) experience. Learners were building their knowledge of school mathematics and obtaining progressively more formal representations by considering mathematical and social constraints on the situation. The make-believe situation supports the understanding while still in context. This will ultimately lead to the learner being able to transpose their thinking to more abstract scenarios, even if this needs time and for some learners cannot happen in only one lesson.

The teacher also observed that some of the learners who never ask questions or volunteer answers were fully engaged with this lesson. Sasha, for example, is a very high achiever who always gets top marks in the tests but never volunteers to answer. However, during this lesson she was instrumental in persuading the rest of the class that the cost depends on how long you have the boat for. The teacher told us that in the lesson she saw a different 'face' of Sasha; this in itself is considered a success.

Lesson study process

We have observed that very often during the post-lesson discussion we say that the next lesson is going to be even more interesting than the one we are discussing. Impact cannot always be observed in one lesson but the groundwork made in one lesson can be shown in subsequent lessons. In fact, one might argue that this is a desirable way of learning since it is more long lasting. The pre-service teacher was very satisfied with the lesson and felt she had built a strong foundation upon which to develop algebraic thinking. She felt that in future lessons, when dealing with algebra, she could remind the class of this lesson to develop their abstract thinking. She very much saw this LS cycle as an opportunity to develop her practice; particularly the planning meetings when reflecting on expected student responses. In particular, having taught this lesson before in a group as part of the ITE course, she was able to predict expected responses and reflect on possible misconceptions. She was also grateful to be able to discuss and reflect with others on her learners' actual responses. In fact, beginning teachers are often too preoccupied about other factors, such as the practical organisation of the lesson and behaviour management, to reflect on the pedagogy. She also felt that this LS cycle gave her an opportunity to try an activity she might have not attempted in isolation.

Next steps

By observing children learning and engaging with this lesson we confirmed that allowing learners to imagine a real-life scenario and keeping the social context alive through the lesson allows them to rely on their informal mathematical understanding (street mathematics) to make progress. Solving a problem in this case requires choosing a model, making a decision about how to proceed as well as applying it. Thinking in this way learners developed pragmatic schemas, i.e. context-sensitive mathematical ideas, that allow them to test for the reasonableness of their answers. Some learners in this lesson could have been encouraged to generalise further with the use of questioning. As observed in the lesson analysis the teacher could have guided those learners who were ready to observe that after 4.5 hours Billy is always cheaper. This could have been achieved by drawing a graph or using a table of results. It would be interesting to consider how to encourage learners to draw a graph when there is no apparent reason to do so and when the graph is not easy to draw since priority has been given to using figures that are realistic. Also, agreeing on an algebraic formula with the class might have made the link between the context-sensitive boat hire task and the more abstract activity at the end of the lesson. This could, however, be a very good way to begin the following lesson and give learners time to develop their understanding.

Pause for thought

Try the lesson with one of your classes. If you can use it as a research lesson using lesson study with a colleague, even better!

References

Hart, K. M., Brown, M. L., Kuchemann, D. E., Kerslake, D., Ruddock, G., & McCartney, M. (1981). *Children's understanding of mathematics: 11–16* (p. 212). London: John Murray.

Hodgen, J., Küchemann, D., & Brown, M. (2014). Learning experiences designed to develop algebraic thinking: Lessons from the ICCAMS project in England. In *Learning experiences to promote mathematics learning: Yearbook 2014 Association of Mathematics Educators* (pp. 171–186). Singapore: World Scientific.

Hodgen, J., Küchemann, D., Brown, M., & Coe, R. (2009). Children's understandings of algebra 30 years on. *Research in Mathematics Education*, 11(2), 193–194.

Mason, J., & Sutherland, R. (2002). *Key aspects of teaching algebra in schools.* Sudbury: Qualifications and Curriculum Authority.

Nunes, T., Schliemann, A. D., & Carraher, D. W. (1993). *Street mathematics and school mathematics.* Cambridge: Cambridge University Press.

Skemp, R. R. (1976). Relational understanding and instrumental understanding. *Mathematics Teaching*, 77(1), 20–26.

Watson, A., Jones, K., & Pratt, D. (2013). *Key ideas in teaching mathematics: Research-based guidance for ages 9–19.* Oxford: Oxford University Press.

Appendix A

Lesson plan and resources

Lesson summary

Learners decide which outlet is better when hiring a boat for a day. They consider social and logical rules as well as calculation involved in choosing a price plan.

Focus on student learning

a   Develop the concept of variable and understand that the best value for money depends on how long the boat is hired for.
b   Understand that the cost is the same at 4.5 hours.
c   Be able to communicate their decisions on the best plan using mathematics as well as social and logical rules.

Lesson preparation

Learners will need time and some prompting to read the task and imagine they are at the lakes and wish to hire a boat. Images are used in this case to help them.

The lesson

Stage 1
Introducing the context. The teacher asks the class where they like to go on holiday and shows them some pictures of the Lake Districts. Then the fictional scenario of a school trip is introduced to the class.

Year 7 is spending a day in the Lake District and wish to hire a boat for the day. Billy's Brilliant Boat charges £27 up front plus £10 per hour and is open weekdays and weekends. Sally's Super Sails charges £16 an hour with no extra cost and can provide lunch on request.

It is possible at this stage that a learner might answer that the better value outlet depends on how long we wish to hire the boat for. This will not, however, affect the success of the lesson since they will be encouraged to justify their answers using mathematics.

Stage 2

Learners work independently on the following question:

◆ Whose boat should you hire and why?
◆ What is the most important thing we need to consider in order to answer the question?

The teacher circulates around the room observing the strategies employed and making notes of possible critical moments. Learners are encouraged to record their findings.

It is expected that the learners will try various values and eventually begin to appreciate the need to work systematically. Some will possibly begin to draw a table of values. At this stage the learners are not expected to write an algebraic expression or to use linear graphs.

Learners are given time to think about the problem. No table is given to them as this might close an open problem too much, guide learners towards one representation and stop independent thinking. The class teacher is, however, aware that some learners might need to be guided forward using a table or try the cost for a different number of hours. Learners are expected to discuss what happens if we hire the boat for one more hour. Maybe they will start considering if it is possible to hire the boat for half an hour. The teachers will be looking for different representations. In particular, if observed at this stage, examples of systematic work, use of tables, graphs and algebraic expression will be shared with the class.

Stage 3

Learners work in groups to prepare an argument to persuade the school to hire from one of the two outlets. They are expected to use everyday language as well as their mathematical representations to make their point. Possible difficulties include wanting to reproduce what has been discussed with the class. The teacher will prompt the learners to use algebraic representations.

Possible prompts for the discussion in groups:

◆ Do we all agree?
◆ Can you repeat what X said?
◆ Did anybody write something different?
◆ Can you think of a different way to say the same thing?

Whole class discussion – the teacher asks: what happens if we hire the boat for 4.5 hours?

Stage 4

Plenary. Learners are encouraged to decide which one is bigger, 3n or n+3. Most learners are expected to draw on their understanding of today's lesson to decide that the answer depends on the value of n. However, the understanding of algebraic representations is only starting to develop for these learners and some misconceptions might still appear.

Possible extension

◆ Use alternative models to describe the scenario. For example, graphs could be used to link time spent on the boat and cost of hire.

Suggestions for lesson study focus

◆ How can a real-life scenario motivate and engage disengaged students?
◆ How can a real-life scenario be used to develop learners' confidence?
◆ How can students build on their own existing understanding to develop abstract thinking?

9

Sustaining argument about randomness

Introduction

Within this chapter, we describe a lesson where students were asked to reflect on the idea of randomness. Learners write two lists, one that results from having flipped a coin ten times and one that is made up. They then play against each other; the aim of the game is to correctly guess whether the list shown is real or fake.

The context allows the teacher to manage class discussion and promote understanding through talk. The teacher initiates discussion by asking if guessing correctly is due to luck or to skill. At the end of the game learners position themselves in the class according to their answers; those that believe that winning the game is mainly due to skill move to the right and those that believe that it is more due to luck move to the left on a scale. Learners are then encouraged to persuade each other to change sides.

The context for this lesson is a state-funded secondary school in the north of England catering for learners aged between 11 and 16. The class involved with this lesson study was a high achieving year 10 class (ages 14–15) with 23 students. They had limited previous experience of whole class dialogue and we focus here on how the teacher encouraged the use of discussion in order to construct mathematical understanding.

The authors planned the lesson with a pre-service teacher at the end of his teacher training course. He had been working with this class for around six weeks before teaching this lesson and described the class as very quiet. He was expecting to have to work hard to facilitate discussion. This pre-service teacher, who was developing into a very successful teacher, had also previously conducted a lesson study cycle on this lesson as part of the Initial Teacher Education (ITE) course. He used the earlier experience as a point of reference for this lesson.

The research focus here is on sustaining argument in a classroom with students not generally accustomed to discussions and group reasoning. We discuss how the student teacher successfully managed to achieve this and analyse in some detail the student discussion and resulting reasoning.

Background to the lesson

This lesson was designed by one of the authors (DS) to stimulate discussion and help learners reflect on the meaning of probability, and randomness in particular. Using coin tossing within probability teaching is very common, and judging real from made-up lists has also been used by many others (see, for example, https://nrich.maths.org/7250).

Probability is intrinsically linked to real life and most real-life decisions involve a degree of chance, for example, what to wear or which activity to undertake based on the weather, or more important decisions around one's health. A doctor might, for example, give patients statistical information regarding the side effects of a certain medication. The patient who does not understand uncertainty will be at a disadvantage (Watson, Jones & Pratt, 2013).

Understanding of probability is linked closely with understanding of language. In fact, one of the difficulties associated with the learning of the topic is the fact that there are many words used in everyday language to describe uncertainty. These words do not always reflect the language of probability and can, in some cases, cause misconceptions. Clarity can be achieved by allowing learners plenty of time to articulate and unpick their understanding, for example by discussing how to place such words on a number line from 0 to 1 (Graham, 2006), see the pause for thought at the end of this section.

One of the first misconceptions learners have is that all outcomes are always equally likely, as would happen for the score on a fair die. According to Graham (2006), this misconception might be caused by a lack of understanding of the difference between theoretical and experimental probability and over-exposure to symmetrical cases, for example the un-biased die or spinner. The abstract nature and symmetry of these objects excludes the effect of other variables and the lack of context allows for all events to seem to be equally likely. However, in real life this is almost never the case, for example the probability of rain on a certain day is influenced by the time of the year, the weather the day before etc. and so the events 'raining' and 'not raining' are not equally likely. Learners might believe that the probability of getting two heads when tossing a coin twice is 1/3 since they consider the three possible outcomes: two heads, two tails, and one head and one tail as equally likely, forgetting that this last event includes both one head and one tail, and the reverse one tail and one head.

Other very common misconceptions when working with uncertainty include:

◆ A six is less likely than any other number to get when rolling a die (in particular, if six is the desired number in a board game)
◆ If you get a number on the first roll you are less likely to get the same number on the next roll ('the gambler's fallacy').

In the first case learners might be considered to be correct since the probability of rolling a six is only 1/6 while the probability of not rolling a six is 5/6. However, this might lead to the misconception that a six is a rare score to get, compared with a one, for instance. Similarly, people might believe that if a number has not appeared for a while in the lottery, it is very likely to come up soon. This misconception is caused by a lack of understanding of independent events (Graham, 2006). Learners might even believe that a real list of coin flips cannot contain too many heads (or tails) in a row. This lesson tries to involve other factors when making decisions about the theoretical event of flipping a coin and we will see in this chapter how strings of either heads or tails are, in fact, very likely.

While conversations about chance enter our lives quite early on (Fischbein, 1975, observed some intuition about relative frequencies in children as young as pre-school), probability is not formally studied in the UK until the learners are in high school, and many of the same difficulties observed in children's understanding of probability continue into adulthood (Watson et al., 2013). In order to understand such apparently contradictory statements it is useful to consider the Tversky and Kahneman (1974) definition of *heuristics*. Heuristics are defined as a useful intuitive understanding that can guide decision-making in the presence of uncertainty but without the involvement of formal understanding or procedures. As such they can cause errors and misconceptions. Heuristics can be divided into the following three different types (Tversky & Kahneman, 1974).

◆ Availability – intuition based on the recall of similar events from long-term memory. For example 'it is a common experience that the subjective probability of traffic accidents rises temporarily when one sees a car overturned on the side of the road' (p. 1127).

◆ Representativeness – which expects outcomes to be representative of the perceived sample space. For example, when considering a short sequence of coin tosses, 'people regard the sequence H T H T T H to be more likely than H H H T T T which does not appear random and also more likely than the sequence H H H H T T which does not represent the fairness of the coin' (p. 1125). This agrees with Watson and Moritz (2003) who found that students disregard experience and judge fairness according to appearance of symmetry.

◆ Adjustment and anchoring – where estimates are made by starting from an initial value that is then adjusted in some way to produce a final answer.

Within this chapter we will mainly focus on the representativeness heuristic as will be seen later in 'Lesson reflection and analysis'.

Watson et al. (2013) suggest that new approaches to teaching could better nurture early intuition and avoid misconception. As always, a robust understanding of what students already know can provide the starting point from which to construct more formal understanding. Learners arrive at high school with intuitive naïve ideas about probability but might not recognise the limitations of their perceptions. We believe the role of the teacher is to expose learners to these limitations by causing cognitive conflict and to draw on learners' intuitions to aid development. This lesson attempts to address this by creating a lived experience for the learners to discuss and unpick.

Shaughnessy and Ciancetta (2002) demonstrated that giving learners the opportunity to play a probability game and seeing what happens helps in developing understanding. In addition to this development, the game scenario here is also used to motivate learners and harness their curiosity. The competitive aspect of the activity is used to support the development of mathematical dialogue. From their direct experience of the game, it is expected that some learners will have used some strategy and been successful and will therefore argue the case for skill, while others may have guessed, and therefore link more strongly with the arguments for it being luck. We have analysed mathematical dialogue in other chapters in this book (for example, see Chapter 5). Here, however, the type of dialogue is slightly different since learners are encouraged to defend their (often) polarised positions.

Swan (2001) suggests that understanding created by discussion is more robust and longer lasting. In this particular lesson the teacher creates a tension by presenting contradictory opinions (is it luck or is it skill?) The intent to persuade others about their own ideas gives learners an opportunity to examine their own reasoning.

In this context, the teacher takes the role of a facilitator who values everyone's opinion and does not try to push their own; they do, however, work hard to ensure at least two different perspectives are in the room. Occasionally, the teacher might also intervene, if the discussion is flagging, by following up a point of view, playing devil's advocate, or asking students to consider other's arguments; 'why do you think X thinks it is all skill?' and 'what do you think the other side's best argument is?'

In analysing how this lesson allowed learners to develop and sustain mathematical discussion we use Mercer's (2002) distinction of three types of discussion.

- ◆ *Cumulative* discussion, which supports learners in building on each other's ideas in a positive non-critical way
- ◆ *Disputational*, which is characterised by disagreement and individual decision-making and is characterised by the unwillingness to take the other person's point of view
- ◆ *Exploratory*, which allows learners to build on each other's ideas in a collaborative and critical manner when different points of views are contrasted and alternatives are considered. Children who have developed their ability to construct knowledge by explanatory talk often use words such as 'because', 'if', 'why' and 'I think' more often than other children who have not developed these skills.

Mercer (2002) argues that most talk in classrooms is disputational rather than cumulative or exploratory and sees exploratory talk, driven by the desire to new understanding as opposed to trying to protect one individual identity and interest, as the preferred type of talk. Mercer also observes, however, that no talk happens in isolation and often learning episodes present aspects of all three. We will see in this chapter how the three types of talk coexist in this lesson and how they are used in different ways to build understanding. Discussion is, in fact, used in the lesson to generate and hopefully resolve a motivating kind of disputational talk.

> **Suggested reading**
>
> Batanero, C., Chernoff, E. J., Engel, J., Lee, H. S., & Sánchez, E. (2016). *Research on teaching and learning probability*. Hamburg: Springer.
> Graham, A. (2006). *Developing thinking in statistics*. London: Sage.
> SMILE probability resources. This includes games, investigations and practical activities. www.stem.org.uk/resources/elibrary/resource/32186/probability

Lesson outline

The expected outcome of the lesson is that the students will develop their understanding of randomness by arguing their side of the argument.

The task involves arguing whether being able to guess if a list is the result of tossing a coin ten times or if it is made up. Is it down to skill or luck? This game allows learners to reflect on the idea of randomness. Learners recognise that the theoretical probability here is not enough to make a decision (as often happens in real life) about the list. Some of the types of arguments relate to what a real list would look like (patterns, length of strings) and whether the person writing the fake list is able to fool the other player by making a 'good' fake list. Other factors can sometimes arise, for example people's handwriting might give away which list is fake and which one is real.

Stage 1
A starter can be used if the teacher feels it is necessary to quickly focus the class on probability. However, you might wish to start directly by watching a video where a coin is tossed ten times giving ten heads in a row (see link in the lesson plan in Appendix A).

Stage 2
Learners create two lists, one real (resulting from tossing a coin ten times) and one fake. It is essential that learners understand the rules of the game so that they know what they are trying to do with their fake lists and, for example, keep their two lists secret. The order of creating the lists should be

considered; it is possible to allow either order, as this will influence the nature of some fake lists, producing more variety.

Stage 3

Learners play the game in pairs. If they guess correctly they stay where they are and if they don't 'win' they move to the other side of the class; it's a knockout competition.

After the first round there is a brief class discussion where the teacher asks two of the learners from each side to explain why they believe they have lost or won. The teacher at this stage can get a good picture of the learners' level of understanding of randomness. The game is continued until there is one winner. After each round the teacher collects opinions on why people believe they won or lost. The idea of skill and luck is slowly introduced by the teacher, highlighting responses that link to skill in some way or to luck.

Stage 4

Whole class discussions. After presenting their opinions, learners are asked to position themselves on an imaginary number line using a 'luck versus skill' scale. Again, the teacher's role here is that of facilitator and opinions are not challenged. This should allow learners to challenge each other. At this point we will expect the class to be polarised. Learners are asked to prepare an argument to try and move more people to their side. We expect more exploratory talk, as described above, when learners plan the defence of their position in small groups. Arguments are presented and learners are asked if they wish to move.

Stage 5

If the trick was shown at the start of the lesson and there is enough time learners can watch the video where the trick behind getting ten consecutive heads is explained (see link in the lesson plan in Appendix A).

Pause for thought

Think about teaching this lesson to *your* class.

- ★ Do you think the Derren Brown or alternative video would stimulate discussion at the start of the lesson?
- ★ Could you design an alternative probability game to uncover student's understanding of randomness?
- ★ What prior learning do your students have that would feed into their potential arguments of whether winning the game is skill or luck?

Lesson reflection and analysis

The lesson began with a brief starter used to encourage students to focus on probability. The teacher then shows a Derren Brown video (2012) called '10 heads in a row' (www.youtube.com/watch?v=XzYLHOX50Bc) and asks 'is this possible?' there are a few nods of the head, and not wanting a discussion yet, the teacher moves on.

The task is explained (Figure 9.1) and students create two lists of ten coin tosses (one real and one fake) recording heads and tails, on the sheets of paper provided. The decision by the planning team was to create the fake list first, encouraging the idea of skill and the possibility of the 'string' argument that we describe later.

The teacher stresses the importance of making the fake list look 'real' and that this is a game that they want to win. Students then pair up and choose one of their lists to show to their opponent for them to guess whether it is real or fake (Figure 9.2).

They then reverse roles. The teacher emphasises that both can win and both can lose; it's not just one winner and one loser. The winners are directed to the left-hand side of the room and the losers to the right. Below we describe, and begin to analyse, the outcomes after each round of the game.

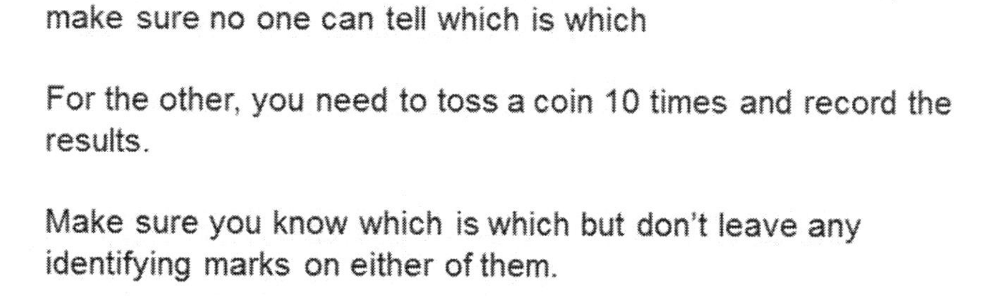

Probability

You are going to make two lists:

For the first one, you need to make up a fake list of 10 coin tosses. Write it out as a list: H T T H H... etc. Do it secretly and make sure no one can tell which is which

For the other, you need to toss a coin 10 times and record the results.

Make sure you know which is which but don't leave any identifying marks on either of them.

Figure 9.1 The task

Figure 9.2 Playing the game

Round 1

Win

Lose

After round 1 there were only four students that did not guess correctly and 'lost', and 19 that had correctly guessed whether the list was real or fake and 'won', and the teacher commented that he had never had that many people win at once, 'that's impressive'. Congratulating those that 'won' is a way that the teacher is beginning to plant the idea that there is some skill to the game. He asked a student why they had lost. 'Jack, you think Archie had a convincing list, why was his fake list convincing?' Jack replied 'because of how many heads were in a row, that made me think maybe it was real, but then I found out it wasn't real'. When asking the winners if they had used any strategy, responses varied, Ben replies that it's a '50–50 chance, so I just guessed' and Olivia commented on order of heads and tails 'when writing the fake list, I wouldn't put lots of the same thing in a row as I don't think people would believe it'. At this stage, students are describing their strategies; all are building on their prior knowledge of probability in some way. Ben says the probability of getting a heads or tails is 50–50, and Jack and Olivia consider the number of the same thing in a row and what they would expect to happen in that situation (they seem to be saying that there should be some heads in a row but not too many). All three are using intuition in some form and the heuristic 'representativeness', as discussed earlier.

The teacher encourages students in the losing group to discuss what they think is happening in the game, while the winners play the next round.

Round 2

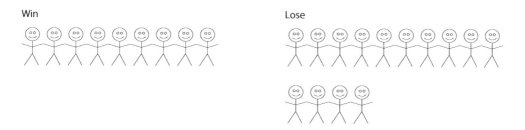

An additional ten students 'lose' after this round, with the teacher describing it as a dramatic round. When asked about his game, Finley agrees with Ben that it is a 50–50 chance, the teacher re-iterated 'so pure luck' (emphasising the idea of luck). The role of the teacher during this part of the lesson is to highlight ideas that link with luck and skill to enable a good discussion later and for students to see that both skill and luck could be viable. He continues to do this by asking if everyone agreed (with pure luck) or did anyone have a good strategy (bringing the idea of skill in to the mix again). 'Sophie, you have won twice, do you have a strategy?' she replies 'Because they had a lot of the same ones in a row and I didn't think they'd write that down.' The teacher suggests 'so you guessed real each time and you were right' and she agrees. At this point the teacher emphasises that Sophie has a strategy; hers is similar to Jack and Olivia's ideas earlier 'length of strings of the same thing'. He encourages everyone in the class to try to figure out the game and what they think, particularly those on the losing side.

Round 3

Win   Lose

After round 3, a further three lose, and the teacher points out the differing numbers losing and winning each time and recaps the numbers that have lost so far and asks for comments. Finley comments 'purely random, if there is more people then there is more chance of them going out'. Nathan responds describing a pattern, 'four then loads then two' so he thinks 'possibly loads will lose again this time'.

The conversation moves back to strategy and a winner (Zara) describes her strategy as looking for long strings of the same thing (not defining how many that is though), repeating Sophie's strategy from earlier. The teacher suggests that they (Sophie and Zara) should be able to keep winning (as they both have a strategy) so we'll find out. One of them replies, 'a lot of pressure!'

While the 'winners' continue the game, the 'losers' watch the games being played out on the other side of the classroom. Some pair up with another 'loser' and play the game again to see if they can catch them out with one of their lists. A few discuss the idea that some of the students must have been cheating, so they don't believe they lost.

Discussions linking to the task involved comparing their lists, for instance looking at the real ones and being surprised by length of strings and 'fairness' of the coin; 'I got six', 'I got four', 'I only got two tails' (we are assuming here that the student was surprised by the fact they got eight heads and only two tails in total, again building on heuristics mentioned earlier]. Someone else adds (referring to 'only got two tails') 'it's the flipping method, the way they flip, depends which way they land'. The talk here is cumulative 'exactly', 'it's skill, yeah', students listening to each other and linking this with their own experience.

Round 4

Win   Lose

A further three lose this time and the discussion initially focuses on the two 'strategists', one of whom lost. When describing what happened, Sophie said 'it had a list of three, so it was a string but not long or short, so not enough to tell whether it's real or fake'. This shows a limiting factor in her mathematics, she does not know if having a string of three is likely or unlikely to happen. In fact, the probability of having at least one string of three heads is approximately 0.51, i.e. just more likely than not, however at least one string of three (heads and/or tails) is approx. 0.82 (for more details about the mathematics see Appendix B). One of the remaining winners, Ella, explained that she had guessed that Zara's list was fake because it just looked like a 'nice' pattern. The teacher suggests that if you were writing a fake list there may be a pattern to it (again emphasising possibly an element of skill both when writing but also when analysing a list).

Round 5

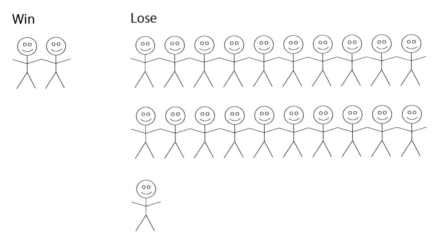

One more loses, Ella, so there are two winners left. The teacher asks 'Ella, what happened this time, your strategy worked last time but not this time?' She replies 'He [Ben] had a long list of heads so I thought it would be real as I didn't think he'd make that up' but Ben had made that up.

Round 6: a winner!

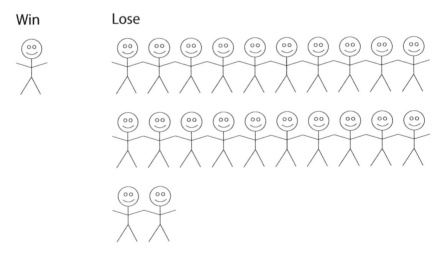

The teacher encourages the class to give Zara a round of applause (does this imply there is skill to the game or is Zara just a lucky winner?)

The lesson moves to the next stage with the teacher directing students to consider the game and decide where to position themselves on a scale from pure luck to pure skill (Figure 9.3); these everyday terms are deliberately employed here.

When we have taught/observed the lesson previously students tend to spread out along the line with clusters in a few places. In this lesson students move to three groups, there are 11 on (or very close to) the pure luck side,

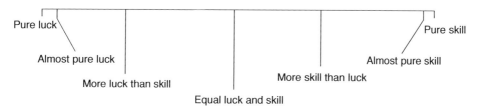

Figure 9.3 Luck/skill scale

seven on (or again close to) the pure skill side and five (Chloe, Nathan, Jack, Emily and Ruby) in the middle. The teacher begins the whole class discussion with asking students about their positions.

'Jasmine, why are you edging towards the skill side?' She responds 'you can kinda trick people with patterns … like more than one of the same thing in a row'. The teacher comments that her comment is quite a common theme coming through now. Caitlin who is positioned on the pure luck side shares her argument 'because I didn't use any strategy for it and I don't think there's any way of working out whether it is fake or real' and Chloe, who is positioned in the middle, adds 'because it's luck but then you can also look for patterns and look for whether it is neat or scruffy'. At this point, the teacher decides to split the group in half and asks everyone in the middle to choose a side; all initially decide to go to the pure skill (perhaps to even out the numbers) but when asked if they are happy with their choice, two students (Emily and Ruby) change their minds and move to luck. In these new groups, students are encouraged to discuss their ideas and try to come up with their best argument to convince the other side. There is animated discussion with the teacher listening in. During the post-lesson discussion the teacher told us that he was trying to pick up on the most passionate arguments to feed into the whole-class segments.

On the luck side there is an argument about whether it is pure luck or mainly luck with some skill. Ben tries to use mathematics to look at combinations, mentioning 200 (10 flips and 2 choices per flip so Ben multiplies to get 200 rather than calculating $2^{10} = 1024$). He also begins to consider that there may be a little bit of skill when he mentions 'trying to guess what they'd put in their fake list', but still believes mainly luck. Caitlin is not happy with that and still believes that it is pure luck. The teacher stresses that even if you argue with people on the same side as you, it's not a bad thing. On the skill side, discussions involve where they came in the game as this may back up their argument. Someone came fourth, one lost in the first round, but the winner is on their team too. They move on to discuss whether others lied to them when playing the game. There is also a lot of comparing of each other's pair of sheets and playing the game again. During these group discussions the talk tends to be cumulative.

The class is brought back together and the teacher asks the skill group if they are pure skill or more skill than luck

> Archie [on skill side, keen to respond]: Because you can trick people by putting strings of heads or tails or mix them up … or stare them in the eyes and intimidate them! [Here, the student recognises that there are other factors that can affect the game as well as the randomness within the coin flipping]

> Teacher: Any counter argument from the other side?

> Ben [on luck side]: There is 50–50 chance of whether you get heads or tails, combine that with the flips you do, there are two outcomes for each flip and 10 flips so there are 200 different that you could make, so the chance of guessing is 1 in 200 but that is quite low. [The teacher decided not to pick up on this mathematical error at this point, in order to remain focused on the luck/skill debate, and summarises the position as slight bit of skill but mainly luck.]

> Ella [luck side]: There is skill to it, as you can use chains and patterns but it's also luck whether the person used that skill in a way to trick you or it actually happened. [Here, Ella comments on being able to judge, in some way, the mathematical understanding of the opponent. The teacher summarises again and suggests that students can change sides if they hear something convincing].

> Caitlin [luck side]: It's pure luck. I don't understand what skill you could have to be able to understand the thought process of another person to decide what to put in each list.

> Amber [luck side]: It *is* pure luck.

> Teacher: Who can convince Caitlin and Amber that there must be some element of skill? [At this stage the teacher is encouraging everyone to listen to each other's argument and, in particular, trying to persuade Caitlin and Amber to see other's points of view (to move towards exploratory talk)].

> Sophie [skill side]: We've said everything: handwriting, layout and different strings. When they are making it up they will write it neater; when they actually do it they will be rushing and it will be messier.

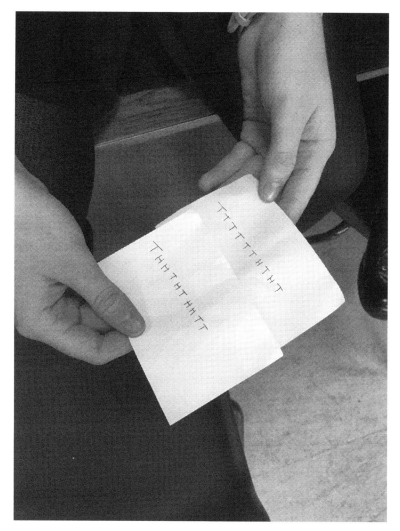

Figure 9.4 Caitlin's lists

The teacher summarises Sophie's point and Caitlin challenges the teacher to decide which is which from looking at both of her lists and purely looking at the handwriting (see Figure 9.4).

Pause for thought

★ Can you tell, from the handwriting alone, which is real and which is fake?

There is lots of animated discussion over Caitlin's challenge to the teacher, with the teacher initially choosing one and then another, after some confusion over which would be neater. He is not able to guess correctly. Caitlin states 'so that proves Sophie's point wrong' (this deviates from the game a little, as you do not see both sheets together during the actual game). Zara, the winner of the game (and on the skill side) comes in,

> we've been taught that there's a 50–50 chance of getting heads or tails, so when we have to write a fake list we'd naturally think to write H T H, but we can't write it that way so I wrote my fake one as H T H H T it would be obvious it's fake if we do H T H and all that … first thing that would come in to your mind is it's not possible to get like three or four tails in a row … so need to make it more convincing.

The argument and disputational talk has motivated all students to sustain the discussion and possibly deepen their understanding. Ben raises his hand to counter Zara's argument

> you say one is more convincing, you can't really have one that is more convincing, cause the one you write is still a possible outcome from flipping the coin. Any outcome is possible … there's a small chance that you can write the same one that you flip. While you're saying, it looks more convincing to get strings or less convincing get a pattern, the coin is so random you could end up with all heads, like we saw in the video, or all heads or H T H T H or you could end up with H H H H … and then one T, it's completely random. Either one could be right … neither one can convince someone more, it's pure luck.

The teacher asks if anyone from the skill group is convinced by Ben's point and no one is so the teacher directs the groups to go back into their two separate groups to come up with their final convincing arguments for the concluding statements. On the luck side, Ben discusses what he will say and asks if there's anything else. Caitlin wants him to ask them what skill there is. After a couple of minutes they are ready. In the skill group, Archie gets a briefing from his team, with many sharing their ideas. These include: the majority wrote heads first in their made-up list because you commonly say 'heads and tails' in that order; and Zara was the winner and she used strategies to win. Archie mentions that the only way of knowing is repeating the game again, and someone stresses 'don't say *all*, say *majority*'.

The teacher decides to flip a coin to see who will go first, the class like the irony of this and someone from the luck side comments on 50–50 chance; Archie wins and wants to go second.

Ben starts by saying that no one in the room is telepathic so they can't read minds. He summarises earlier points by highlighting the randomness of flipping the coin and that skill doesn't come in to it. Final comment: 'you're wrong, at the end of the day it's a 50–50 chance, you're either lucky or you're not, you guess right or you guess wrong'.

Archie mentions that 'the coin flips may be random, however the way people write their fake lists isn't, we can predict it. Because the majority of people we found have written heads first on their fake list'. Ben, interjects 'I wrote tails' leading to class laughter. Archie continues:

> However, we can also change the amount of strings of heads and tails and put spaces in between them and then look at the patterns in them and predict other peoples. Only feasible way of testing this is by re-peating it again and seeing if we get the same winners.

Archie has considered the other side's point of view but dismisses it (begin-ning of exploratory talk); however, the majority of talk within the lesson has been disputational. We believe the benefits of disputational talk within the les-son have been in sustaining dialogue, and engaging all learners in the debate. Through the dispute, students feel the need to express and sharpen their rea-soning (the type of discussion goes beyond being purely disputational) and the organisation of the periods of talk by the teacher facilitates this.

At the end of the lesson, the teacher shows a second Derren Brown video (2012) with the explanation of the 'ten heads in a row'. We don't want to spoil the illusion but it can be viewed on www.youtube.com/watch?v=n1SJ-Tn3bcQ. The teacher then asks students to complete a form with two points; what have you learnt this lesson and which argument did you find the most convincing? These will be discussed, along with other features of the lesson, in the next section.

What we have learned

We begin by reflecting on the lesson study focus of sustaining dialogue within the class and within this discuss the type of talk used. The discussion then moves on to the lesson study process, including a brief analysis of the student comments (this is different from the other chapters) and then possible next steps.

Sustaining argument

During this lesson, we believe that the teacher sustained the argument and discussion very well. One way in which he did this was by trying to emphasise during each round ideas that linked to skill and luck. The importance of reading the room should not be overlooked, too. He listened in to conversations and chose students carefully to input to the whole class, meaning that some students were convinced by the luck argument and others by the skill.

Ensuring there are two sides worked really well here too, with some students at, or near, the pure luck position, and others at, or near, pure skill. Occasionally, when we have taught this lesson with pre-service and in-service teachers the dividing line has been between 'pure luck' and 'almost pure luck' but even then the actual arguments polarise in a similar way between luck and skill. It also could be worth considering keeping a third middle group (if this arises, as it did here) to encourage students to build on each other's opposing ideas more and hence include more exploratory talk.

To get even more exploratory talk in future lessons, it would be good to ensure there is more time spent in group discussions, with students discussing their side's arguments. This can be shaped by the teacher through questions to the groups such as, what is your best argument; how do you specifically counter their best argument; what is their best argument; what is a mathematical argument for your position; and are we (the class) really arguing over nothing and just saying the same thing in different ways, etc.

The aim within the lesson is for students to gain a better understanding of the situation and recognise that there is some merit in both sides of the argument. Asking students whether they think they would be more successful if playing against a primary school student, may allow some to realise that skill could come in to it, as from experience they are much more likely to write a 'fair' list for their fake one, e.g. H T H T H T T H T H.

We also witnessed a high level of engagement throughout the lesson, with the teacher commenting on the fact that two students in particular were much more involved than in most lessons. The significant level of disputational talk and cognitive conflict fostered an environment where students were keen to share their ideas and listen to others. Here we see that arguments in mathematics classrooms can be used successfully to recognise (possibly not agree with) other's views.

> the word 'argument' has more than one meaning: as a persuasive monologue, as a competitive dispute and as a reasonable dialogue. We can perhaps now see why these three meanings co-exist. All are concerned in some way with the competition of ideas, and all (even

dispute) may have the ultimate aim of creating a broader consensus, a situation in which more people think similarly about some topic or issue than was the case before the dialogue commenced.

(Mercer, 2002, p. 104)

Lesson study process

There are some similarities between this lesson study experience and that described in Chapter 5. Here the authors work with a pre-service teacher who knows the lesson, and ideas behind the lesson, very well through the modelling of it at university and from working with other pre-service teachers to teach the lesson much earlier in the ITE course.

This lesson study differs from others within the book due to the inclusion of student voice. All the students at the end of the lesson were asked to respond to two questions: what have you learnt this lesson and which argument/point did you find most convincing? (Figure 9.5). Analysing the student voice shows that ten students thought that there was more skill than luck, five students thought that there was more luck than skill and eight students thought that it was pure luck. There were some students that could see that there is an element of both but chose one of the two sides when answering the second question.

Also, some students were persuaded by the content of the arguments presented while a few were persuaded by the manner in which the argument was given 'the only reason the other side could be convincing is because of the delivery of the arguments not the actual content or valid reasons'. We planned the questions prior to the lesson but after analysing them we felt the second question

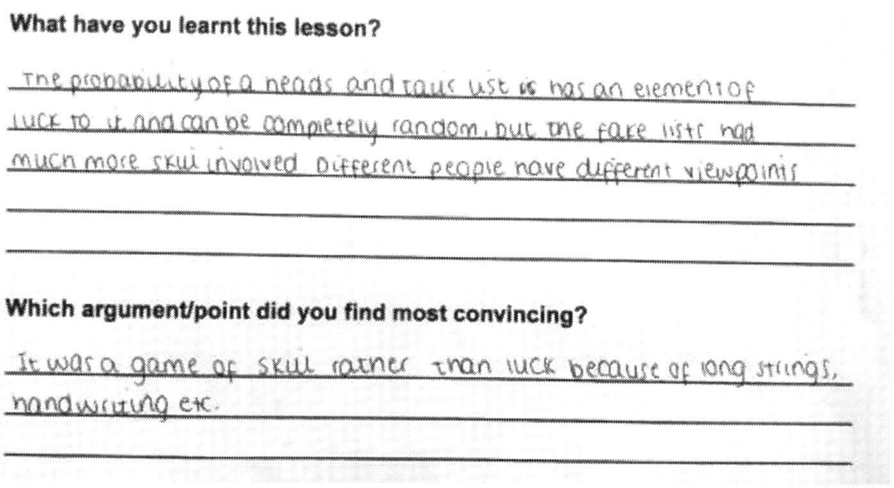

What have you learnt this lesson?

The probability of a heads and tails list is has an element of luck to it and can be completely random, but the fare list had much more skill involved. Different people have different viewpoints

Which argument/point did you find most convincing?

It was a game of skill rather than luck because of long strings, handwriting etc.

Figure 9.5 Example of pupil voice

directed them to choose one side mainly based on the concluding remarks. If repeating the process we would ask 'after hearing all arguments, write down your own "best" argument based on everything that you have heard today'.

Next steps

If we were teaching the lesson again we would give students two long strips of card, so they can fold the bottom and write real or fake on it; this would ensure that no one could cheat or believed that they had been cheated.

To further understand the way in which students think, we would collect the students real and fake lists in at the end and analyse them. The ideas of randomness and strings, dominated much of the arguments related to skill, with students using their heuristics to decide whether the string presented to them was likely to be real or not. It would be useful to collate both lists and compare the length of strings in the real lists and then in the fake lists and compare this to theoretical probabilities of these events happening. This could form a second lesson where the understanding of probability and randomness based on the length of strings could be explored further. We think younger students are more likely to see H T H T H T as real than ones with strings of two or three. Within this lesson we had rejection of H T H T H T, two strings being possible, uncertainty over three strings and above that probably fake; those with more understanding may recognise strings of four are actually quite likely to occur (see Appendix B).

Some of the mathematics linked to flipping ten coins (Appendix B) could be discussed depending on the age and attainment levels of the class. This lesson could also be used at later stages of schooling, for example post-16. Developing the connections between the 50–50 chances of tossing a coin, and of guessing real or fake (if it was pure luck), and generalising from and between these two real-world examples of the same mathematics can lead very nicely into the binomial distribution for students.

Pause for thought

Try the lesson with one of your classes. If you can use it as a research lesson using lesson study with a colleague, even better!

★ How is the use of dialogue similar to and different from that in Chapters 3 and 6?
★ How would you develop the mathematics within the problem with a class?
★ Have you seen students using heuristics when discussing probability?

References

Fischbein, H. (1975). *The intuitive sources of probabilistic thinking in children* (Vol. 85). Dordrecht, The Netherlands: D. Reidel.

Graham, A. (2006). *Developing thinking in statistics*. London: Sage.

Mercer, N. (2002). *Words and minds: How we use language to think together*. London: Routledge.

Shaughnessy, J. M., & Ciancetta, M. (2002). Students' understanding of variability in a probability environment. In *Proceedings of the sixth international conference on teaching statistics: Developing a statistically literate society, Cape Town, South Africa*. Voorburg, the Netherlands: International Statistical Institute.

Swan, M. (2001) Dealing with misconceptions in mathematics. In P. Gates (Ed.), *Issues in mathematics teaching* (pp. 147–165). London: Routledge Falmer.

Tversky, A., & Kahneman, D. (1974). Judgment under uncertainty: Heuristics and biases. *Science, 185*(4157), 1124–1131.

Watson, A., Jones, K., & Pratt, D. (2013). *Key ideas in teaching mathematics: Research-based guidance for ages 9–19*. Oxford: Oxford University Press.

Watson, J. M., & Moritz, J. B. (2003). Fairness of dice: A longitudinal study of students' beliefs and strategies for making judgments. *Journal for Research in Mathematics Education, 34*(4), 270–304.

Appendix A

Lesson plan and resources

Lesson summary

Students write two lists, one that results from having flipped a coin ten times and one that is made up. They then play each other trying to guess whether the list shown is real or fake. After the game they engage in a discussion about whether winning the game is due to skill or luck. Understanding of randomness is developed through the passionate discussion that often results from having played the game.

Focus on students learning

a   Challenge their understanding of randomness by defending their position with others.

b   Communicate reasoning effectively to justify their position.

Lesson preparation

Learners will need two strips of thin card to write their lists on. You may wish to clear the room to make space for learners to line up in an imaginary number line according to their position in the argument (more luck or more skill). The teacher will need slides and access to the videos mentioned below (if using).

The lesson

Stage 1 (optional): diagnostic question

You might wish to begin with a diagnostic question, which refreshes probability. Some misconceptions might arise here, time should be allowed for students to write down their answer and thoughts before sharing their answers but ensure there is enough time for the main part of the lesson.

Stage 2: introduction

Show the class a video where a coin is tossed and the result is ten heads in a row. There are several videos available on free websites. The one we used for this lesson is a short clip of Derren Brown flipping a coin (2012) www.youtube.com/watch?v=XzYLHOX50Bc. After watching the video learners create two lists, one resulting from tossing a coin ten times and one invented. It is essential that learners keep their two lists secret so later they can ask people to guess which one is real and which one is fake. Rosencrantz & Guildenstern Are Dead (1990) – Heads Scene (2017) (www.youtube.com/watch?v=C_TfdNAXOwE) could be used as background while students are creating their lists. Consider carefully the order of creating the list; we have found that if they do the real one first some students create their fake list from swapping the heads and tails of their real list.

Stage 3: playing the game and developing ideas around luck and skill

Students begin playing the game, pairing up and taking it in turns to show their opponent one of their lists. They win if they can guess correctly whether the list shown to them is a fake list or is real. Both players can win, both can lose or one can win and one can lose.

After each round the teacher asks one person who has lost and one who has won to explain what happened and whether they have a strategy. Learners are expected to share a variety of strategies related to the mathematics and not. They might comment on the symmetry of the list and their perceived randomness but can also comment on how the lists are written or presented (many often think that the list is real if the handwriting is scruffy). The teacher will encourage the idea of luck and skill during this part, at the same time as gaining an understanding of the class's perception of randomness allowing the students' ideas to develop independently.

Stage 4: discussion

Learners are asked to position themselves on a 'luck versus skill' scale, which is projected on the board (or pinned on the wall) to help. The teacher will not challenge opinions or provide a 'correct' answer. Discussion can be ignited at this stage by using direct questioning and asking learners who seem very passionate about their position to justify it. At this point we will expect the class to be polarised in their opinion. After a few of the learners have justified their position they are asked to prepare an argument to try and move more people to their side, at this point they should be encouraged to work in smaller groups. After the arguments are presented learners sit down and are asked to position themselves again on the number line. Sitting down and standing up again might give some of the learners, who don't want to be seen as moving, time to think. In the final discussion, facilitated by the teachers, learners explain if they have moved and why. Some learners will comment on their class mates' presentation skills while others will focus more on the mathematical reflection.

A question that can be worth asking early on is 'has anyone got a good fake list?' as this reinforces the idea of some skill in the task. Other useful questions to the groups are, what is your best argument; how do you specifically counter their best argument; what is their best argument; what is a mathematical argument for your position; and are we (the class) really arguing over nothing and just saying the same thing in different ways.

Stage 5: reflection and explaining the trick

Learners complete a brief reflection by answering two questions:

◆ What did I learn today?
◆ Based on what you have heard this lesson, write your own 'best' argument.

Both questions should give you an insight not only on their mathematics but also on their thinking skills. How their thinking of randomness has changed and what allowed them to develop their understanding. What do they value in class discussion?

If there is enough time learners can watch the end of the video where Derren Brown (2012) explains the trick behind getting ten consecutive heads (www.youtube.com/watch?v=n1SJ-Tn3bcQ), the explanation starts after 50 seconds.

Possible extension

The lesson could be followed up by exploring some of the mathematics further, using either theoretical expectations or the experimental data from the first lesson. Can they write a better fake list after the first lesson? What would they include? Further discussion of strings for instance.

Suggestions for lesson study focus

You might want to consider these aspects of students' thinking:

◆ How do students try to convince each other, what persuasive language/mathematics do they use?
◆ What changes when students discuss in smaller groups compared to the whole class?
◆ How do students' heuristics influence their understanding of the game?

Useful links related to this lesson

★ Numberphile – Randomness is random (2018)
  ○ https://*youtu.be*/tP-Ipsat90c
★ Flipping coins – ABC
  ○ www.abc.net.au/science/surfingscientist/pdf/lesson_plan19.pdf

Appendix B

Mathematics linked to flipping ten coins

This appendix looks at the probability of having strings of heads (or tails) or either when flipping a fair coin.

You might want to start by looking at the probability of simpler cases with students, by listing all the possible outcomes we can see that:

Table 9.1

	Flip a coin 1 time	Flip a coin 2 times	Flip a coin 3 times	Flip a coin 4 times	Flip a coin 5 times	Flip a coin 6 times
Probability of at least 2 heads in a row	0	$\frac{1}{4}$	$\frac{3}{8}$	$\frac{8}{16}$	$\frac{19}{32}$	$\frac{43}{64}$
Probability of at least 3 heads in a row	0	0	$\frac{1}{8}$	$\frac{3}{16}$	$\frac{8}{32}$	$\frac{20}{64}$
Probability of at least 4 heads in a row	0	0	0	$\frac{1}{16}$	$\frac{3}{32}$	$\frac{8}{64}$
Probability of at least 5 heads in a row	0	0	0	0	$\frac{1}{32}$	$\frac{3}{64}$
Probability of at least 6 heads in a row	0	0	0	0	0	$\frac{1}{64}$

Listing all the outcomes for ten flips (1024) is possible, either by hand or using a spreadsheet. However, this is not a trivial task. We therefore suggest trying to use a different strategy; this might involve looking at the longest run and partitioning, using Fibonacci or another method.

We found that the probability of having at least 3 heads in a row in 10 flips is $\frac{520}{1024}$ = 0.5078125 (approx. 51%), which might be surprisingly high for many students.

[The chance of having at least one string of 3 equal outcomes (of either heads or tails) is 83%.]

We have also calculated that the probability of getting a string of 4 or more of either heads or tails is almost 0.5 (approx. 46%) and hence about 50–50. This is something that would be even more surprising for some of the students in the lesson.

Table 9.2 shows the total possible outcomes for each longest run, enabling you to do further calculations, for instance the probability of a longest string of 5 is $\frac{222}{1024}$ = 21.7% (to 1 dp).

Table 9.2

Longest string (for 10 coins)	Total
10	2
9	4
8	10
7	24
6	56
5	126
4	254
3	370
2	176
1	2
Total	1024

We omit the details of the methods and calculations used in order to leave it as a challenge for you (or your students)! However, we would love you to contact us if you are interested in having detailed solutions or comparing your own solutions to ours.

10

Experimental design
Connecting statistics to student experience

Introduction

In this lesson students explore the links between music and mathematics. In particular, they study the Mozart effect,[1] which claims that listening to music improves performance on reasoning tasks. Students take part in an experiment to test the Mozart effect (attempting a form of 'intelligence' test before and after listening to Mozart) and then critique the experiment and look for ways to improve it.

This lesson originated in a university course for social science students learning statistics and quantitative methods. It was later adapted for use with similar students at an earlier stage of their education, in a post-16 sixth form college. One of the authors (DS) did the initial work of adapting the materials, and then worked with two college lecturers from a college in the North West of England to analyse, teach and adapt the lesson further with two of their classes.

The primary focus of the lesson study was to see how connecting mathematics to experience in various ways, such as analysing the links between mathematics and music and participating in the experiment to be critiqued, would encourage engagement and influence reasoning. Ultimately, the designed lesson was successful in engaging students in analysing the connections between music, mathematics and intelligence and in critiquing the design of the experiment. What follows will explore how it did that.

Background to the lesson

This lesson originated in undergraduate lecture and tutorial materials designed by Alan Marshall as part of the QStep initiative (see www.nuffield-foundation.org/q-step). QStep is a programme that aims to increase the numbers of quantitatively skilled social science researchers through integrating training with the needs and approaches of particular disciplines. Many students who go to university to study social science have chosen to do so over alternatives such as mathematics or science courses. Sometimes, perhaps even often, they are doing so because they are keen to avoid mathematics. Yet mathematics, particularly in the form of statistics, can play a weighty role in their subjects of choice. Universities try to ensure social science students are therefore informed of quantitative methods but this has often involved courses detached from the core concerns of the students' chosen subjects, and many students have tended to struggle through such courses and then abandon quantitative methods when they can. QStep is designed to break that pattern.

This lesson was adapted from the original materials as part of a project to connect QStep with Core Mathematics, a level 3 course in post-16 schools and colleges (see www.stem.org.uk/core-maths). Core Mathematics (CM) is a relatively new course in England, which focuses on applications of previously learned mathematics rather than the introduction of new higher-level materials, and is designed for students who wouldn't want (or perhaps wouldn't be allowed) to do the standard A-level mathematics course. There is clearly therefore some crossover in the aims of both QStep and CM, and potentially also a crossover in students, as many studying CM at college may go on to study humanities, or some science subjects at university.

The aim of both educational endeavours is to connect mathematics to other educational subjects of interest to students, and the lesson described here does something similar in connecting mathematics to students' experience, in two different ways: first, through making connections to students' knowledge and interest in music; and second, through creating direct experiences within the classroom to provide a grounding for the statistical understandings which are developed.

There are many valid and important reasons why mathematics should be connected to student experience. One element that contributes to the anxiety often aroused by school mathematics comes from its detachment from students' lives outside of school. Teaching that aims at breaking down that division, or which begins with, and privileges, students' own understanding, has been seen not to cause, and even reduce, such anxiety (Pampaka et al., 2019). More positively, beyond doing no harm, connecting mathematics is also seen to increase motivation and engagement in students. There is evidence that basing teaching in 'students' pre-existing understandings, interests, culture and real world experiences' can make the curriculum more meaningful for them, and that they stay engaged when they are allowed agency and to use their own resources in the learning process (National Research Council, 2003, p. 3). Moll, Amanti, Neff & Gonzalez (1992) and others have shown that there are more than sufficient resources or 'funds of knowledge' even within the most disadvantaged of households to feed into schooling, and to allow teaching to have this emphasis.

We have discussed in this book (including in Chapter 8) how the connections to experience that are important for engagement are also seen as being important for understanding mathematics; in fact, they can be seen as being essential to mathematics itself. For example, in Realistic Mathematics Education (RME, see Van den Heuvel-panhuizen & Drijvers, 2014, and Chapter 3), it is often stressed that mathematics is a human activity rather than an object, and that one essential element of that activity is the progressive mathematisation of reality. Therefore, mathematics education should begin with rich contexts, meaningful to students, from which they can develop mathematical concepts and structures.

Mathematical concepts and relationships are first and foremost generalisations of the relationships found in the world of human experience (although we say this boldly, it is of course much debated historically, see De Lange, 1996, for an overview). Just as we wouldn't teach children other generalisations, such as the concept 'animal', without reference to any particular types of animal, e.g. lion and tiger, or experiences of particular animals, e.g. their pet cat, it is important not to try to transmit the concepts of mathematics without some connection to the real-world processes and experiences that they are ultimately generalised from (see Chapter 11 for a more theoretically developed version of this idea). Either we should begin with these and allow some student agency in mathematising the experiences (as in RME), or if the concepts have been learned previously through more traditional, transmissionist approaches, we should attempt to fill these formal concepts with real-world experience.

In the lesson that follows, both these processes may happen. Students are encouraged to critique a well-known experiment (and its results), which look at the relation between listening to music and intelligence. Therefore students' own experiences of music are brought into the classroom, and the class directly participates in the experiment, to allow a basis for their reasoning and their critiques. In the other direction, as this is a Core Mathematics class that explores applications of previously learned mathematics, some of the formal understanding of sampling and experimental design may already be known to students, and the connections made to experience can then infuse those existing conceptions.

Following the lesson outline and analysis, we will return in 'What we have learned' to the question of how the lesson provided opportunities for such processes, by looking at how student experience provides a potential grounding for the critiques they raise about the Mozart effect experiment.

Suggested reading

Gainsburg, J. (2008). Real-world connections in secondary mathematics teaching. *Journal of Mathematics Teacher Education*, *11*(3), 199–219.

Glaister, P. (2017). What is Core Maths and why is funding it so important? *FE Week*, 27th Nov 2017 Available online at https://feweek.co.uk/2017/11/27/what-is-core-maths-and-why-is-funding-it-so-important/

Wake, G. (2010). *Connecting mathematics with reality – Connecting reality with mathematics.* London: QCDA. Available online at www.ncetm.org.uk/public/files/15982437/14532-Connecting_mathematics_with_reality_connecting_relality_with_mathematics_Geoff_Wake_Universtiry_of_Manchester.pdf

---

Lesson outline

The expected outcome of this lesson is that students will be able to critique, and suggest ways to improve, an experiment. Students are expected to do this through bringing together their prior statistical understanding with their outside-school experience and understanding of music, and their direct experience of participating in the experiment.

Potential key moments to consider and expected responses are discussed below.

Task 1: discussing the connections between mathematics and music

Play any music video, asking students to individually make a note of anything mathematical they can see while they watch. Following the video ask students to discuss in groups and produce a list of all they have found.

Circulate to encourage discussion and the sharing of particular answers in the class discussion. A large variety of student suggestions are possible here, and any and all can be relevant. Use the class discussion to probe students deeper on their own understanding and experience, and try to get students to build on other students suggestions. The aim of this section is to make students' own experiences as prominent in the room as possible. This will help encourage some possibility that the Mozart effect is true, and feed in to some of the potential critiques of the experiment. Focussing on students who play music themselves or care deeply about music can help here.

Task 2: initial discussions of the Mozart effect

Share newspaper reporting of the Mozart effect, either on a whiteboard or handouts.

> A scientific study published in 1993 in the respected journal *Science*…
>
> It showed that teenagers who listened to Mozart's 1781 Sonata for Two Pianos in D major performed better in reasoning tests than adolescents who listened to something else or who had been in a silent room.
>
> (The Telegraph, 2015, see Appendix B)

Ask students to discuss in pairs whether they believe it, and to come up with reasons why, or why not. Again, circulate to engage, encourage and pick up on interesting arguments. In the class discussion share some of this reasoning. If there is sufficient numbers on both sides of the debate, extend the discussion encouraging each side to convince the other. If possible, try to connect the reasoning here to the discussion in task 1.

Task 3: the experiment

Explain the experiment and how the spatial reasoning test works and ensure students are happy with the example (see lesson plan and resources, Appendices A and B). Stress that the purpose is to genuinely test the Mozart effect and that no one else will ever see the individual scores. Conduct IQ test 1, play Mozart for 5 minutes, and then conduct IQ test 2. Ask students to swap to mark and read out answers then return the test, and collect in the answer sheets.

Task 4: critiquing the experiment

Ask students to discuss, in groups, ways to use the collected data to test the Mozart effect while you quickly enter the data on a prepared spreadsheet before circulating. Take suggestions and use the spreadsheet to discuss further. Use the results to argue that the Mozart effect has been proved correct or incorrect and ask the class if they agree. When one or two criticisms of the experiment have been aired, ask students to create a list of all the potential problems. Circulate to encourage contributions to the class discussion, and use the class discussion to probe and build on student responses, and discuss how the experiment could be redesigned to correct the problems.

The main problems with the experiment and therefore the expected responses include the size and representativeness of the sample; that performance on the tests may improve through practice; that attitudes toward Mozart effect may influence the results (e.g. given participants have discussed the Mozart effect prior to do doing the test, thinking about how it is affecting performance during the test may influence performance, confounding the results); that other music or no music may have same effect (or may work differently for different people), and that there is a need for a control group; that other types of IQ tests may give different results, and the general limitations of IQ tests in measuring 'intelligence'.

Pause for thought

Think about teaching this lesson to *your* class.

★ What type of music video would you use to stimulate discussion in task 1?
★ Could you design an alternative test marking process where neither the teacher nor other students know any individual's score, but students know their own score, without any self-marking of the test?
★ What prior learning do your students have that would feed into their potential critiques of the experiment?

Lesson reflection and analysis

In this section, we describe and analyse the lesson, which resulted from the lesson outline above. This lesson was taught twice though, with the first attempt based on a less developed outline, following an initial adaptation of the original university lecture and tutorial materials, and a brief meeting between the lesson study (LS) participants. We therefore briefly share the experiences of that first lesson, and the adaptations that were made through the post-lesson analysis resulting in the plan for the second lesson described above. In both lessons described here, it should be noted that other activities took place within the hour designated for the classes, and the central activity of the IQ test (including explaining and marking) took up around 20–25 minutes of the remaining time, so the analysis here rests on briefer classroom sequences than in other chapters.

The first attempt

The first lesson begins with a general discussion on tables, and then among the full class, on the links between mathematics and music. Many students struggle to see any links but some do arise including things such as timing, the vibration of strings, and half notes and quarter notes. The LS team felt that the limitations of this discussion had meant that the students' own experiences of music could not really feed into and underpin later discussions. It was felt that the question had perhaps been too open and it was decided to make it more concrete next time by showing the students something musical and asking them to say what mathematics they could see in it, and to focus discussions by asking groups to produce a list of what they see. It was also felt that there should then be a discussion, and predictions, about the Mozart effect itself. This would help to connect whatever the students come up with about links between music and mathematics to the experiment (partially through providing some basis for potentially believing in the Mozart effect) and would encourage the students to be more invested in the outcome of the experiment.

In the Mozart effect experiment itself, which immediately follows, many of the students 'cheat' a little by checking the answers of their neighbours or by changing or adding answers when self-marking after the IQ test? This was perhaps due to frequently being judged through high-stakes testing, and/ or through not wanting to appear unintelligent to their classmates. The team decided they needed to stress more the non-judgemental nature of the experiment, ensure the tests were not self-marked, and promise, as much as is possible, the anonymity of results.

Following the experiment there is a brief discussion about the Mozart effect. Many say they didn't feel more or less intelligent during the second IQ test and that they don't believe the theory, but some think the music maybe calmed them down, allowing them to perform better afterwards (this insight provides a potentially testable explanatory factor, an essential element to the scientific method, which goes beyond analysing the mechanics of experiments). In the second IQ test some had improved radically (two students), some had increased a little (three), some stayed the same (three) but the majority scored less (nine). To test the theory using the collected data the students suggest taking the averages and find these to be identical pre- and post-music, with the large individual increases cancelling out the larger numbers of decreases. This seems to confirm for the students that the Mozart effect isn't true, which hints that the design of the experiment was perhaps sufficiently convincing for them. When asked to critique the experiment, however, some are able to come up with potential problems such as the small sample size, the nature of the sample (mathematics students), and suggestions that the choice of music may only work for some people ('it has to be music you enjoy to calm you down and help you think'). Again, the team felt that ensuring there were group discussions, structured through the production of a list, before the class discussion, may have allowed wider critiques to emerge, and that making some of the changes discussed earlier would also contribute to this.

The second lesson

Following the post-lesson analysis, some of which is captured above, the teacher of the second class, which occurred a few weeks later, adapts the plan based on the discussion. The teacher begins by playing a video of a DJ playing, while others dance, in what looks to be a disused office high in an office block. Before starting the video he asks each table to watch and come up with a list of anything mathematical they can see, or connect to, the video. This leads to a variety of suggestions, which are shared in the class including the number of people dancing; how many storeys high the room is; the volume; beats per minute and time delays; the costs of equipment; the length of songs; and frequency and decibels.

Students are then asked to read an extract from a newspaper article on the Mozart effect, and to discuss in pairs whether they believe it, and why (or why not). It is stressed that they should make a note of their reasons. The teacher then circulates to join in discussions and encourage particular students to contribute what they have said to the class discussion when it happens. A minority (4 out of 13) believe there would be some effect. The first reason suggested is that the music would calm you down and help you perform better, although 'it would have to be something like Mozart and not Eminem if it was going to do that', as more intense music makes it harder to concentrate. Other students argue that it depends what music you like, as they find more intense music does calm them down.

The discussion then drifts onto another aspect of the article, which mentions a celebrity playing music to their unborn child to make them more intelligent. One student argues that the sort of people who would do this would be more likely to push their children academically too so it probably isn't true. Another student notes that the article has this in the headline but then doesn't discuss it any further, and there is a brief discussion of how newspapers can distort scientific stories.

The teacher then suggests that the class try out the experiment and some students seem very engaged by the idea. One says 'Why Mozart though? The whole thing is based on prejudice', that is that the musical preferences of a particular section of society are being presented as somehow superior or more intelligent. The teacher suggests 'that's why we need to test it'. He stresses that their results in the experiment will just be used to check if there is a difference before and after listening and that no one else will see the results. He then talks them through how to do the spatial reasoning test (see Appendix B). This time there are no visible signs of students checking others' answers, and scripts are swapped before being marked and are then collected in by the teacher.

As in the first lesson, the class is then asked to discuss in groups how we can use the data to test whether the Mozart effect works. Suggestions that arise include looking at the percentage of people who improve and by how much they have improved, finding the averages before and after and comparing ('the mean, because it's the best average'), using line graphs or scatter graphs to compare, and looking at the standard deviation.

The teacher has entered the data in the spreadsheet while students have been discussing, and he now shows this to the students. This time 6 out of 13 have improved, 2 have scored the same and 5 have a lower score on the second test. The spreadsheet has calculated that the mean score has increased by 0.77, from 5.38 to 6.15. When the teacher asks whether that has convinced the class, one student immediately starts critiquing the experiment, saying that the second part might have been easier due to getting used to doing the tests, adding that they felt that themselves, despite their score on the second test being lower, a very direct (if contradictory example) of experience feeding in to reasoning. A student then points to the bar chart that has been produced and says that the axis doesn't start at 0 and another adds that that accentuates the change, which impresses the rest of the class.

The teacher asks a student to put a line of best fit on the scatter graph, but another student then says it isn't convincing because of the small size of the test group. The teacher asks whether anyone is convinced that the Mozart effect is real, or convinced it's not, and the students generally say 'not'. When asked 'why not?' the first response is that 'it's an awful test'. Another student suggests that it would have to be done with two different groups of subjects (i.e. with a control group). Some of these critiques can arguably be seen to be grounded in the experience of doing the test, and we analyse this further in the following section.

The central aim of the lesson is to generate critiques of the experiment, and many have already been raised, even without explicit prompting. The teacher then asks for each table to produce a list as long as they can of all the reasons the test 'was awful' and how it could be improved. Additional suggestions which arise through this are (i) that people will be more used to it the second time so should do better (the test used is designed to compensate for this though); (ii) that different genres of music would need to be tested, and silence; (iii) for any particular music, results may depend on whether you know the music, or like the music; (iv) that the sample was too small here and would need to be much larger; (v) that the tests should be repeated and then averaged; (vi) that individuals should have been tested separately to avoid being able to see others' answers; (vii) that the sample should have included a variety of people, gender and age; and (viii) that different types of IQ test should be tried.

The teacher then summarises and relates what they have done to hypothesis testing more generally. He then brings the class to an end, and the students leave the class still engaged in discussions about the Mozart effect and classical music.

Pause for thought

Consider the above lesson reflection and analysis.

★ How else could students' experiences of music be brought in to the discussion in the early stages of the lesson?
★ How do the critiques of the experiment raised by the student relate to their direct experience of the test and their outside-school experience?
★ What would you do next with this class?

What we have learned

In this section we first analyse the relationship between the students' own experience, whether of music in the real world or of the experiment in the classroom, and the critiques of the experiment that they raised. We then discuss the lesson study process, in particular the potential involved in re-teaching a lesson, and draw parallels between the importance of experience within student and teacher learning.

How experience feeds in to reasoning

In the section on the background to the lesson we discussed two of the main reasons for connecting mathematics to experience. The first was in terms of motivation and engagement, and here, connecting to students' ideas about music, and taking part in the Mozart effect experiment, certainly seems to have engaged the students in meaningful reflection and discussion. The second reason was to make formal mathematics more meaningful, and more deeply understood, through interrelating the type of mathematics learned in schooling with rich experiential content. This process can go in two different directions, with either consciousness of experience generalising and reaching toward the formal mathematics, or with already learned formal mathematics being filled with the rich experiential content.

In this lesson, both directions are possible. Students in this class will have encountered some ideas about sampling, for example, in their previous schooling, and this previous knowledge may then interrelate with the experiential aspects of the lesson in diverse ways that we cannot evidence from the resulting student contributions. We are not therefore in a position to say, for example, that this or that experiential aspect led to any particular critique of the experiment. What we can analyse, however, is whether there is an experiential grounding for any of the critiques raised (or those absent) and thus the potential for the formal mathematics to become entwined with concrete experience in either direction.

In 'Lesson outline' we outlined the most common critiques of the experiment that we would expect to potentially arise. Almost all of these arose within the two lessons. In both lessons, the size and nature of the sample are criticised, and the potential that simply repeating the test may lead to improvements are raised. These critiques clearly have an experiential grounding in participating in the experiment. For example, some students were likely to have felt unsure of how to solve the spatial reasoning questions early on in the first test but more sure of what they were doing in the second, and the nature and size of the sample are clear to all. Similarly, in the second lesson, the suggestion of testing individuals separately to avoid copying could have grounding in either witnessing its occurrence or feeling the temptation or possibility during the test.

Although the potential for different types of music to have different effects on different people arises briefly in the first lesson, this critique feels more fully developed within the second. It leads to the suggestion of testing different types of music, and none, which then also feeds into the idea of having a control group. This increased emphasis has potential grounding in the more involved discussions about music, where students' own experiences come to the fore more, and where there are critical discussions about the privileging of particular types of music (i.e. not generally the type of music the students themselves listen to).

In the second lesson there is also some criticality shown in relation to the IQ tests, for example that they could be made more reliable by repeating the tests and averaging, or that different tests may give different results. Again, these have potential grounding in the experience of doing the tests, where awareness of chance elements, and the test's particularities, may noticeably contrast with any portrayal of the test as an objective measure of general intelligence. These critiques represent the beginnings of a questioning of IQ tests more generally. This was one of the two foreseen potential critiques, which didn't arise here, but we can see that the embryo of such a critique existed, grounded in the experience of the tests. With this, there was the possibility of building on the student responses to pose this question more directly. The second missing critique relates to noticing the potential confounding factor of having discussed and formed opinions on the Mozart effect before doing the test. This does have some potential grounding in their experience but perhaps not sufficiently so. One way to add emphasis to this potential grounding would perhaps be to move those students who see some validity to the Mozart effect together and extend the debate on it, before doing the experiment. Then differences may arise in either results or post-test reasoning between the two groups which might be noticed by students.

Lesson study process

The participants in the lesson study team were conscious that they had perhaps not prepared sufficiently for the first attempt at this lesson, with just the initially adapted materials and a brief meeting to talk through them, which occurred several months before the lesson itself. In an ideal world, with lower teacher workloads, and more space for developmental rather than judgemental approaches to improving teaching, it would have been possible to do such things differently. Adapting LS to the demands of local contexts is important however, and the resulting LS process in this case actually confirms the potential benefits of a more widely applicable strategy, which involves re-teaching as a means of purposeful reflection.

There is a danger in lesson study that post-lesson analysis and reflection can remain superficial, or unnecessarily tied to the particular experiences, and not move to deeper and more general learning that can be applied to wider situations. Re-teaching a lesson to a different class can play a role in forcing participants to analyse what occurred in the first lesson in a deeper, more meaningful way due to being driven by the need to better address the issues related to the research focus (e.g. in making more of what you want to see happen occur). This seemed to work here in leading to the development of the lesson and the outcomes seen in its second iteration. Comparison of both lessons then also allows greater opportunity for generalisation, through exploring what is the same and what is different in both experiences.

Within this process parallels can be drawn between students learning mathematics and teachers and researchers learning about teaching and learning. In the lesson students attack a problem (critiquing the experiment) and experience (of doing the experiment) assists them in doing that by making the problem more concrete. Meanwhile, the lesson study team also attack a problem (designing a lesson that encourages and enables students to critique the experiment) and experience (of teaching the lesson the first time) again assists them in doing that by making the problem more concrete.

Next steps

One possibility for going beyond this lesson is touched on above, which is to begin discussions about the usefulness and appropriateness of IQ tests more generally. This would take the lesson even more in the direction of a 'critical mathematics' (see Skovsmose, 2011) direction, even to the point where students can begin to challenge the unfairness of their own frequent measurement by testing within schooling.

Other approaches to building on the lesson include reinforcing some of the understanding developed so far by asking students to redesign and write up an improved experiment to test the Mozart effect. It would also be possible to ask the class to collectively conduct an improved design of the experiment with a larger sample from the school or college. Another option, which continues to connect to student experience, is to build on what has been learnt and ask students to design and conduct a new, different experiment. An example is included in the lesson plan in Appendix A where a variation of the classic 'lady tasting tea' experiment (see Fisher, 1937) can be designed to test an individual's ability to tell one soft drink from another. This experiment allows for more mathematical aspects, such as calculating the possibilities of guessing correctly a certain amount of times by chance, and comparison of what would be theoretically convincing with what convinces in practice. This experiment is also fun for students to design and take part in, although is also arguably a little unhealthy as it involves sugary drinks!

Note

1   See https://www.sciencedaily.com/releases/2010/05/100510075415.htm

References

De Lange, J. (1996). Using and applying mathematics in education. In A. J. Bishop, K. Clements, C. Keitel, J. Kilpatrick, & C. Laborde (Eds.), *International handbook of mathematics education* (Part I, pp. 49–97). Dordrecht, The Netherlands: Kluwer.

Fisher, R. A. (1937). *The design of experiments*. London: Oliver and Boyd; Edinburgh.

Moll, L. C., Amanti, C., Neff, D., & Gonzalez, N. (1992). Funds of knowledge for teaching: Using a qualitative approach to connect homes and classrooms. *Theory into Practice, 31*(2), 132–141.

National Research Council. (2003). *Engaging schools: Fostering high school students' motivation to learn*. Washington, DC: National Academies Press. Available at www.nap.edu/catalog/10421/engaging-schools-fostering-high-school-students-motivation-to-learn

Pampaka, M., Swanson, D., Williams, J., Ralston, K., Hernandez-Martinez, P., Carter, J., … Tyndsley, K. (2019). *Unsettling understandings of mathematics anxiety: A critical synthesis to inform policy and practice*. London: British Academy. In press.

Skovsmose, O. (2011). *An invitation to critical mathematics education*. Rotterdam: Sense Publishers.

The Telegraph. (2015, March 28).'Mozart effect': Can classical music really make your baby smarter? Available at: www.telegraph.co.uk/news/health/children/11500314/Mozart-effect-can-classical-music-really-make-your-baby-smarter.html

Van den Heuvel-panhuizen, M., & Drijvers, P. (2014). Realistic mathematics education. In S. Lerman (Ed.) *Encyclopedia of mathematics education* (pp. 521–525). New York: Springer.

Appendix A
Lesson plan

Lesson summary

In this lesson students explore the design of experiments to test hypotheses. Students discuss the links between music and mathematics, and music and intelligence, and take part in an experiment to test the Mozart effect. They then critique the experiment and use what they have learned to redesign the experiment, try the redesign on others, or design and try out a very different experiment (on telling two soft drinks apart). This lesson relates to a range of mathematical content, including data collection, sampling, interpreting data and experimental design, alongside more critical skills such as argumentation.

1) Music and intelligence: eliciting student views (approximate time 15 minutes)

1a) Class discussion: music and mathematics
Begin by playing a music video and ask students to make a note of anything mathematical they see. Circulate to encourage discussion and pick up on interesting answers. Use the class discussion to probe more deeply and bring students' musical experience into the classroom.

Some questions that could be asked within this discussion include: Do you think there is a link between music and mathematics? Who plays an instrument? Where is the mathematics in what you do? Does being good at music mean you are also good at mathematics?

1b) Pair discussion: Mozart effect
Show slide or distribute handout on the Mozart Effect.

Ask: 'Do you believe it?' 'Can listening to music make you smarter?'

Ask students to discuss in pairs, whether they believe the Mozart effect or not, and to make a note of the reasons why, or why not.

Share some of this reasoning within the class, and if there is potential for debate try to sustain this by getting each group to convince the other.

2) Mozart effect experiment (approximate time 20 minutes)

Introduce the experiment.

Use a presentation slide to explain how the IQ test should be tackled – check everyone is happy, warn that the questions can be more complicated than the example, and stress the non-judgemental nature of the tests and that no one else will see the results.

Distribute IQ tests [Paper folding test (or alternative). Printed single sided and stapled.]

Start experiment, ask students to turn over paper to page 2, and give them 3 minutes to complete. Play [Mozart Sonata for Two Pianos in D major – via YouTube or other source] for 5–10 minutes. Ask students to turn over paper to page 3, and give them 3 minutes to complete.

3) Mozart experiment data processing (approximate time 10–15 minutes)

Ask the students to swap their tests with a friend. Read out the answers to the paper folding test so students can score test A and B. Collect in the results.

Questions that can be asked as you collect in the data include: How did you do? Do you think the Mozart effect is true now?

Ask pairs or groups to come up with suggestions of what to do with the data. During their discussions, you can add the data to the prepared spreadsheet. Spreadsheets can be designed in advance to make calculations and draw bar charts and scatter graphs, and calculate mean, SD, etc. automatically on entering the data. However, you may wish to do this on the spot based on student suggestions from the on-going discussion.

Option for smaller classes, or large classes with insufficient computer access

Distribute the data collection [Paper folding test score] sheets (or if a small class and students don't mind, get them to shout out their scores). Use the data to fill in a spreadsheet pre-prepared to make statistical calculations and draw graphs from the data (see Figure 10.1 for an example). Show the mean score chart and the scatter diagram.

Discuss the data as presented and what it represents. Possible questions include: How were these means calculated? Can you put in words why the scatter graph looks that way? Are there any outliers? Does anyone think they were an outlier? (Looking at table below) Can anyone explain what these are? Why have they been calculated? How are they calculated? Etc.

4) Critiquing the experiment (approximate time 10 minutes – can be shortened)

Declare the Mozart effect to be proved or disproved (depending on results).

Ask the class 'Is that true?', 'Have we proved/disproved it?' When critiques begin to arise, move to asking the students in groups to write down as many criticisms of the experiment, or ways to improve it, they can think of (if critiques initially fail to arise, and much time passes, prompt directly with 'Can you think of anything wrong with that experiment?'

Return to a whole class discussion, gather all the different objections and check whether everyone agrees/disagrees. If there is disagreement encourage debate. Ask for ways to get around each problem.

Typical issues raised (or that you may want to encourage in their absence): Maybe people just get better through practice? Is it Mozart or would anything work, including silence? Small sample size and nature of sample. Placebo effect (believing in it?). Is this an appropriate IQ test? Should there have been a different IQ test the second time? Is IQ a real thing?

Extending

The above lesson could take approximately 45 minutes to 1 hour, depending on the choices made and the learners' age and attainment. There are a variety of options on where to go next if there is time in the lesson or if spread over a few lessons:

Option 1: redesign the experiment

Asking the students to redesign the experiment to test the Mozart effect allows them to apply what they have learned so far, and adds practice of report writing and logical structuring. You may wish to scaffold the task by providing a pro-forma that they can complete.

Option 2: test a larger sample

If the students have completed Option 1, this could then be used to engage in a wider data collection process with students outside their class. You could just ask them to plan how they would go about doing that in order to discuss practical issues and sampling questions further. If students do carry out a new design, they may want a different IQ test so that test 1 and 2 are different.

Option 3: design a new experiment – testing whether someone can tell two soft drinks apart

Having dissected an experiment and looked at its flaws, it is useful to then design a completely different experiment. Much of the critical approach from the first experiment should carry forward into the new design.

A nice experiment to design is one to test whether an individual can tell two similar soft drinks apart. The original experiment on which this is based was an important milestone in the development of statistics 'The lady tasting tea' which tested whether someone could tell if milk had been added first or last to tea. There is a video here www.youtube.com/watch?v=lgs7d5saFFc, which could introduce the task (but stop at 1.18 before the experiment is described). Other variations of this experiment are of course possible, so feel free to adapt.

For testing two common soft drinks you will need a bottle of each (both diet, or both non-diet), some water (for clearing the palette) and some plastic cups. Ask the students in groups to design an experiment to test someone who is confident they can tell them apart. Get a group who are happy with their plan to present it to the class and ask the other groups to point out any problems/add elements from their design. Perfect the design as a class, and then test on an individual.

Questions that should arise: How many cups to test? Cups in matched pairs or random? A practical system for knowing which cup is which, without the participant knowing. How many do they have to get right to convince they can tell them apart, all or some (e.g. four out of five or five out of six pairs or eight out of ten overall, etc.)?

This last question is an opportunity to engage with the mathematics of the binomial distribution. Break off to spend time working out the probabilities of various results if they are random (you can scaffold this task if necessary by starting with the probabilities for one pair, then two etc.). Get the students to share their methods with the class until they agree the probabilities before agreeing success criteria. It is worth returning to the success criteria after the test, comparing what is convincing in practice to what they claimed would be convincing beforehand.

Appendix B

Lesson resources

An example newspaper article on the Mozart effect can be found here. It is useful to use an edited version of such articles so that the evidence doesn't seem too clear against it: www.telegraph.co.uk/news/health/children/11500314/Mozart-effect-can-classical-music-really-make-your-baby-smarter.html

The spatial reasoning paper folding test can be found here: www.cs.otago.ac.nz/brace/resources/Paper%20Folding%20Test%20Vz-2-BRACE%20Version%2007.pdf

Other spatial reasoning tests are available here (although please read all licensed use information at the beginning): www.ets.org/Media/Research/pdf/Kit_of_Factor-Referenced_Cognitive_Tests.pdf

Solutions to paper folding test

Test 1		Test 2	
Question	Answer	Question	Answer
1	A	1	C
2	D	2	B
3	B	3	A
4	D	4	E
5	B	5	E
6	E	6	A
7	A	7	E
8	C	8	D
9	E	9	D
10	E	10	C

Student answer sheet for test

Question	Answer
1	
2	
3	
4	
5	
6	
7	
8	
9	
10	

Example of prepared spreadsheet for entering data

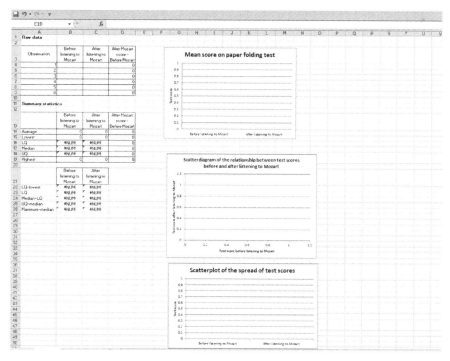

Figure 10.1 Example spreadsheet

11

Teaching logarithms through problem solving

Introduction

Within this chapter, we describe a lesson where students learn about logarithms through problem solving. These problems include investigating how many times a piece of paper can be folded in half; how many folds it would take to reach the moon; and how the teacher is able to give the log of any number without using a calculator.

> **Pause for thought**
>
> Try to answer at least one of these problems before proceeding further:
>
> ★ How many times can you fold a piece of paper in half, and why is there a limit?
> ★ If you could keep folding in half forever, and if the moon is 384,400 km away and paper is 0.1 mm thick, how many folds would it take to reach the moon? (Write down a guess first before calculating).
> ★ Using a calculator to spot patterns, find a trick to solve $\log_{10} x$ without a calculator.

The lesson study took place in a sixth form college with students aged 16–19 in Manchester, UK, with an A-level (post-16 university entrance level) mathematics class of nine students. The teacher who worked with us had previously studied with us on our initial teacher training (ITE) course. He had been a very impressive student and was now an impressive teacher with deep pedagogical and mathematical understanding. Two of the authors took part in the lesson study.

Lesson study is not about creating the perfect lesson, but rather about developing pedagogical understanding. Often though, we can develop pedagogical understanding through trying to perfect a lesson and that was the approach we took here. The aim, more fully explained in the following sections, was to find a way to develop conceptual understanding of logarithms through students solving problems rather than through more traditional explanation/illustration and practice. The research focus was on to what extent, and how, students had developed conceptual understanding of logarithms through problem-solving, and how the lesson could be developed to do this further.

The lesson was very successful at engaging (and at times entertaining) the students who came up with, and shared, important insights throughout. Through this process they developed understanding of some key aspects of the concept of logarithms, but without yet reaching full conscious systematic understanding. The lesson and lesson study process provided us with much to think about, and led to suggestions as to how to take the lesson further.

Background to the lesson

There were three overlapping motivations for the initial design of this lesson (by one of the authors – DS). The first, and most important, was in relation to one argument about problem solving (see Lesh & Zawojewski, 2007): do you have to teach people the concepts and skills they need *before* they use them to solve problems, or can you learn the concepts and skills you need *through* problem solving? The lesson aims to show that you can do the latter. The second motivation is an extension of that: given that there seems to be a lot more problem-solving material available at lower school levels, is it equally possible to do this for higher-level school mathematics (where most teaching is seen to involve traditional transmissionist pedagogy, see Pampaka et al., 2012)? The third motivation arose from a slight feeling of guilt at the freedom we have as initial teacher educators in comparison to classroom teachers and our students. Often, we will try to model (and then collectively reflect on) good mathematical learning experiences with our trainee teachers. In doing so we are free to start with any good problem or important aspect of pedagogy we want to illustrate, and don't suffer the curriculum restrictions that classroom teachers often face in having to teach a particular mathematical topic on a particular day. For this lesson we therefore started with that restriction, and picked a topic that is often taught in a traditional way and can be seen as a difficult concept: logarithms.

In this section we outline some general guidelines on designing lessons, which aim to develop concepts through problem solving, and look at some of the implications for developing conceptual understanding of logarithms. In the following section, 'Lesson outline', we will outline the main phases of the lesson as usual, but will also take time to relate some of the ideas here to the particular problems used.

Developing mathematical concepts

To explain the approach taken in the lesson, we begin with a perspective on concept development based on the work of Vygotsky (1987). The starting point for this perspective is to think of concepts as the totality of their connections. At first this definition can feel oddly recursive, as if something is missing. What makes it work is the existence of words (like *logarithm*), or symbols, that act like the stick in candy floss/cotton candy and allow connections to gather around them.

There are two main types of connections that matter for us here. One is the connection of the concept to structured relationships within experience (where experience can be physical, visual, social, mathematical, etc.), the other is connection to other concepts, and to structured relationships between concepts. These two realms of systematic relationships that we are trying to embed our concept within are intimately connected. Our systems of concepts, even the most abstract of mathematics or logic, are ultimately grounded in human experience. All our experience is mediated by the concepts and systems of concepts we have, so that we see the world through our understanding of it. However, thought and experience are also different and it is useful to separate them as both types of connections are important in concept development in different ways.

There are various approaches to relating mathematics to experience that we can take within education. One is to ignore experience and just memorise processes and the formal shell of mathematics; however, this doesn't lead to very well-developed concepts. Another is to start with definitions and the relationships between concepts and then, once we have some grasp of those, try to make them more meaningful by relating them to experience through problem solving. This can work, but the initial phase of learning detached from experience can be alienating and difficult for many, and often we don't then make it on to the second phase. Here, instead, we want to start with experience of the concept in engaging problem situations, and then aim to abstract, generalise and draw out the essence of the concept through that problem solving.

Using this latter approach through one problem is usually insufficient to carve out the concept as a conscious useable mental object though, at least to the extent we desire. Developing concepts through problem solving also requires seeing the concept from multiple perspectives to build up an image of it, in particular through seeing its place within a wider system of concepts. If the concept can be seen as a generalisation of some essential structure within the original problem, we need to find a way, again through a new problem, for the concept instead to be the object which is being generalised. These inverted processes of generalising and being generalised combine to make useable concepts, which interrelate both experience and the mathematical system. The concept can then be further developed through its connection to other experiences, and its embedding within different aspects of conceptual structure.

There are various ways to encourage the generalising of a concept within problem solving through posing new problems. The easiest new problem is asking students to communicate their solution or understanding to others. This in itself creates a new perspective on the concept for students and can encourage the development of connections to previous and wider understanding. Similarly, asking students to meaningfully compare different solutions and different methods can do this. Beyond this, we can also develop new problems that connect the concept to other parts of mathematics, or embed it in wider mathematical processes.

To summarise: concepts develop through their connections to experience and other concepts. We want students to first, experience the concept, in some sense. We then pose problems related to those experiences which aim to draw the concept into consciousness, employing problems in which the concept is required for a solution. We then pose new problems that connect this emerging concept to other concepts.

So, to develop a sense and understanding of logarithms, we need to allow students to experience aspects of the concept and its varied connections and relationships, whether physically or mathematically, and then pose problems that can make sense of those experiences. The most important aspects will be a sense of exponential growth, logarithmic shrinking and the inverse relationship between those (and within that awareness of their being two different types of inverse of powers). Next most important (arguably) is then the relationship log xy = log x + log y, and the role that relationship plays. In the next section we outline the problems designed to allow the experiencing, and then drawing into consciousness, of these key aspects.

The different elements of this lesson have been used, sometimes together, sometimes separately, within our own immediate context of initial teacher education. However we were keen to see how it worked in the context of a classroom of mathematics learners who hadn't as yet encountered logarithms. Our lesson study focus here was on understanding to what extent, and how, the lesson helps develop understanding of logarithms through problem-solving within that context, and how it can be further developed to do so.

In practice, the end result was an inspiring lesson where we witnessed learners' thinking develop through the activities. Careful reflection on expected responses within the collective planning allowed the teacher to pick interesting strategies to share with the class without shutting down the opportunities for discovery and mathematical thinking. The lesson was very successful in developing learners' mathematical thinking and in enthusing them; however, one (75-minute) lesson was insufficient to test out all aspects of the plan. We touch on some of the ideas that we couldn't get to in the next section but the experience of the lesson developed our thinking of what could come next so we return to that question in the section 'What we have learned' and within the accompanying lesson plan.

Suggested reading

Clark, K. M., & Montelle, C. (2010). Logarithms: The early history of a familiar function. *Loci, 2010*(6), 1–11. Available on line at http://dx.doi.org/ 10.4169/ loci003495.

The Lesson Study Group. (2018). Teaching through problem solving. [online]. Retrieved July 5, 2019, from https://lessonresearch.net/teaching-problem-solving/overview

---

Lesson outline

The expected outcomes of the lesson are that the students will develop their understanding of logarithms through problem solving activity.

Problem 1: *how many times can you fold a piece of paper in half?*

It is best to begin by asking students what they think first to get them invested in finding the answer. There is a common misconception that you can only fold a piece of paper in half seven or eight times, whereas it actually depends on the size and thickness of the paper and the figure can be higher. The teacher can then distribute paper for the students to try themselves. In the lesson we describe next, we only distributed regular A4 sheets as we didn't want to spend too much time on this, but if you want to take more time you can have a range of paper of varying thickness and size (e.g. tracing paper, A1 flipchart paper, toilet rolls …). After this experience you can ask the students the question again to see if they have changed their mind and then show a video (see the lesson plan for a link to an example) where some paper is folded more than eight times (in the video they manage 11).

Again depending on how much time you have you can now have a discussion (or an even longer problem solving session) on whether and why there is a limit and what that limit is. Very complicated equations exist but the simplest explanation is that the paper at the fold can be seen as a semi-circle with a radius equal to the thickness of the paper before folding. As the thickness doubles and the length of paper halves (sort of), eventually there will be insufficient paper to allow enough for half a circumference for the relevant radius plus have anything left over (see Korpal, 2017). Again, as we didn't want to spend time on this here, we moved to the next problem instead.

The aim of problem 1 is to get the physical sense of repeated doubling (the layers and thickness) and halving (the size of the paper) into the room. These are the simplest forms of exponential growth and logarithmic shrinking. The problem doesn't quite get the full power of these across yet but provides a physical experiential basis for the next question where the power of the exponential comes across more clearly.

Problem 2: *if you could keep folding a piece of paper forever, how many folds would it take to reach the moon?*

Again, it is good to begin by getting students to write down and then share their own guesses. Most guesses are likely to be much larger than the actual answer. The next step is to take suggestions from the students of what information do we need to know. It is very likely they will suggest 'distance to the moon' and 'thickness of the paper', but you can nudge them if necessary.

There are choices to be made here. We would like the powers of two to be visible through this problem for later use. We could get these from the number of layers of paper after each fold but students may not incorporate this variable directly within their solutions so we would have to add them artificially when sharing and discussing those. Alternatively, a common type of paper, 80 gsm, is 0.1 mm thick so it is useful to agree to take that as our thickness of paper. Then after n folds the paper will be $2^n \div 10$ mm thick. The second choice relates to units. Do you want the distance to the moon to be given in km, and add the complexity of using two different units, or do you want to convert one measurement into the other and have longer numbers, or use standard form? Finally, do you want to get all these ideas into the room and then let students decide what they will use within the problem?

Overall, problem 2 is to an extent still grounded in their experience of paper folding, but moves to an imaginative version of that experience. This kind of step is an important part of mathematics and its history. For example, we see it in the language of powers, with squaring and cubing, with their basis in experience of squares and cubes, then being extended to dimensions beyond the three we commonly experience. We also see it in moves such as 'what if we could take the square root of –1?' where the role of imagination in the process is enshrined in the resulting name of imaginary numbers.

In this problem, students also experience the real power of the exponential given how few folds it takes, as the paper's thickness rapidly accelerates. But most importantly, in solving this question we also get experience of exactly the thing we are interested in – logarithms, although, importantly, without giving it a name. 'How many folds?' is a real world version of the question 'what power are we raising two to?'

Problem 3: the log to the base 10 trick

Here we shift from log to the base two to log to the base ten. This problem requires some preparation and practice by the teacher, who will ask the class for numbers and will then work out the log to the base ten of the number in their head, letting students then check the result on their calculator. It is useful first to show students how to use the button and try some examples. This will help make the trick seem as impressive as it actually is (even to those who have an idea of what logs are). It is possible, although far less entertaining, to just let the students investigate what this button is doing. Perhaps use this if you have practised and always get it wrong. If you are just nervous of getting it wrong then that is very natural, so just have a go at the trick version.

Summary of the log trick (for a fuller discussion see Appendix): we would recommend investigating and discovering the trick yourself. If you wish to do that you should skip to the next paragraph now. The trick uses the scale of the number to give the whole number part of the answer and relies on memorisation of the logs of the first 9 integers to get the decimal part. As log (ab) = log (a) + log (b), writing any number in standard form will give you a power of 10 (easy to find the $\log_{10}$ of), and a number between 1 and 10 (the $\log_{10}$ of this will be between 0 and 1) multiplied together. So if, for example, x = 25 900, x = 2.59 x10^4 in standard form. And so $\log_{10}$x = $\log_{10}$ 2.59 + $\log_{10}$ 10^4. The second part gives us the whole number part of our answer, 4. Then, 2.59 lies a little over half way between 2 and 3, so $\log_{10}$ 2.59 will be (approximately) a little more than half way between $\log_{10}$ 2 and $\log_{10}$ 3, i.e. between 0.3 and 0.48. Therefore, you could guess $\log_{10}$ 25 900 = 4.41, which is correct to 2 d.p. (additional ways to ensure accuracy in your answer are suggested in the Appendix for this chapter).

To begin the problem, start by asking students to work out the log of a random number to get them used to using the button. Share some of these numbers and their logs to make everyone in the room aware that the answers are complicated (i.e. that it would be unlikely anyone could work them out without a calculator but you don't have to be explicit about this). Then say you can work out the log in your head without a calculator. Go round the room taking suggestions and, using the trick, give the answers (this will take you time for each one). After a few, encourage them to give you more difficult numbers. After a few more correct, or very close to correct answers, the students should be very impressed.

The problem for the students is now to work out how you are doing it. You can leave this open and build from whatever they come up with, or you can have hints ready if they are struggling (see final lesson plan – Appendix). Students should notice things such as the logs of positive numbers of the same length having the same first digit. Work with what you get to push for more until it is clear that they could do the trick themselves if they know the logs of the integers 1 to 9. Then get them to practise doing the trick themselves.

In this part of the lesson we are explicit about logarithms to the base ten and attempt to find a practical way of working them out. By embedding this within a problem students can discover aspects of logarithms for themselves. Most of all we want them to experience base ten logs as having some sort of inverse relationship with powers of ten; and to have some sort of experience of log ab = log a + log b. Depending on what students have produced this may be more or less explicit in the room.

Problem 4: *comparing the log$_{10}$ experience to the original problem from stage 2*
For the final stage of the lesson, we were unsure when planning how far the class would get, and what would be best to do at this stage. We wanted

somehow to return to the moon problem so that we could make connections between $\log_{10}$ and $\log_2$ to help generalise awareness of what logs are.

Returning to the original problem, show a table with column headings: number of folds; number of layers of paper; and thickness of folded paper (see Figure 11.4 for an example). Ask the students how to get from one column to the other (students can fill in numbers to help them). Once it is established that number of layers is $2^{\text{number of folds}}$ and thickness is the number in column 2 multiplied by 0.1, ask how to go backwards, e.g. for 384,400 km or 3.84×10^{11} mm. Going from column three to column two should be easy, but going from column two to column one is more difficult. Return to $\log_{10}$ where when a number was multiplied by ten its log increased by one, and ask what is the equivalent that is happening in this case. Try to draw from the room that if that was log to the base ten this might be log to the base two. Get students to work out $\log_2 3.84 \times 10^{11}$ on their calculators to confirm it is 41.8.

Here, we are focussing on what is the same and what is different between the two number patterns with the aim to make students more aware of what logs are, in general.

Lesson reflection and analysis

The teacher had been teaching this class for only a short time but he was very experienced in using problem solving within the classroom. Following our planning session, which included a long discussion of the various elements, and several exchanges via email, he went away to adapt the lesson for his context, making various choices in how each problem would be presented and used. The class was scheduled to last 1 hour and 15 minutes.

The lesson started with the teacher giving the class a piece of A4 paper and asking them how many times they could fold it in half. Some learners predicted seven and some eight folds, saying they had heard of this before but couldn't explain any further. When attempting it themselves, one student manages six folds, and the students all laugh as another student claims seven while standing up and applying much force as he tries to make the seventh fold.

The teacher asked the learners which factors would contribute to helping get to seven folds; the students are quick to suggest that the thickness and the size of the paper would both influence the answer. The video is then shown where a very large sheet of paper is folded 11 times with the help of a fork-lift truck and a steamroller for the final folds.

If we could keep folding forever, how many times before it reaches the Moon?

Distances

Earth to Moon	384 400 km
Thickness of paper	0.1mm

Extension: **Further Distances**

Earth to Sun	1.496×10^8 Km
Earth to next nearest star	4.01×10^{13} Km
Length of visible universe	4.32×10^{23} Km

Figure 11.1 The paper-folding to the moon problem

The teacher then poses the next problem: 'If we could fold the paper as many times as we wanted, how many folds do we need to make in order to reach the moon?' (Figure 11.1), while acknowledging that this is an abstract/ mathematised question. One of the students comments that they would need to know how thick the paper is. The teacher reveals this on his slides to be 0.1 mm, and asks what else would need to be known. The class suggests they need the distance to the moon; this, too, is revealed as 384,000 km.

Before starting work on the problem the learners were asked to write a guess, and some of these were shared. As expected all guesses were over-estimates, with suggestions including one billion, one million, 300 and 100. However, these last two are not too far away from the correct answer of 42^1, showing some of the students already have a sense of the power of repeated doubling.

The teacher now encourages learners to get down to doing some calcu-lations, while keeping a record of what they are doing. He refrains from giv-ing hints at this stage and limits his interventions to asking questions. He does, however, pick up on interesting and significant strategies as they arise in order to share them with the rest of the class.

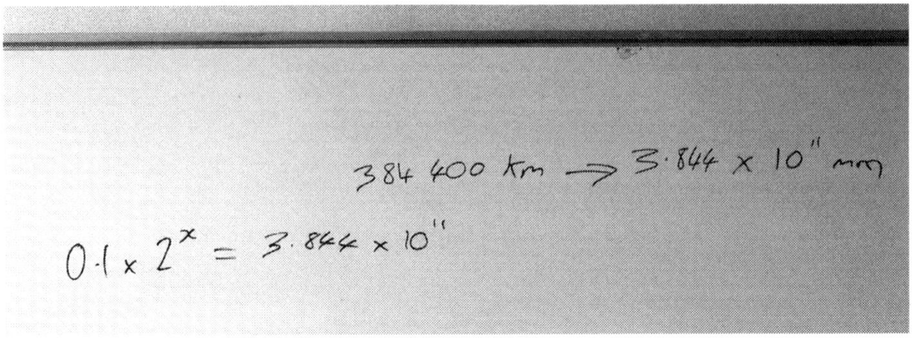

$$384\,400\ km \longrightarrow 3.844 \times 10^{11}\ mm$$

$$0.1 \times 2^x = 3.844 \times 10^{11}$$

Figure 11.2 An attempted solution

One student begins by simplifying the problem to reaching the height of the room and another says the problem reminds him of compound interest, making connections with the mathematical topic they had previously seen, which involved exponential growth while lacking the general concept or language. A few minutes later another student then claims he has an answer and comes to the board to share his ideas (see Figure 11.2).

He explains that he, too, had used compound interest. In his explanation he first converts the distance to the moon into millimetres and writes the equation to solve, which he then rearranges to give $2^x = 3.844 \times 10^{12}$. But then he says, 'I don't know how to solve that!' and instead he says he worked out an answer of $x = 50$ by using iteration of x2 on the calculator until reaching the figure on the right of the equation.

Having had this significant strategy shared, but with a not quite correct answer, the teacher asks all the learners to try it. He also asks them to keep a record as they work through it, partly so that all students have some awareness of the pattern of increasing powers of two (based on starting at 0.1 rather than 1, but with the same recognisable digits), and an example of the subsequent student work can be seen in Figure 11.3.

While the teacher circulates, one student suggests using the square root to solve the equation directly. Here we observe the common confusion between the two inverses of powers that we discussed earlier. The teacher asks him to test his theory and he quickly abandons it. This is a great pedagogic method of overcoming misconceptions without stifling the independent learning of the student. As this misconception is so important though, it would perhaps also have been useful here to widen this discussion to the whole class. Meanwhile, the other students continue with the approach of repeated doubling,

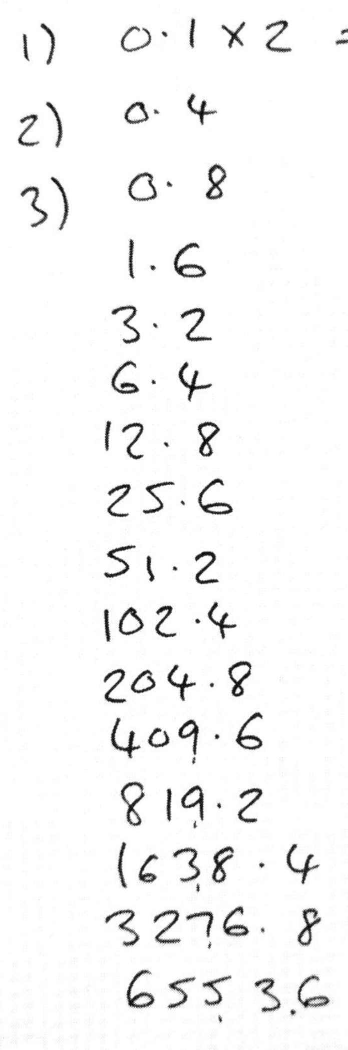

1) $0.1 \times 2 = 0.2$

2) 0.4

3) 0.8

1.6

3.2

6.4

12.8

25.6

51.2

102.4

204.8

409.6

819.2

1638.4

3276.8

6553.6

Figure 11.3 (Almost) the powers of 2

and reach consensus that the answer is 41.8 and so there needs to be 42 folds (41 is said to be insufficient, and 'you can't have half a fold').

The teacher now moves on to the log trick, first showing them how to use the log button (representing $\log_{10} x$) on the calculator, asking them to try their own numbers, and sharing some of the results. He then asks the students to test his magic ability, by giving him numbers that he can guess the log of without using a calculator. The first numbers that are suggested are 49, 420, then 497, and having practised at length the night before, he gives the correct answers to two decimal places. The students look a mix of impressed, confused and astonished and there are scatterings of applause each time. He then suggests they give him a harder number. What a harder number is in this context is, of course, not really known by the students, but one goes big and suggests 3.844×10^{11}, taken from the paper folding task (and perhaps hoping to find the solution this way). A correct answer earns a loud round of applause this time. Other suggestions include 2.6232, 1000 and the genuinely more difficult, 0.005. When asked about doing negative numbers the teacher says 'error'.

Students are then asked to figure out the trick and they are immediately intensely focussed on the task, experimenting with numbers on their calculators. After a while one student says that, 'every time I add zero the log increases by one'. He writes the logs of 9, 90 and 900 on the board (0.95, 1.95, 2.95). Another shares that he did something similar and puts the logs of 1, 10, 100 and 1000 on the board (0, 1, 2, 3 – see Figure 11.4). Here we are very close to seeing the powers of ten and their logs as being the inverse, which gives you the exponent of ten in each case. The teacher makes a point of asking about the decimal part ('there isn't one') to draw extra attention to the importance of these numbers. A third student then suggests that the size of the numbers give you the first digit of their logs, 'if it's hundreds its two, if it's thousands it's three). After a little more thinking time, a fourth student then suggests writing numbers in standard form and adding the logs of each together.

At this point the teacher asks if any of them think they could do the trick themselves, but some students say they still wouldn't know the logs of the first part of the standard form. One student suggests the teacher has memorised them, that he has memorised the logs of one to nine. As the teacher admits this is indeed what he has done, there is a great sense of satisfaction in the room at their collective solving of the problem. He asks them to try to learn to do the trick themselves by writing down the logs of one to nine and memorising them. At this point, if there had been more time, it would perhaps have been useful to explore the relationships between these numbers, and to make connections with the idea of adding logs for multiplied numbers that had already appeared in one form, to make this more conscious (the logs of two, four and eight may stand out as being linked, then those of three and nine, and then two, three and six). While trying to practise the trick, students ask about numbers in between such as 6.84. The teacher talks them through

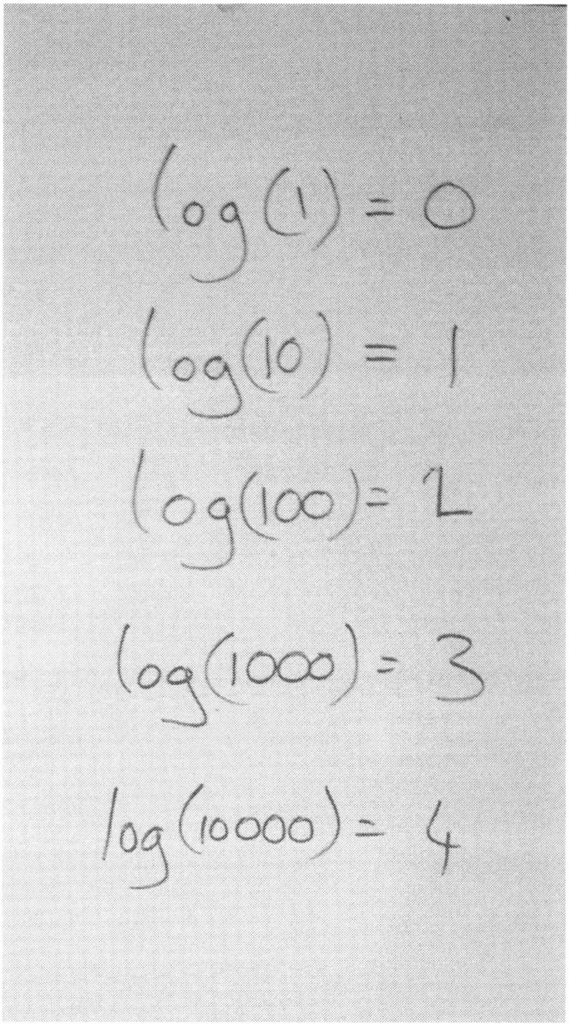

$$\log(1) = 0$$

$$\log(10) = 1$$

$$\log(100) = 2$$

$$\log(1000) = 3$$

$$\log(10000) = 4$$

Figure 11.4 The logs to base ten of powers of ten

the process of interpolating and how giving answers to 2 d.p. (or even 1 d.p. if necessary) makes the task easier.

Again, if time had allowed, it would have been useful to spend more time on this, as it connects to many other areas of the syllabus. It was evident, however, that the teacher had captured their imagination with this activity and had kept them engaged and enthused for the whole lesson. In fact, when the teacher suggested going back to the folding paper problem one of the learners refused because he was determined to master the log trick.

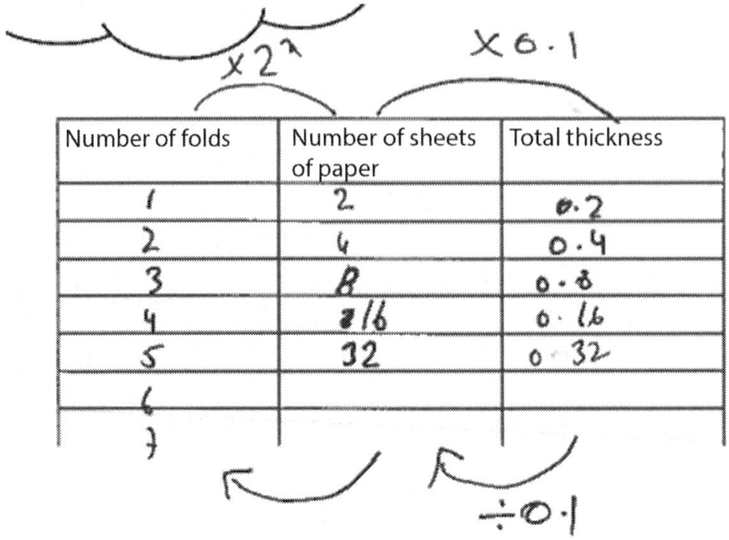

Figure 11.5 A student's version of the known relationships

The teacher returned to the moon/paper folding problem to link the two activities. He asked the learners to think about the relationships between the number of folds, the number of sheets of paper and the thickness on the paper (see Figure 11.5).

A student manages to fill in the table on the board, and the class are collectively able to work out the relationships required to move from left to right, including

number of sheets $= 2^{\text{number of folds}}$.

Going in the other direction proves much trickier (the missing relationship in Figure 11.5), and perhaps too much at this stage and with the short time remaining. One student goes back to suggesting taking the square root, but the class can see that will not work. The teacher reminds the class that in the previous problem when we multiplied by ten the log goes up by one. Here the students can see that now the number of folds goes up by one when we multiply the number of sheets by 2. At this point a parallel was made between powers of ten and powers of two, however the missing piece of the jigsaw is the explicit understanding that the base ten log is the inverse of the power of ten. Since time had essentially run out, the teacher summarises by telling the learners that the inverse here of 2^x is $\log_2$ and he gets them to try finding $\log_2$ of 3.844×10^{12} on their calculators to confirm their original answer of 42.

The lesson ends, leaving further developments until the next class on logarithms.

Pause for thought

Consider the above lesson reflection and analysis.

★ What aspects of the logarithm concept are still missing for the students?
★ If you were teaching this lesson to your class, which tasks would you want to spend more time on, and which less?
★ Did the teacher tell the students anything? At what points? What strategies would you use to hold yourself back from telling?
★ Choose a different concept and think of problems in which that concept could develop for students.

What we have learned

In this section we outline where we think the students had got to at this stage, and where the lesson could be taken next. We also share some thoughts on the lesson study process, and offer suggestions for designing problem-solving lessons to develop different concepts.

Developing the concept of logarithms further

By the time the log trick problem had been solved, the students have arguably, and to varying extents, some experience and consciousness of the following (among other things): the rapid acceleration of exponential growth; the particular powers of 2; examples of doing what the logarithm does in practice (e.g. finding x in $2^x = 3.44 \times 10^{12}$); the particular powers of 10; that $\log_{10}$ is somehow related to the powers of 10; the connections of $\log_{10}$ to standard form; and examples of multiplied numbers being equivalent to the adding of their logs. What they haven't developed yet includes explicit awareness that logarithms are the inverse of powers, that they are one of the two distinct inverses of powers, and that $\log (ab) = \log (a) + \log (b)$. It would be possible for a teacher to simply tell the students these things at this point, relating the explanation to the problems they have already solved. Given their previous engagement and the understanding they have already developed they would be maximally receptive to such an intervention, and it should effectively crystallise their thinking. However, as we set out to avoid telling the students anything, what else could be done to encourage the class itself to come up with these crystallisations?

With more time for the original lesson there were some opportunities to push a little further within the original tasks. For example, we could have spent a little more time looking for patterns within the logs of the first nine positive integers to create more examples related to log (ab) = log (a) + log (b), which we could then have attempted to generalise. We could also have more explicitly asked what the log button does after the log trick, as there is a possibility some students could guess this at this stage. Before doing this though, it would perhaps be better to pose a new problem: Given that log means $\log_{10}$, can we find a trick for logs of a different base, i.e. $\log_2$? After showing students how to use their calculator to find logs to different bases, students can play around as they have already done for $\log_{10}$. This time they are highly unlikely to find a trick for doing them without a calculator (but please get in touch if you ever find one). What will arise though are the numbers that give single digit answers, that is, the powers of 2. This is likely to be connected directly to the paper folding problem by students, and should, through generalisation between their experiences of $\log_2$ and $\log_{10}$ allow the answering of the question of what are and what they do.

If students still don't make that final leap, (and even if they do) this can be followed by a simpler problem that also makes more explicit and conscious that logs are one of two possible inverses of powers: What are the two inverses of a) $2 \times 5 = 10$, b) $2 + 5 = 7$, c) $2^5 = 32$, d) another mathematical operation of your choice. This problem could lead to interesting discussions, particularly around the operators of − and ÷ which they are likely to choose for d). In this problem we also come very close to simply telling students that log is the (other) inverse of powers. If this is an extreme case, it should also be noted that this is true to an extent of all problems. Answers are always partly contained in their questions (which is why coming up with questions is often the hardest thing to do, and is something we ultimately want students themselves to be able to do).

Therefore, when we promote not telling as we do in this chapter (and in most of this book) we should be clear we are not against implicit telling in this way, i.e. through posing the right problems. We are also not against students telling each other things as part of collaborative problem solving. We are social creatures, and most problems in the real world we solve together with others, not on our own. As we saw in this lesson, as long as students are actively involved in this collaborative process their understanding will develop as part of that, they will also feel as if they are part of having solved the problem rather than having just been told (because they are). Also, if we are honest, we are not against teachers occasionally 'telling', and being the ones who sometimes help crystallise understanding, or, for example, as we have often seen in this book, providing the terminology for the concepts which students are forming. But, ultimately, we would argue students can develop conscious conceptual understanding through collaborative problem solving without the need to be (explicitly) told anything, and this is the ideal we should strive for.

Lesson study process

This lesson study followed a similar pattern, in various ways, to those of other chapters in this book. Most of the initial research was conducted in the original design of the lesson, and the testing of various elements in initial teacher education sessions over a number of years. The lesson study team included one of our ex-students on that course who contributed various design elements in adapting the core ideas for his class, following collective discussions on the lesson with the two authors who also made up the lesson study team. The lesson was filmed, audio recorders were placed around the room, and materials produced by students were collected. An initial post-lesson analysis took place immediately after the lesson with the whole team and then we authors conducted a closer analysis through immersion in the collected data, resulting in this chapter.

The class teacher described the experience from his perspective:

I gained a great deal from participating in the lesson study, and so did the students. I liked the idea that a topic could be introduced concretely though a problem and brought to life through some number magic, rather than dead abstract rules for pushing symbols around the page. I gained some confidence through learning the log trick. I prepared as much as I could and decided to just try my best, letting go of control to the students who chose the numbers freely. How can I set an example to my students to do the same with a problem, if they never see me in a position of trying and not knowing the answer immediately without having previously prepared it? I had to let go of any idea that this was going to be perfect, but close enough to a couple of decimal places.

The folding to the moon problem was well anticipated and seemed to flow well, and this was the part that we had talked most about in the planning stages.

The main stumbling block was facility with inverses. The square root function and the logarithm to base 2 evaluated at 4 coincide.

I told the students to try more numbers in their calculators to be sure, but I can see that if I were to do this again that I could have had the numbers of folds and the number of pages tabulated and addressed that misconception by asking the students to take the square root of other numbers in their table.

Next steps

Potentially, we could build on this lesson with new problems. For example, since students now have strong awareness of powers of two and ten, and $\log_2$ and $\log_{10}$, we could pose the problem of how to convert between the two in either direction, and then to generalise to a formula to convert logs of different bases. But as the initial part of this 'what have we learned' section, has already focused enough on next steps, we will instead similarly subvert this space also, to encourage readers to develop their own lessons that develop concepts through problem solving. A starting point for doing so is to do a little of what Freudenthal (1983) has called 'didactical phenomenology'. Didactical phenomenology of a mathematical topic involves 'describing it in its relation to the phenomena for which it was created, and to which it has been extended in the learning process of mankind … as far as this description is concerned with the learning process of the young generation' (p. ix). That is, it addresses mathematical topics and concepts in terms of their formal logical structure, but also from the perspective of the human activities from which these generalisations arise, alongside the particular issues of their development within teaching and learning.

In essence, this means analysing the concept; its inner connections and sub-concepts; its relationship to other concepts and parts of mathematics; current understandings of pedagogy related to the concept including, for example, common misconceptions; how the concept appears within your curriculum and what students are expected to be able to do; and, most importantly finding where the concept is involved, explicitly or implicitly, in current or historical human experience. This list seems intimidating but this task doesn't have to be done exhaustively. Much will be available in books or online, for example, useful starting points for understandings of most topics in school mathematics can be found in Nunes, Bryant and Watson (2009); and the series that includes Mason, Graham and Johnston-Wilder (2005).

The next step is to think up problems, based on experiences that the concept is part of, and that require the concept to solve. Also, think up problems involving comparison, connections or other forms of generalisation, which help make the concept more conscious for learners. These can be thought up from scratch, or again through using online resources. The NRICH website (https://nrich.maths.org/) is one good place to find problems which you can adapt, as is the National Stem Centre (https://www.stem.org.uk/), particularly if you search their historical mathematics resources from the 1970s and early 1980s. The log trick at the heart of the lesson described above was adapted into a problem from something found by searching Google for *logarithm* and *amazing*. Most importantly, if you do develop anything that works well – find a way to share it!

Pause for thought

Pick a narrow topic in your curriculum that is difficult to teach in an interesting way.

★ Find a real-world example where the topic features, or is consciously used.
★ List three concepts that appear in the topic
★ List three common misconceptions found for the topic
★ Find another area of the curriculum where something similar happens.

Note

1   Fans of *The Hitchhiker's Guide to the Galaxy* (Adams, 1979) will recognise this number as also being the answer to the ultimate question of life, the universe and everything. This may or may not be a coincidence.

References

Adams, D. (1979). *The Hitchhiker's guide to the galaxy*. London: Pan Books Ltd.

Freudenthal, H. (1983). *Didactical phenomenology of mathematical structures*. New York: Kluwer.

Korpal, G. (2017). Folding paper in half. *At Right Angles*, 4(3), 20–23.

Lesh, R., & Zawojewski, J. S. (2007). Problem solving and modeling. In F. Lester (Ed.), *The Handbook of research on mathematics teaching and learning* (2nd ed., pp. 763–804). Reston, VA: National Council of Teachers of Mathematics; Charlotte, NC: Information Age Publishing. (Joint Publication).

Mason, J., Graham, A., & Johnston-Wilder, S. (2005). *Developing thinking in algebra*. London: Sage.

Nunes, T., Bryant, P., & Watson, A. (2009). *Key understandings in mathematics learning*. London: Nuffield Foundation. Retrieved from www.nuffield-foundation.org/key-understandings-mathematics-learning

Pampaka, M., Williams, J., Hutcheson, G., Wake, G., Black, L., Davis, P., & Hernandez-Martinez, P. (2012). The association between mathematics pedagogy and learners' dispositions for university study. *British Educational Research Journal, 38*(3), 473–496.

Vygotsky, L. S. (1987). *Thinking and speech. The Collected Works of L.S. Vygotsky, Vol. 1*. New York: Plenum.

Appendix

Lesson plan and resources

Lesson summary

Students work on a variety of problems in order to develop conceptual understanding of logarithms.

Focus on students learning

a   Recognise the relative power of exponential growth and logarithmic shrinking
b   Develop understanding of logarithms including: the particular examples of 2^x, 10^x, $\log_2 x$ and $\log_{10} x$; logarithms as the (other) inverse of powers; $\log xy = \log x + \log y$ and its use in simplifying calculations; and converting logs with different bases.

Lesson preparation

Learners will need A4 sheets of paper to fold, or a range of paper of different sizes and thicknesses, and calculators. The teacher will need slides (or an alternative) with distance to moon/thickness of paper; and an example table including number of folds, number of sheets and thickness columns. The teacher will also need to practice the $\log_{10} x$ trick in advance (see box below for tips).

The lesson

Task 1: how many times can you fold a piece of paper in half?

Begin by asking students to write down then share what they think. Distribute paper for the students to try themselves (either regular A4 sheets or a range of paper of varying thickness and size, e.g. tracing paper, A1 flipchart paper, toilet rolls etc.). After this experience you can ask the students the question again to see if they have changed their mind and then show a section of video where some paper is folded more than eight times e.g. YouTube MythBusters video (https://www.youtube.com/watch?v=kRAEBbotuIE).

Follow up with a brief discussion (or an even longer problem-solving session) on whether and why there is a limit and what that limit is.

Task 2: if you could keep folding a piece of paper forever, how many folds would it take to reach the moon?

Begin by asking students to write down and then share their guesses. Then ask students what information would be known to actually calculate. Share the distance to the moon = 384,400 km and thickness of paper = 0.1 mm. Circulate to encourage and to identify strategies to share. Ensure the final solution is illustrated using a table with columns with number of folds, number of sheets and total thickness. Compare results with initial student guesses and discuss.

Task 3: the log trick

In this problem the teacher asks the class for numbers and then works out the log to base ten of the numbers without using a calculator. The students then have to work out how the trick is done.

Begin by showing the students the log button on the calculator and try some examples together, so students are confident in using the button (and so it is clear to the class that logs are complicated). Tell the students that you can work out the log in your head without a calculator. Take suggestions for numbers and, using the trick (see box below), give the answers. Encourage students to suggest more difficult numbers. Once you have done a few and the students seem sufficiently impressed ask the students to work out how you are doing it. Circulate to encourage, and to identify student strategies to share. If this process is insufficient in itself, possible hints for the class or individuals include: change one thing at a time; try two-digit numbers then three digit numbers; try 5.5, 55, 550, 5500; can you make the decimal part of the answer disappear?; try writing the number in standard form. Aim to get to the point where at least one student can do the trick (allowing them to refer to notes rather than memorise particular log values).

Tips for doing the $\log_{10}$ trick

Finding the $\log_{10} x$ means finding the power to which 10 to has been raised to make x. We outline here how to get a good estimate of the answer without using a calculator.

Finding the whole number part of the answer

Let's begin with two examples. 10^2 and 10^3, equal 100 and 1000 respectively, therefore $\log_{10} 100 = 2$ and $\log_{10} 1000 = 3$.

This also means that anything between 100 and 1000, i.e. any three-digit number, must come from ten being raised to the power of something between two and three. So for $100 < x < 1000$, $\log_{10} x = 2.\text{something}$. This pattern continues for other powers of ten, e.g. for $10^5 = 100{,}000 < x < 1{,}000{,}000 = 10^6$, $\log_{10} x = 5.\text{something}$, i.e. to get the whole number part of our answer we just need to count the digits after the first digit of our number.

This is perhaps easier to see if we write any number in standard form, e.g. $34{,}562 = 3.4562 \times 10^4$. By the rules of logs (which we will assume for now), $\log_{10} xy = \log_{10} x + \log_{10} y$, so $\log_{10} 3.4562 \times 10^4 = \log_{10} 3.4562 + \log_{10} 10^4$. As 3.4562 lies between 1 and 10, i.e. between 10^0 and 10^1, $\log_{10} 3.4562$ will lie somewhere between 0 and 1. As $\log_{10} 10^4$ is by definition 4, $\log_{10} 3.4562 \times 10^4$ will equal 4.something.

Finding the decimal part of the answer

For the last example, we still need to find $\log_{10} 3.4562$, or in general the $\log_{10}$ of the number between one and ten when written in standard form. This we do by memorising the logs of whole numbers from one to nine and interpolating.

The logs of whole numbers from one to nine

Technically, we only need to memorise the log of 2, 3 and 7 (≈ 0.3, 0.48 and 0.85 respectively), as other numbers we can work out from those. For example, $\log_{10} 4 = \log_{10}(2 \times 2) = \log_{10} 2 + \log_{10} 2$ and $\log_{10} 5 = \log_{10}(10/2) = \log_{10} 10 - \log_{10} 2$. Similarly we can use the fact that $6 = 2 \times 3$, $8 = 2^3$ and $9 = 3 \times 3$ or 3^2. This gives us:

$\log_{10} 1 = 0$; $\log_{10} 2 \approx 0.3$; $\log_{10} 3 \approx 0.48$; $\log_{10} 4 \approx 0.6$; $\log_{10} 5 \approx 0.7$; $\log_{10} 6 \approx 0.78$; $\log_{10} 7 \approx 0.85$; $\log_{10} 8 \approx 0.9$; $\log_{10} 9 \approx 0.95$

Interpolating

For numbers between these we have to interpolate. Unfortunately, the log function is not linear, which makes this a little harder, but it can be taken to be so for most of the gaps between known values. So for example, $\log_{10} 8.7$ is approximately 7/10 of the way between $\log_{10} 8$ (=0.9) and $\log_{10} 9$ (=0.95), giving roughly 0.935, or 0.94 to two decimal places (the actual answer is 0.939519 to

(Continued)

six d.p.). The combination of estimating via assuming linearity and limiting the number of decimal places to two and, if you are unsure one, will usually get you there.

The hardest gap is between $\log_{10} 1$ and $\log_{10} 2$ as the function is least linear here. For this gap you can just add a little on for the earlier numbers as the function increases most rapidly here, and/or you can reduce the number of decimal places you give to one.

It is also possible to use the addition rule of logs for this, and other, gaps. For example $1.6 = 4 \times 4 \div 10$, so $\log_{10} 1.6 = \log_{10} 4 + \log_{10} 4 - \log_{10} 1 \approx 0.6 + 0.6 - 1 \approx 0.2$.

Complication: if you are given a negative number then (assuming we are ignoring complex numbers) the log is undefined. But if the number given is between zero and one then we are into the area where powers of ten are negative. The trick still works but be careful with the addition that puts the whole number and decimal parts together. First, work out the negative power that would appear in the standard form version, then add the approximate log of the other part of the standard form number, but remember this will involve a more complicated calculation than just appending the digits as in the examples above. For example, $\log_{10} 0.007 = \log_{10} 7 \times 10^{-3} = \log_{10} 7 + \log_{10} 10^{-3} \approx 0.85 + -3 = -2.15$

Some examples:

$\text{Log}_{10}\, 65\,000$

1   There are 4 digits after the first digit so the whole number part will be 4.
2   6.5 is half way between 6 and 7, so $\log_{10} 6.5$ will be approximately half way between $\log_{10} 6 \approx 0.78$ and $\log_{10} 7 \approx 0.85$, and so ≈ 0.82 to 2 d.p.
3   Therefore $\log_{10} 65\,000 \approx 4.82$ (actual answer is 4.812913357 to 9 d.p.)

$\text{Log}_{10}\, 0.00004392$

1   $0.00004392 = 4.392 \times 10^{-5}$, so the whole number part would be -5, but when we adjust for the decimal part it will be $-4.\text{something}$
2   4.392 is roughly 4/10 of the way between 4 and 5. So the log of 4.392 will be roughly 4/10 of the way between 0.6 and 0.7, so let's say 0.64
3   $\text{Log}_{10}\, 0.00004392 \approx -5 + 0.64 = -4.36$ (actual answer = -4.357338 to 6 d.p.)

Task 4: $\log_2 x$ trick, and what logarithms are

Explain that the log button stands for $\log_{10}$, and that other logs to other bases exist. Show students how to use their calculator to find logs to different bases. Ask students to find an equivalent trick for $\log_2$. Once students find that powers of two give numbers without a decimal part, compare this for the base ten and base two trick and ask the students what this means logarithms are.

Via slides or handout ask students to find the two inverses of a) $2 \times 5 = 10$, b) $2 + 5 = 7$, c) $2^5 = 32$ d) any other mathematical operation/calculation of their choice.

Complete this task by returning to the table from task 2 and asking students how you get from one column to the next in the table in both directions. Get students to work out $\log_2 3.84 \times 10^{11}$ on their calculators to confirm it is 41.8.

Possible extension

Using knowledge of the powers of two and ten, find a way to convert between $\log_2 x$ and $\log_{10} x$. Generalise to converting between logs of any two bases.

Suggestions for lesson study focus

◆ Focus on shift from instruction to facilitation of student problem solving; how do you and the students respond.
◆ Focus on scaffolding. Vary the timing and content of scaffolding and hints for the various problems; what impact does that have?

12

Conclusion(s)

Mathematics, pedagogy, professional development and research

Introduction

At the core of this book are ten lessons in mathematics. Each of the chapters explaining, describing and analysing a lesson could be picked up and used by novice or experienced teachers, without reference to the others, to think through, adapt and use in their own classrooms. Through doing that, individuals might also develop more general ideas about mathematical understanding, pedagogy or lesson study (LS) that they can apply beyond the particular lesson they use, but, of course, they might not. As authors we are particularly keen on general understandings, so long as they are infused with the rich details of particular examples. When ideas are general they are connected in systems, and when systematic ideas are connected to practice (connected in the sense of being inside each other) then they are at their most powerful and useful. So we want to take some time in this concluding chapter to discuss some of the more general understandings developed within the book.

In writing the book we wanted to tell three interrelated stories: one about *mathematics* and mathematical understanding; one, closely related, about *pedagogy*, or teaching and learning; and a third about *LS* and professional development. Given the chapter/lesson format, and the varied focus of each, it is useful to pull these different stories together here. Having written the book, and in the process of spending many hours discussing the meaning of what we are doing, we would also add a fourth element to the list, which is *research*.

The world we authors work in straddles two domains, the world of schools and teaching, and the world of research. These two domains have their own logic and can seem quite detached from each other at times. For example, one of the initial impetuses for this project was our search for literature to share with our pre-service teachers that wasn't either overly simplistic or overly abstract and realising there was a real lack of such material. All three authors work in both teaching and research, but the work we do together in teacher training lies very much at the interface of the two. Our teaching on the course is informed by research and research plays a prominent direct role in the course, whether in the articles we read together, the theoretical discussions we have critically reflecting on mathematics and pedagogy, or the research on their own practice that the student teachers themselves do. Given the understanding we have of both domains, we think this book, too, lies at the interface of research and teaching. The research element is, of course, seen in some of the literature that is discussed, particularly in the background sections, but much more than this it is seen in the processes of conducting the LSs. In the 'Research' section we discuss the LS we have conducted here as a form of research in terms more common to academic literature.

Before that, in the 'Mathematics and pedagogy' section we draw out some of the knowledge we have developed about mathematical understanding and pedagogy through the various chapters. We then use these to say something more general about both. We situate this knowledge within a wider framework of pedagogy and discuss what may be missing from the types of lesson seen in this book and why those things are missing. In the 'Lesson study' section we summarise the variations in LS seen within the chapters and how they relate to the elements generally seen in traditional versions of LS. We ask whether what is described here can be called LS and whether that matters. We also focus briefly on one important aspect of the LS process we have used, the role of writing and disseminating findings in developing generalisation, and argue that the format modelled here could be useful in various professional development contexts to encourage the same.

Mathematics and pedagogy

In this section we outline some of the key features of mathematics and pedagogy found within the lessons in this book. Many of the lessons have a lot in common with each other in this regard, and little in common with traditional mathematics teaching where a teacher models, an example is worked through together, and then students practice independently. We take time to outline some of the commonalities in mathematics and pedagogy found within the lessons, and then explore some of the further insights developed through the various LSs.

The lessons in this book span a range of curriculum content including number, shape and space, and algebra, from primary/elementary through to post-16 levels. As we have said already in some of the chapters, many of these lessons could be used across a wide range of ages and attainment levels, sometimes as they are, and sometimes with some adaptations, scaffolding, or extensions and additional problems. The reason for this is that most of the lessons focus on one, or a small number of, problem(s) (or, rich tasks, see https://nrich.maths.org/11249), which, at their best, are open to a range of attainment levels, and which have sufficient potential depth to stretch even the most confident students.

The openness of such tasks can be substantial, such as in the virus out-break task in Chapter 7, or the drawing game in Chapter 5, where there is no correct approach or final answer. The openness may primarily be in the method, or the extent to which generalisation occurs, such as in the perim-eter, enlargement and logarithm tasks of Chapters 2, 6 and 11. It could also be within the reasoning around different answers (which may be correct, or potentially correct) as in Chapter 3's sharing of sandwiches or arguments about luck or skill in the coin tossing game of Chapter 9; or the openness may mainly be in how the mathematics is connected to real-world experience as in Chapter 8's boat hire task or Chapter 10's critiques of an experiment.

The openness of problems is very helpful in moving away from the anxi-ety inducing right or wrongness of much mathematics education, which can lead many students to develop a fear of being wrong, looking stupid and even being ridiculed by their peers or teacher. Openness also allows begin-ning with, and valuing, student knowledge and understanding. This enables students to feel like the mathematics is their own (rather than just memoris-ing other people's mathematics), but it also provides a meaningful basis for building an individual's understanding upon, and brings a wealth of differ-ences in knowledge, and methods, into the classroom as raw material for all to potentially engage with.

Three other commonalities in the lessons connect to this last point. First, is the frequency of connecting mathematics to the real world whether through real world scenarios and/or outside school experience in Chapters 3, 4, 7, 8 and 10 and direct experience (including manipulatives) in Chapters 2, 5, 6, 10 and 11. As well as engaging students and providing the concrete content of mathematical concepts, these connections with experience help enable the beginning with, and use of, students' own understanding, in developing further mathematical understanding. A second common feature, in all the lessons, is the use of dialogue through paired or small group work, and class discussions. Such dialogue is vital for ensuring the different experiences, methods and answers become shared raw material for further development. The third and final common feature we want to stress flows from the second, and that is generalisation. This occurs when the different experiences, methods and answers are thrown together in a meaningful way, often through a new problem. So, for example, in the sandwich lesson of Chapter 3, different ways of cutting up sandwiches are not just shared, but new questions such as 'are these the same?', or, 'is it $\frac{3}{5}$ or $\frac{3}{15}$?' are raised; and in Chapter 9 where different perspectives on skill or luck in guessing real from fake lists of coin tosses are not just stated, but the contradiction of the different answers drives students to elaborate and develop the reasoning to defend their position.

This generalisation and deepening of understanding through the re-problematising of different answers and methods can take other forms, such as when connections are made more explicitly between particular problems or parts of mathematics and other problems or mathematics, or when students are asked to take a new perspective on their own methods through sharing with others in dialogue, or in writing it down. All these forms appear (to a greater or lesser extent within the lessons), but we would often expect to see them even more in the lessons that follow and build on the ones in these chapters. In studying one lesson it made sense for us to explore the early stages of the materials, but we wanted to stress the potential for greater explicit generalisation as the lessons are built upon.

On reading the book, some may feel other aspects of mathematics teaching are missing too. Most commonly, perhaps, the repetitive practice many feel is necessary for securing memory and understanding. Partly this is missing because it wouldn't make for a very interesting book, but mainly it is missing because we believe it is in lessons with the sort of pedagogy described above that students develop their understanding the most. We even believe that such teaching is all that is needed (with the proviso stated above, of the need for building on open task lessons, with problems that emphasise mathematical connections and generalisation). We realise though that in many contexts shifting wholesale to such an approach may be difficult. The current emphasis on high-stakes testing, and the atomisation of curricula shaped by that, often encourages the use of traditional teaching methods (see, e.g. Gainsburg, 2012). Chapter 2 on mastery teaching outlines one model of how to structure a more mixed approach with a four-part lesson including formative pre-assessment; open and collaborative 'anchor' tasks' and journaling; more traditional instruction and practice (although building on developments in the anchor task); and an individual assessment task. Other models are, of course, possible, and in more resistant cultures it may just be possible to introduce occasional lessons of the type found in this book, or even just segments of lessons initially. If a mixed approach is to be used though, we would also encourage the use of intelligent forms of practice, such as forms of procedural and conceptual variation (see Gu, Huang & Marton, 2004; and https://variationtheory.com/), rather than random, repetitive practice.

Many of the elements of the brief outline above of the general pedagogy found in this book are expanded upon in the background sections of the chapters. This understanding was built upon in various ways through the analysis and 'what we have learned' sections, leading to various insights. Many of these insights will hopefully contribute to the pedagogic understanding of those reading, and some will have wider significance and originality, particularly in illustrating general ideas within particular contexts.

The various findings connect to, and build on, the main themes described above, i.e. open problems; connecting to experience, and beginning with students own understandings; using dialogue and collaborative reasoning; and generalisation through mathematical connections. So, in relation to openness of problems we found that, in different ways, openness often requires forms of structure (Chapters 7 and 10), or teacher facilitation (Chapter 6) to support productive developments. In relation to connecting mathematics to experience we learned and illustrated various ways in which direct and indirect experience can provide a grounding for concept development (Chapters 7, 8, 10 and 11). Related to dialogue we found new ways in which different forms of dialogue can interrelate (Chapter 9). And on the generalisation that can emerge from bringing different student answers and models together, or through connecting mathematics we found that problems involving comparison (Chapter 11), or particular types of questions (e.g. on uniqueness in Chapter 2) are often required for explicit generalisation. In relation to these processes we also developed understanding on the need for attention to the practicalities of sharing and journaling when using manipulatives (Chapter 2), and gained greater clarity on the benefits of particular models of proportion and how to use them with students (Chapter 3 and 4).

Alongside our own findings, the teachers that we worked with in our LS teams also developed their own pedagogical understanding in various ways, as illustrated in some of the vignettes we have provided. Examples of this include that openness and not confirming or closing down *does* encourage engagement and discussion (Chapter 3); and, that there are enormous potential benefits in encouraging students to ask their own questions, rather than just answering ours (Chapter 5).

Although in reality it is hard to separate pedagogical understanding from the mathematical understanding of our students, some of what we have found perhaps can be allocated to the latter category. These include a deeper understanding of the variations in heuristic approaches to probability, and how that interrelates with other aspects of activity (Chapter 9); the examples of the relationship of language and concept development, and the potential for meta-awareness and reflection at lower/younger attainment levels (Chapters 3 and 5); and illustrations of the complexity of van Hiele levels in practice (Chapter 5), and of the relative ease of solving situated problems versus their formal equivalents (Chapter 8).

This new mathematical and pedagogical understanding was formed due to the commitment of those involved with the LS, their willingness to try something new and the mutual trust within these groups. We discuss more about the lesson study experience in the next section.

Lesson study

The primary essence of LS is to develop the pedagogical understanding of teachers, and (possibly) develop general understanding about teaching and learning (Stigler & Hiebert, 2016), through studying and implementing a lesson or lessons. Given the findings we have outlined in the section above, we think we can justly claim to have conducted activities that capture the essence of LS. There is some debate in the literature, however, as to what exactly counts as LS, with some giving lists of elements which must appear (e.g. Fujii, 2018), and others lists of elements which are important if it is to be effective (e.g. Takahashi & McDougal, 2018). In this section we look at some of the typical elements, based on these lists and the outline given in Chapter 1, less to justify that what we have done is LS (although we would argue that we have conducted LS, it wouldn't upset us for others to think differently), but rather to explore the (sometimes very different) form that those elements took here.

Initial research

Takahashi and McDougal (2018) argue for a sustained period of research into the needs of the class, the curriculum, and the research theme etc., something often lacking in translations of LS to contexts outside of Japan (Fujii, 2018). As noted in Chapter 1, the lessons in this book have been designed, borrowed, adapted and used, often over a long period of time, to study and illustrate particular pedagogical aspects within initial teacher education or teacher professional development. We also took a general perspective on the needs of mathematics classes and curriculum, i.e. in the need for more open, accessible problems that connect to real world experience, build on students own understandings, and emphasise dialogue, reasoning and connections in mathematics. Working with teachers to adapt the lessons for their particular classes was then sufficient to generate rich data. These aspects of our approach therefore shortcut some of the processes involved for us. We would argue, however, not to generalise from the good fortune of our particular context in this, and to devote as much time as possible to this phase. In fact, we would stress the need to add further phases of research, once the data has been gathered and is being analysed, and particularly, when the experience and analysis is being written down to be shared with others, something we will expand upon below.

Research focus

Although we did have a clear research focus for each of the lessons, the focus presented in the book for each study is not always exactly the same as the one we began with. Openness to the possibility of adapting the question asked is something we bring from our role as educational researchers. In qualitative research, it is generally accepted that the research question may change in the process of conducting research, in response to the emerging data (see Creswell, 2012). We would argue that, in general, there is always a dialectical relationship between question and answer. In research, questions are initially formed based on the researchers understanding at the beginning of the process, but as understanding develops through the research, for example, if awareness grows of the limitations of what can be learned, then the question must be adapted. Sometimes answers even appear to questions that the researcher hadn't intended to ask at all, or, at least, interesting things emerge from the collected data that are worthy of investigating further. In this book, both of these types of adaption of research focus occurred at times, and we would recommend a similar flexibility in focus for others who conduct LSs, particularly once they have gained experience in LS.

Lesson planning; teaching, observing and collecting data; and initial post-lesson analysis

We group these phases together as they are generally the phases in which we were joined by class teachers within the lesson study process. They are also the phases commonly seen in limited translations of the Japanese LS experience to other contexts (Fujii, 2018). Therefore, we can't in general claim that the teachers involved fully participated in what would be accepted as LS. However, solely taking this perspective would miss much.

First, the LSs in this book simply couldn't have occurred without those teachers, and their ability to make the ideas in the lessons concrete, adapting them to their contexts and the needs of their students. The teachers also provide a vital resource for us in checking details of our later analysis of the data. Some of the teachers did also participate in other phases to an extent, for example, where they had taught and thought through the lessons previously within initial teacher education, or engaged with discussion about the research behind the lessons in ITE or professional development (Chapters 6, 8 and 9); and, where they had determined the needs of the class and been part of the collective shaping of the research question (e.g.in Chapters 2 and 3). We have also shown, we think, that even participating in a slightly restricted version of the process, can be beneficial in developing an individual's pedagogical understanding, as illustrated by some of the insights seen in the occasional vignettes. For all these reasons we would encourage engaging others in any phase or phases of the process, so long as there is sufficient numbers for collaborative practice also in the phases where they do not participate.

Role of knowledgeable other

We authors are perhaps the sort of people who would be seen as knowledgeable others who could join in with other teachers' LSs. In some ways we could therefore rely on ourselves to provide this role within the activities described in this book. This is not a helpful model though for those teachers who feel less confident but cannot access a knowledgeable other to work with them. However, for us, it wasn't just that we had some understanding of research to bring to the activity but rather two other factors that were equally or even more important. First, is that, just as in a mathematics classroom, collaborative dialogue and reasoning enables higher level thinking than an individual can often achieve on their own. We think it is important to view the lesson study collective therefore as a form of knowledgeable other. Second, as described further below, we found that the need to share our findings pushed us to analyse our experiences in greater depth, including returning again at various phases to research literature, to help us make sense of and develop our understanding. We would argue that previous research and mathematics educational literature can be the collective knowledgeable other that we can all access (at least to an extent), and that this too is a helpful strategy for other teachers conducting their own lesson studies.

Reflection and dissemination

Elsewhere, we have written about various means to ensure LS goes beyond the particular context (see Swanson & Morgan, 2020), for example, where different LS teams come together within professional development and are pushed to generalise through comparison with others' experiences. We also suggested other means for doing this connected to lesson study, such as writing up and sharing with others, and our own experiences with this book confirm, for us authors at least, the usefulness of the pressure of having to share something meaningful, and to express our findings in coherent and convincing ways, which made us delve deeper into the analysis of the lessons shared here, and deeper into the existing literature to find, and understand, similarities and differences.

Writing has played an important role in the historical development of human consciousness as it is more enduring than spoken word, allowing greater potential for accumulation of understanding. For each individual too, writing plays a key role in the development of their consciousness. Vygotsky (1987) discusses various aspects that lead to writing requiring a higher level of abstraction, including, for example, the lack of intonation or expression which can bring additional meaning in spoken language; the absence of the person addressed means that all potential readers have to be imagined and considered sufficiently; the absence of a shared immediate context requires that much detail can't be taken for granted and has to be spelled out in written language; and the absence of the general flow of conversational language requires that language is more self-motivated and generated, and more consciously constructed when written rather than spoken.

In the mathematics classroom, some of the more abstract requirements of written language are also present in dialogue which involves justification and reasoning, when compared to more conversational forms of speech. Writing can itself be used in the classroom though to help develop more abstract thinking, as is seen for example, in the outline of the approach to mastery in Chapter 3, where student journaling follows the open and collaborative anchor tasks.

All these benefits of writing also apply to lesson study. First, writing up and sharing LSs can provide the basis of a cumulative development of understanding for the teaching community. Secondly the additional requirements of writing encourage a more detailed spelling out and justification of findings, in relation to existing literature, which necessitates a more conscious and systematic understanding on the part of those writing. In Japan, where LS is more systematically integrated into a collective development of the curriculum, the writing up of lesson studies is common practice, and many are published (Takahashi & Yoshida, 2004). Producing such reports would be beneficial in other contexts such as our own, and we hope we have provided a model for doing so in the chapters of this book, and we will return to this question in the conclusion of this chapter.

Research

LS is a form of action research (Lewis, Perry & Friedkin, 2009), and has been used not just to improve the pedagogical understanding of participants, but also to investigate aspects of teaching and learning more generally (Stigler & Hiebert, 2016). There has been much debate historically on whether action research by practitioners really counts as research, mainly due to questions of rigour, but it has become more widely accepted in recent years (Hendricks, 2019). In this section, we justify that what we have done in this book is research, in academic terms, by being more explicit about various aspects of the research process. This section will primarily be of interest to academic researchers but may also be useful for others engaged in practitioner research.

Given the many and varied perspectives on qualitative research, Meyrick (2006) has developed a useful framework for judging the quality of qualitative research, based on literature from across a range of academic fields. We use the elements, and sub-elements, from that framework here to provide a structure for discussing some key aspects of the research.

Researcher epistemological and theoretical stance
Our general epistemological and theoretical stance has been made explicit within the chapters of this book in our discussions of mathematical and pedagogical knowledge, and our perspective on knowledge in relation to research is the same. So for example, we have argued that mathematics is an activity

not just an object; that mathematical understanding represents a particular form of generalisation from experience; that experience is inside concepts and vice versa; that the systematic connections between mathematical concepts are also inside those concepts; that knowledge is profoundly social; and that we develop understanding through problem solving. Therefore in research, too, we believe that we can come to understand the world through attempting to change it (solving problems), in close relation to practice, in ways that are collaborative, and that connect to wider systems of understanding (i.e. here mathematical educational research).

An engaged stance such as this does bring potential dangers of a lack of objectivity distorting the analysis. These dangers are mediated here through being explicit about our process and choices (as we do here and elsewhere in the book); our avoidance of sharing only perfect lessons; the sharing of detailed data from the lesson; and researcher reflexivity (collaborative reflection is frequently provoked in joint activity and co-authoring). We also worked hard to create distance at points in the process. For example, following LS planning sessions we would leave the class teachers to finalise the lesson plan, including adapting it for their students, and switch to researcher mode. We also ensured that at least one author did not take part in any particular LS, including the primary analysis phase, so that one of us would bring some critical distance to the analysis in the chapter.

Methods and data collection

For each lesson we have given the objectives and research question. In lesson study each of these is directly related to a particular lesson, and thus data collection focuses primarily on the classroom and the lesson in action (although all data generated in the preparation of the lesson was also collected including recordings of any planning sessions). Each lesson study can be viewed as a form of explanatory qualitative case study (Yin, 2018), and as such they require multiple sources of data to enable triangulation. In all LSs (except the Japanese lesson in Chapter 4) we audio recorded the classes, including typically the local interactions of four to five pairs or small groups of students (including a range of attainment levels); we photographed student work in progress, and collected in student productions; and we made observation notes of the whole class and small-scale interactions. Around half of the lessons were also video recorded. Data collection was conducted by the two authors who were part of each lesson study team (apart from Chapters 4 and 10 where only one author was present).

Sampling

We used a combination of purposive and convenience sampling (see Etikan, Musa & Alkassim, 2016) within the research. We primarily chose teachers to work with who either had rich experience in, or openness to, the type of pedagogy found within the lessons, in order to maximise learning from the experience. We also wanted to ensure that some of the teachers were at an earlier stage of experience in relation to such pedagogy, so that different issues would arise that would be relevant to those beginning to adapt their teaching in this direction. We therefore worked with some student teachers from our initial teacher training course. Particular classes were then chosen by the teachers involved, partly on the basis of the content of the lessons, and partly on timing and availability of the participants.

Analysis

We have included all cases or lesson studies that were undertaken for this book to avoid criticism of selecting cases that confirm our own prejudices. Two Chapters (4 and 10), based on experiences prior to the research and writing of the book, were included simply due to us having sufficient data from these other lesson study experiences.

There were various stages to the process of analysis. These included a feedback session immediately following the lesson with the lesson study team, which was recorded to add to later analysis. After transcription of all relevant data, both of the observer authors would then begin to independently analyse all data in terms of how it related to the research focus. There would then be an iterative sequence of collaborative analysis to develop the analysis based on emerging themes, and contradictions in analysis, through a series of meetings, individual analysis and written communication. This iterative process included re-engaging with existing literature on the emerging themes. Once those authors participating in the LS had written up the initial analysis, the remaining author would then critique and challenge the emerging findings and a new iterative process would begin. After this process was complete, the analysis would be shared with other participants in the LS team and with educational researchers, teacher educators and teachers to challenge its interpretation and to challenge its analysis, interpretation and/or descriptive detail, beginning a third iterative cycle of review.

We have highlighted within the chapters where alternative explanations are possible, or where explanations given are seen only as possibilities. As mentioned above in the section on lesson study, it should be noted that sometimes the focus of analysis would change as a result of the data collected. Usually this involved a narrowing of focus, or the addition of new elements, and is made visible in the chapters through observation of the stated research focus and what is discussed in the 'what we have learned' sections.

Results and conclusions

We have tried to include as much relevant data as possible within the lesson study reports, including quotes and photographs to allow readers to see the path between data and conclusions. The processes of analysis and critique we describe above brought challenge to debateable or unjustified conclusions being drawn, but readers are encouraged to find more that can be challenged, and we hope we have provided sufficient data to enable that. The detail we have provided is particular to each individual lesson and context, yet we have drawn more general understandings from those individual experiences. In doing so, we follow the elements of the process from individual case study to theoretical generalisation laid out by Eisenhardt (1989). We have given some detail on many of those elements already in this section, but we would stress the importance of the aspect of 'enfolding literature' (p. 544), whereby similarities and contradictions between the data, emerging analysis and existing literature, and the reasons for them, play a central role in the forming of generalisations. Again, we have aimed to present sufficient details of the results of this process within the 'background', 'analysis' and 'what we have learned' sections of each chapter.

From a subjective perspective, the primary difference between the research conducted for this book, and other research we have participated in, particularly that which involves theoretical generalisation from qualitative case studies, is the form in which the results have been shared. In writing we have erred towards accessibility and engagement. Teachers, a central audience of this book, are generally dismissive of educational research, partly because of its distance from practice but also due to its inaccessible language (Gore & Gitlin, 2004). Therefore, we have tried to use clear language, we have avoided overwhelming the text with citations, and we have at times stated perspectives more boldly than we typically would in academic writing.

Final words

We hope that this book is found useful by a wide range of readers: that pre-service teachers gain some insights into planning and reflecting on lessons; that pre-service and in-service teachers benefit from thinking through pedagogy and mathematical understanding a little more deeply; that those in teacher professional development see, or add to, their understanding of the role LS can play in developing pedagogical understanding; that those who train teachers also see the benefits of this for their students, alongside gaining some useful materials that connect research to practice for their students; and, also, that researchers gain from these examples of action research, or seeing how mathematics educational research translates into classroom activity. We hope, most of all that this book inspires teachers to conduct and write up their own LSs.

In many contexts, including our own, the workload that teachers face perhaps makes conducting a LS feel like a daunting task for any individual. The beauty of LS though is that you don't do it on your own. Also, just imagine if you had access to hundreds of lessons like the ones in this book, covering any conceivable topic; where some research has been done into the lesson and the thinking behind it shared with you; where the experience of the lesson in a real classroom is described and analysed, so you get an idea what to expect from your students; and where the final lesson plan has been developed, based on new understanding gained through the analysis of the experience of the lesson. Having access to such materials could imaginably have a large impact on your workload as a teacher. To make those hundreds exist, you along with a few colleagues perhaps only need to contribute one or two. Through the process of conducting a LS, we can also guarantee that you will develop and deepen your understanding of teaching and learning mathematics; even more so through the act of writing up and sharing with others.

So if this book has inspired you to do just that, then go convince some colleagues to join you and start your own LS group. The results don't have to be perfect, or academically written, but just in a form that you yourself would find useful if it was shared with you. If you like, you can send the results of your LS to us, and in return, we promise to share all the others we receive with you, and with the wider teaching community online.

References

Creswell, J. W. (2012). *Educational research: Planning, conducting, and evaluating quantitative*. London: Pearson.

Eisenhardt, K. M. (1989). Building theories from case study research. *Academy of Management Review*, 14(4), 532–550.

Etikan, I., Musa, S. A., & Alkassim, R. S. (2016). Comparison of convenience sampling and purposive sampling. *American Journal of Theoretical and Applied Statistics*, 5(1), 1–4.

Fujii, T. (2018). Lesson study and teaching mathematics through problem solving: The two wheels of a cart. In M. Quaresma, C. Winslow, S. Clivaz, J. P. da Ponte, A. N. Shúilleabháin, & A. Takahashi (Eds.), *Mathematics lesson study around the world* (pp. 1–21). Cham, Switzerland: Springer.

Gainsburg, J. (2012). Why new mathematics teachers do or don't use practices emphasized in their credential program. *Journal of Mathematics Teacher Education, 15*(5), 359–379.

Gore, J. M., & Gitlin, A. D. (2004). [Re]Visioning the academic–teacher divide: Power and knowledge in the educational community. *Teachers and Teaching, 10*(1), 35–58.

Gu, L., Huang, R., & Marton, F. (2004). Teaching with variation: A Chinese way of promoting effective mathematics learning. In L. Fan (Ed.), *How Chinese learn mathematics: Perspectives from insiders* (pp. 309–347). London: World Scientific Publishing.

Hendricks, C. C. (2019). History of action research in education. In C. A. Mertler (Ed.), *The Wiley handbook of action research in education* (pp. 29–51). Hoboken, NJ: Wiley.

Lewis, C., Perry, R., & Friedkin, S. (2009). Lesson study as action research. In S. Noffke & B. Somekh (Eds.), *Handbook of educational action research* (pp. 143–154). Thousand Oaks, CA: Sage.

Meyrick, J. (2006). What is good qualitative research? A first step towards a comprehensive approach to judging rigour/quality. *Journal of Health Psychology, 11*(5), 799–808.

Stigler, J. W., & Hiebert, J. (2016). Lesson study, improvement, and the importing of cultural routines. *ZDM Mathematics Education, 48*(4), 581–587.

Swanson, D., & Morgan, S. (2020). *Going beyond lesson study: Professional development courses and the systematic/scientific development of pedagogical understanding*. Manuscript submitted for publication.

Takahashi, A., & McDougal, T. (2018). Collaborative lesson research (CLR). In M. Quaresma, C. Winslow, S. Clivaz, J. P. da Ponte, A. N. Shúilleabháin, & A. Takahashi (Eds.), *Mathematics lesson study around the world* (pp. 1–21). Cham, Switzerland: Springer.

Takahashi, A., & Yoshida, M. (2004). Lesson-study communities. *Teaching Children Mathematics, 10*(9), 436–437.

Vygotsky, L. S. (1987). *Thinking and speech. The Collected Works of L.S. Vygotsky Vol. 1*. New York: Plenum.

Yin, R. K. (2018). *Case study research and applications: Design and methods*. London: Sage.

Index

Printed in Great Britain
by Amazon